POSTCARDS
FROM THE BORDERLANDS

David H. Mould

PRAISE FOR
Postcards from the Borderlands

"*Postcards from the Borderlands* [is] gracefully interwoven with history and geography, and guaranteed to ignite a bit of wanderlust in anyone who shares Mould's sense of wonder and adventure at our strangely eclectic world of borders."

—Natalie Koch,
Associate Professor of Geography,
Syracuse University, New York

"Mould is an intrepid traveler, often poking his nose in where it isn't welcome… a style of travel that requires a certain toughness and resolution, but which rewards readers with secrets invisible to conventional tourists."

—Alan Wilkinson,
biographer, travel writer and novelist, Durham, UK

"David Mould's writing shines brightest when he combines his personal thoughts and observations with research on borders that were often imposed by foreign powers with the flick of a pen. …The reader will never again take nations and borders as we find them today for granted."

—Elizabeth Sammons,
novelist and journalist, Columbus, Ohio

"David's journey crisscrossing the borders of countries in Asia and southern Africa is enthralling. The conversational narrative is witty and easy to read, especially for the armchair traveler; yet, his third travel adventure book would serve as valuable text for students in high schools and universities."

—Katherine P. Manley,
author of *Don't Tell'em You're Cold*

"In *Borderlands*, Mould addresses questions we might never have thought to ask. When did mapping and delineation of borders begin? When, where and why were passports first used? How are borders felt and understood by the people who live near them? As an experienced guide, he encourages us to shelve our worries, expand our mental borders and explore the unfamiliar. Ride in a rickshaw, try the frog porridge and get to know our fellow humans, wherever they live."

—Margaret Romoser, Ph.D.,
retired university administrator, educator,
community activist and avid traveler, Columbus, Ohio

"With an ear for dialogue and an eye for fresh detail, Mould explores the geopolitics of border regions not only through the lens of history but through his interactions with ordinary people. The result is a book that will inform, entertain and inspire."

—Sharon Hatfield, author of
Enchanted Ground: The Spirit Room of Jonathan Koons

"David Mould is NOT a mints-on-your-pillow kind of traveler. He steps out of the tourist bubble and explores the action, people and history of back alley markets, crowded neighborhoods and bustling wharves. Mould has a remarkable ability to put the present in historical context."

—Lynda Berman,
teacher and artist, Athens, Ohio

"...a book to be savored and reread, not necessarily sequentially, but even at random. This is Mould's third in his 'Postcards' series, and perhaps his best."

—Paul Epstein,
retired public school teacher, writer, musician
Charleston, West Virginia

"Beyond the gated entrance of seaside resorts where the bikini clad models cavort and uniformed waiters bring piña coladas on a tray, there are the towns where people live, or scratch a living. The farms, the fisheries, the unpaved streets, the old mosques or churches or temples, the town markets where women bring fruits from their orchards to sell, the schools where children study and dream of a better future."

—Josep Rota, Professor Emeritus of Communication and Vice Provost Emeritus for International Studies, Ohio University

"Whether you are a confirmed armchair traveler, or someone considering the road less taken, David provides a primer that demystifies many countries and transcends borders, clearing the way for a better understanding of cultures beyond our comfort zone."

—Frederick Lewis, documentary filmmaker, Professor, Media Arts & Studies, Ohio University

"*Postcards from the Borderlands* is a love letter to the world by an 'accidental' travel writer."

—Jean Andrews, award-winning video documentary producer and science writer.

"David [Mould] provides us with a thoroughly entertaining group of stories that fit together into a cohesive commentary on the state of the world."

—Andrew Carlson, Associate Professor of Communication at Metropolitan State University in St Paul, Minnesota

"David Mould has been almost everywhere, but it would be wrong to call him a tourist. He interacts with people, experiences their culture, learns their history, sees how they really live. I'm amazed at his ability to soak up the tiniest details and weave them into engaging stories. Let him take you on his latest adventure."

—Kamellia Smith, former reporter for Indonesia's national magazine *TEMPO* and Cincinnati's Enquirer Media

"David Mould has done it again with *Postcards from the Borderlands* where he describes the complex religious, political, economic, and ethnic considerations involved in drawing boundaries. Anyone who relishes descriptions of other countries and their idiosyncrasies, including borders, will enjoy and learn from this book."

—Paula Claycomb, Senior Advisor, Communication for Development, UNICEF (retired)

Published by Open Books

Interior design by Siva Ram Maganti

Cover image "Mount Mulanje, on Malawi's southern border with Mozambique" © David Mould

Cover image © rangizzz shutterstock.com/g/rangizzz

Interior photos © David Mould

Maps by Ana Mojika Myers, Benjamin Bryan, Anna Stover, and Hunter Uhl

ISBN-13: 978-1948598422

To my wife, Stephanie Hysmith, for being the best companion for travel and life I could ever have hoped to have.

Contents

Chapter 1

Crossing Borders

★ ★ ★

The two cops were loitering with intent when I arrived at Almaty airport in southern Kazakhstan. I was doing my best to merge with the crowd. I was dressed in jeans, a faded T-shirt and sneakers; my chin sported several days of stubble. My dented suitcase looked as if it had been tossed around too many times on the tarmac and chewed up on baggage carousels. I had arrived, not in a taxi or hotel car, but in one of the city's beat-up *marshrutkas* (shared taxis), the crowded minibuses that ply short-haul routes in Central Asia. If I didn't open my mouth and mangle Russian syntax, I hoped I could pass for one of the ethnic Russians, Ukrainians or Germans who made up a sizeable minority of Kazakhstan's population.

The cops were experienced in the art of foreigner spotting. Something about me—perhaps my body language or the purposeful way in which I walked—told them they had a customer.

"*Vash passport, pozhousta* [Your passport, please]," one asked, as his partner shifted his frame to block the sidewalk in front of me.

After the collapse of the Soviet Union in 1991, customs and border officials in the five Central Asian republics—Kazakhstan, Kyrgyzstan, Tajikistan, Turkmenistan, and Uzbekistan—earned a reputation for trying to shake down weary travelers by inventing entry taxes and selling transit visas you didn't need. Other scams involved currency controls. Because of capital flight, these countries imposed limits on the export of currency. However, the official inquiry, "How much money are you carrying?" was often

1

the prelude to a search and an on-the-spot, undocumented fine.

Most attempted shakedowns were minor, and often played like a game. The cop who scanned my passport noticed that my local registration stamp had expired two days earlier. "That's a $100 fine," he declared triumphantly, as if he had just solved a major white-collar crime.

I was not convinced. Perhaps I had violated a minor provision in the Kazakhstan Civil Code, but I figured that the fine, if there was one, would be denominated in Kazakhstan *tenge*, not dollars. "Show me the regulation," I asked. We entered a small office inside the terminal. There was no sign on the door, so I wasn't even sure it was the police office. As the cops skimmed through papers on the desk, failing to find the one that described my offense, I became impatient.

"Even if you're right, I don't have $100," I said, not entirely truthfully. My inquisitors looked crestfallen. "How much money *do* you have?" one asked. "One thousand *tenge* [at that time, about US $12]," I replied. "That will do," the first cop said. "Have a nice flight, and if anyone else in the airport asks, please don't mention this happened."

I handed over the money, shook hands, accepted a shot of vodka, and went on my way. In a country where police do not earn a living wage and routinely stop drivers to extract small fines, it was an additional, and not unexpected, travel expense.

As a traveler who writes about his experiences, I may have come out ahead on the deal. The cops got enough to buy two more bottles of vodka. I got an anecdote about petty corruption that provided a glimpse of life in a post-Soviet society that was undergoing wrenching social and economic transition. As travel writer Thomas Swick notes, travel only becomes interesting (and therefore worth writing about) when things go wrong. I don't go looking for trouble but given the way I've travelled for much of my life, it's sometimes difficult to avoid it. To quote the father of a friend, "Experience is what you get when you don't get what you want." I'm not short of experience.

In retrospect, the shakedown at Almaty airport makes a good traveler's tale. At the time, I had no idea what might happen to me in a country that routinely arrests and imprisons activists, journalists and, occasionally, foreigners working for international and non-governmental organizations. I was in the latter category; I had spent the last two weeks in Almaty conducting a workshop for journalists sponsored by UNESCO. That's perhaps why my heart always races a little when I approach or cross a border. Will my passport and visa be in order? Will one of my entry stamps raise an eyebrow, a question about what I was doing in that country? At the airport, will the immigration officers be suspicious if I switch to a line that is moving faster? Is it worth slipping a small bill into my passport for expedited service? That depends. In some countries, you'll be whisked through with a nod and a wink; in others, you may be arrested.

Then there's the issue of how much to say about what I'll be doing in the country I'm about to enter. I've learned not to volunteer too much information, because it may appear I'm hiding something. Most of the time I'm unnaturally reticent. "Purpose of visit?" "Business." "How many days?" "Ten." If I can get through with a few words, that's fine.

Passport Required

It's tempting to think that before the birth of the modern nation state, political borders, such as we know them today, did not exist or, if they did, were extremely porous. That was the case in some parts of the world where people moved freely, herding livestock to summer and winter pastures, clearing forests to plant crops, engaging in trade, or fleeing from poverty, conflict or religious persecution. For them, the only borders were the natural barriers they had to cross—mountain ranges, deserts, rivers, lakes and seas.

Yet even the oldest civilizations built walls and moats around their cities, partly for defense and partly to control the movement of people. Some were large infrastructure projects, such as the Great Wall of China, the series of forts built across the northern border to protect the empire from nomadic invaders, and Hadrian's Wall, built by the Romans to keep marauding Scots out of England. In pre-colonial West Africa, there were about 10,000 walls, a quarter of them on now-deserted sites, separating kingdoms and political groups between Lake Chad and the Atlantic Ocean.

With or without walls, there were always barriers and costs to travel—road, bridge and ferry tolls and taxes on the movement of commercial goods. However, few people needed a passport or its equivalent. The main exceptions were the equivalent of today's frequent fliers such as royal couriers and foreign merchants. They needed formal letters of authority with stamps and seals to show to guards and customs agents.

The first formal passport system was introduced during the Han dynasty (206 BC–220 AD) in China. To allow citizens to travel through the empire, the bureaucracy issued passports listing personal details including age, height and bodily features. In the medieval Islamic Caliphate, which stretched west from the Arabian peninsula across North Africa to southern Spain and east to India, travelers needed to show a *bara'a*, a receipt for taxes paid, to be allowed to travel to different regions.

The word "passport" is of French origin. In the Middle Ages, it was the document required to pass through the gate ("porte") of a city wall or through a territory. It was issued by local authorities to foreign travelers and listed the towns and cities the holder was permitted to enter or pass through. King Henry V of England, by a 1414 Act of Parliament, created what is considered to be the first passport in the modern sense of the term, to help his subjects prove who they were in foreign lands.

Before the age of mass transportation, passports were still reserved mostly for diplomats, couriers and merchants, whose business required frequent travel. Until World War I, people could travel around Europe by railroad without ever having to show a passport. During the war, European governments introduced border passport requirements for security reasons, and to control the migration of people with useful skills. These controls remained in place after the war, with the League of Nations issuing guidelines and a general design template. Political borders—and the passports needed to cross them—had come to stay.

Passport from Adolescence

Growing up in Britain in the 1950s and early 1960s, I counted myself lucky that my parents took the family on annual camping vacations in Europe. While other families shivered on stony, wind-swept English beaches and promenades, we were swimming and, blithely unaware of the health risks, toasting our pale skins on Mediterranean beaches.

From the age of eight, I faithfully recorded details of these trips in my diary, including the excitement of crossing borders. After taking the car ferry across the English Channel, we disembarked at Calais or Boulogne. French *gendarmes* in stylish, neatly pressed dark blue uniforms and peaked hats inspected our passports, smiled at the two children in the back seat and wished us *bon voyage*. At the Spanish border, the Guardia Civil, with their distinctive black *tricornio* hats and semiautomatic weapons, looked more menacing, but were just as welcoming.

On those childhood vacations, I traveled on my father's passport as an "accompanying child." At the time, I did not think of this as a demeaning category, yet it was a proud day when, in March 1965 at the age of 15, I was issued my first passport. My mother insisted on a haircut and a new shirt and tie for the formal passport photo session. The inside of the passport front cover bore the seal of the monarch, and a stern instruction in elaborate cursive (with random capitalization) not to mess with her loyal subject:

> Her Britannic Majesty's Principal Secretary of State for Foreign Affairs Requests and requires in the Name of Her Majesty all those whom it may concern to allow the bearer to pass freely without let or hindrance, and to afford the bearer such assistance and protection as may be necessary.

Today, this language feels rather quaint, the pompous posturing of a country that since the end of World War II had surrendered its empire in Asia, Africa and the Caribbean but was not yet ready to accept its new, reduced role in the world. The curious phrase, "Requests and requires," seems almost passive-aggressive. The passport was valid "for all parts of the Commonwealth and for all Foreign Countries." The British Empire was gone, but at least we still had the Commonwealth, even though some of its member countries were ruled by autocrats whom the British had thrown into jail during the struggle for independence. The former imperial master was now forced to acknowledge these rascals by inviting them to meetings in London and asking them to put on airport military parades to greet visiting members of the Royal Family.

That first passport was a sign of passage from childhood to adolescence, although my profession was still listed as "schoolboy." Five years later, fresh out of college and ready to start work as a newspaper reporter, I had the passport office cross out "schoolboy" and insert "trainee journalist." I forgot to ask them to adjust my height (I had grown three inches).

In 1975, when I got a new 10-year passport, I was still confusingly described as a "Citizen of the United Kingdom and Colonies." All the large colonies had achieved independence at least a decade earlier. What was left was a scattering of small islands and island groups in the Caribbean, Indian Ocean, South Atlantic and Pacific, and the remote British Antarctic Territory. The best-known remaining colonies were Gibraltar, which Spain claims, and Hong Kong, which was only on lease anyway and was handed back to China in 1997.

After I became a naturalized US citizen in 1991, I let my UK passport lapse and traveled on a US passport for the next 12 years. I applied for a new UK-European Union passport in 2003 after the US invaded Iraq. I hoped I might be more welcome in some countries as a loyal subject of Her Britannic Majesty, rather than as a traveler from the land of Bush and Cheney. In the end, it made no difference because the "old ally" followed the US lead in its foreign policy and military engagements. The UK-European Union passport was only useful for speeding up entry to the UK and France, where my sister lives. Since Brexit, it's probably not worth renewing.

With two passports, I have one more than most people. I am still a long way away from matching the collection of my passport hero, Jason Bourne, the CIA-trained rogue assassin played by Matt Damon in the action thriller movies based on the novels of Robert Ludlum. Picked up by fishermen in the Mediterranean Sea with two gunshots in his back and a device with the number of a Swiss bank account embedded in his hip, the character discovers he is fluent in several languages and skilled at navigation and hand-to-hand combat but has no idea who he is or how he ended up floating in the sea. In Zurich, he opens his safe deposit box to find US $5 million in various currencies, a handgun, credit cards and six passports (Canadian, French, Russian, Brazilian and two US) with his photo, each with a different name and the appropriate visas. He picks the name on the first of the two US passports, Jason Bourne. In future scenes, as he nears a border or as guards move down the train corridor, he sifts through the passport pack and selects his next identity.

Fellow travelers sometimes ask me why I have two passports. No one asks me if I am Jason Bourne.

If It's Tuesday, This Must Be Belgium

If I travel in Europe today, I no longer need to show either my US or UK passport, except at the port of entry. Economic and political integration have signaled the end of formal frontiers. In 1985, under the Schengen Agreement, five of the ten countries in what was then the European Economic Community—Belgium, France, Luxembourg, the Netherlands, and West Germany—began abolishing border checks. Since the fall of the Berlin Wall, former Eastern Bloc countries have joined the European Union and become part of the agreement. The Schengen Area now consists of 26 countries, with a population of more than 400 million. Travelers show passports to enter and leave the Schengen Area, but not at national borders. You can drive from Lithuania to Portugal or from Greece to Norway without ever having to stop at a border crossing. Except, that was, during the Coronavirus pandemic in 2020, when countries fighting to stop the spread of the virus temporarily closed national borders.

Passport-free zones make travel and commerce easier, but they also end the thrill and romance of crossing national borders. No *gendarmes* or Guardia Civil at the border. You zip through on a six-lane highway and, if you don't notice the "Welcome to" sign, you may not realize you've entered another country. The absence of border checks gives new life to the old joke about time-pressed US tourists whizzing around the European continent, counting off the countries where they stop by the days of the week. "If It's Tuesday, This Must Be Belgium."

7

Borders within

Not all borders are where they should be or where you expect them to be. If you are traveling in a conflict zone or entering an area controlled by a guerilla army or a drug cartel, you expect to be stopped on the road, have your documents scrutinized and your vehicle searched. There are also random stops in areas free of conflict and crime, particularly in countries where the legal and administrative system is still, well, maturing. Traveling in Central Asia in the 1990s and 2000s, my car was sometimes flagged down by armed men in uniforms who may or may not have been members of the country's military or law enforcement agencies. Sometimes, they informed me that I was about to enter a special, restricted, or military zone.

"It's not on my map," I would protest. "Of course not," the guard would reply. "If it was on the map, it would be an easy target for terrorists." I would try again. "Well, there's no sign on the road saying we're entering a restricted zone." The guard would start to look impatient and fidget with his semiautomatic weapon which was not a reassuring sign. "Don't you understand? It's a secret zone. If we put up signs, it would not be a secret any more. Now show me your passport. We need to report the names of all foreigners on the road. And you must pay the special transit fee." The "fee," of course, went straight into the guard's pocket, with a percentage paid to his commander at the end of his shift.

Even in countries where the legal and administrative systems work more efficiently and you don't encounter armed militias at traffic intersections, there are borders within. For half a century under the apartheid regime, internal travel in South Africa was severely restricted. Blacks and coloreds (people of mixed racial origin) had to show passes to travel from their homes in designated districts for work or other business and had to return at night or face arrest. Separate rural "homelands" were created for ethnic groups. In the Soviet Union, you needed official documentation to move from one city or district to another for work or education.

All authoritarian regimes erect borders within their countries as a means of social and political control. Before the age of digital media, when a state was able to control and censor radio and television broadcasting, restrictions on the movement of people helped stop information and ideas from spreading. The government could stop the printing of newspapers, magazines, pamphlets, and books, seize illegal copies and ban imports of what it deemed to be foreign propaganda. The Internet and mobile phone network have rendered broadcasting censorship and bans on print materials less effective, so governments have built digital borders to restrict information. They either restrict access to certain websites, as in the so-called Great Firewall of China, or, in extreme cases such as India's crackdown in Kashmir in 2019-2020, simply turn off the Internet and mobile phone service.

Borders within the UK

Until my late twenties, when I moved to the US for post-graduate study, I lived in a relatively free and democratic country that was variously called (depending on one's attitude to Her Britannic Majesty and colonialism) Great Britain, Britain or the United Kingdom (UK) of England, Wales, Scotland and Northern Ireland (the province of Ulster). I lived in the bit called England, which thankfully no longer needed Hadrian's Wall because most recent Scottish invaders were soccer players or investment bankers. I did not need a passport to travel within the UK. That did not mean borders did not exist.

In Northern Ireland, tensions between Protestant Unionists and Irish nationalists demanding civil rights had been simmering for decades. Full-scale communal violence broke out in January 1969, with marches and rioting, primarily in the provincial capital Belfast, and the second largest city, Derry. By August, the Protestant-dominated police force, the Royal Ulster Constabulary, could no longer handle the situation and the British army was deployed. The violence spiraled out of control, with the Irish Republican Army (IRA) setting off bombs in the province and in England. On "Bloody Sunday," January 30, 1972, in Derry, 26 unarmed civilians were shot by the British Army during a massive demonstration against the internment of political prisoners. In March, Northern Ireland's government and parliament were dissolved and direct rule from London imposed.

As a young newspaper reporter, I made my first visit to Northern Ireland in August 1971, crossing the Irish Sea by ferry from Liverpool to Belfast. Although I had followed the so-called "Troubles" in the newspapers and on TV, I was still taken aback when I disembarked. British troops and armored personnel carriers were stationed at the dock. A soldier with a sub-machine gun did a full body search and inspected my press credentials and letter of authorization for the Yorkshire regiment I was assigned to visit. In Belfast city center, I was stopped, searched, and questioned by soldiers at checkpoints, standing under wire enclosures built to repel rocks and Molotov cocktails.

Everyone was on edge. Without having to show a passport, I had crossed a border more formidable than any I had ever faced on those family vacations in Europe.

Who Drew the Borders?

Since those childhood experiences in Western Europe, I have always been fascinated by borders. My interest intensified during my undergraduate program in European Studies. The history courses were served up in predictable chronological slices, starting with the so-called Middle Ages and proceeding through the Renaissance, the Protestant Reformation, the Enlightenment, the French Revolution and the wars and revolutions of the nineteenth century all the way up to World War Two. Our textbooks often had the word "age" in the title—the *Age of the Bourgeoisie*, the *Age of the Puritans*, the *Age of Revolution*, and so on. In line with current academic trends, the temporal slices came with toppings of social and economic history, but the basic recipe was military and political. It was a long list of wars fought between empires, kingdoms, and principalities, or between religious factions, rebellions by nobles, the bourgeoisie, peasants and workers, ceasefires and treaties, an endless succession of kings, queens, regents, prime ministers, and rebel warlords, and just too many dates to remember. The British historian Arnold J. Toynbee, author of the sweeping 12-volume *The Study of History* (published over a quarter of a century) has the misfortune to be credited with the memorable phrase that history is "just one damned thing after another." In fact, Toynbee believed exactly the opposite and used the phrase to critique other historians, who chronicled events of the past but failed to analyze connections between them. For Toynbee, history was all about grand patterns, the rise and fall of world civilizations that transcended nations, races, dynasties, conflicts and changing borders.

I have some sympathy with the "just one damned thing after another" complaint because in order to present the big picture, the grand patterns in history, you need to know the small stuff. Besides all those dates and names, historians face daunting cartographic challenges. As all those empires, kingdoms and principalities fought, made peace, and fought again, the maps kept changing as they grabbed portions of each other's territory. I had to remember and date the changing borders of the Holy Roman, Austro-Hungarian, Napoleonic and Ottoman empires, Bismarck's Germany, the shifting front lines of World War One, the faster moving battle maps of World War Two. Some areas of the map seemed to be constantly changing hands and color. One of my fellow students reached metaphorical exhaustion in a term paper when he described Alsace Lorraine, repeatedly fought over by France and Germany, as "the innocent filling between two hostile slices of bread."

It was challenging enough to keep up with the shifting borders of European countries. When I opened the atlas and turned to other continents, the borders of some countries seemed to make no sense at all. Why were some strangely shaped, with portions of their territory protruding into other countries? Why were there straight line borders, particularly in the Middle East and Africa? Who on earth drew the borders this way, and why?

The main culprits were political leaders sitting around conference tables in European capitals, thousands of miles away from the lands they were dividing. The so-called "Scramble for Africa" began with the Berlin Conference of 1884-1885, where Belgium, Britain, France, Germany, Portugal, Spain, Italy, and the Ottoman Empire, each with its own economic and geo-political goals, carved up the continent into spheres of influence. Over the next half century, cartographic surveys and boundary commissions created the borders that were preserved intact when the countries became independent. They cut across topography, ancient kingdoms, ethnic groups, and traditional hunting and grazing lands. As British Prime Minister Lord Salisbury famously remarked at the signing of the Anglo-French convention on the Nigeria-Niger boundary in 1899: "We [the British and the French] have been engaged in drawing lines upon maps where no white man's foot ever trod: we have been giving away mountains and rivers and lakes to each other, only hindered by the small impediments that we never knew exactly where the mountains and rivers and lakes were."

It may seem obvious, but it's worth stating anyway. Except for some mountain ranges and wide rivers, there are few *natural* land borders anywhere in the world. To quote the well-traveled Canadian writer Kate Harris, whose *Lands of Lost Borders* describes her bicycle trip along the Silk Road, "Borders try to cut across so many differences that don't really exist ... They go against the natural [boundaries] of the world, and that's where they fail us." A border, by its very nature, is demarcated by someone or something—a cartographer or surveyor, a national government, an international agency, a military force, a border commission. The act of demarcation inevitably gives rise to disputes. Borders, especially those with walls and fences, create economic and social barriers, dividing ethnic and religious groups, communities and even families. For aggressive nation-states, the lines on the maps are never fixed or accepted; they simply represent a fragile status quo that can be disrupted by war, economic blockade, or diplomacy.

Around the world, there are hundreds of territories, large and small, that are currently governed by one country but claimed by another. Some disputes are intense, high-profile, historical conflicts: between Israel and Palestine over the West Bank and Israeli settlements; Kashmir, over which India and Pakistan have fought three wars; eastern Ukraine, invaded by Russia and controlled by Russian-backed separatists. There are other long-running disputes that flare up from time to time—over South Ossetia and Abkhazia, two self-proclaimed republics established after the 2008 war between Russia and Georgia, between Armenia and Azerbaijan over the Nagorno-Karabakh region, between India and China over the high mountain borders in Kashmir and Arunachal Pradesh, between Cyprus and the Turkish-controlled north of the island, between Sudan and South Sudan. In the African continent alone, it's estimated that there are currently close to 100 active border disputes.

It's academically fashionable to trace the origins of many border disputes to the economic and political greed of colonial powers. Of course, territorial conflicts have occurred throughout history, as empires and kingdoms battled for political dominance, trade, natural resources and prestige, but there is no doubt that the deals made by the colonial powers and the borders they drew sowed the seeds for many of the conflicts in the world today.

Studying Borders

With so many issues over borders—trade, migration, refugees, sovereignty—border studies has emerged as an academic sub-discipline, or rather, as an interdisciplinary field that bridges geography, history, political science, economics, sociology, international relations, and other disciplines. It has academic journals, such as the *Journal of Borderland Studies, Journal of Borderland Research, Journal of Law and Border Studies*, and *International Journal of Migration and Border Studies*. What they have in common is that they regard the "border" not only as a concrete place or structure—a fence or wall, boundary markers or border guard posts with barriers and national flags flying—but as something more fluid, in terms of physical space, or as a psychological or cultural phenomenon. In a call for papers, the Association for Borderlands Studies argues that "borders continue to be conceived of and represented by mainstream politics and the media in an overly simplistic way. Much recent political and public debate has regressed into nationalistic, state-centric thinking and populist rhetoric, reducing the idea of borders to be mere protective frontlines." Border scholarship "can provide tools to analyze and understand xenophobia, exclusion and inequality."[1]

---

1. Association for Borderland Studies, Call for Papers for 2020 Annual Conference, Portland, Oregon, USA.

Border scholars recognize that although surveyors, commissions and governments draw political borders, their cartography does not always align with the mental maps of those who live along them or cross them for work, school, business, or family visits. The broad conception of a "border" is illustrated by article titles from the *Journal of Borderland Studies*: "Conflicting Imaginaries of the Border: The Construction of African Asylum Seekers in the Israeli Political Discourse," "Securitizing a European Borderland: The Bordering Effects of Memory Politics in Bosnia and Herzegovina," "Quantifying Impediments to India-Nepal Overland Trade: Logistics Issues and Policy Messages," and "The San Diego Chicano Movement and the Origins of Border Art." For the non-specialist, some titles are head-scratchers. I have no idea what to expect from "An Alternative Border Metaphor: On Rhizomes and Disciplinary Boundaries" or "Borderities and the Politics of Contemporary Mobile Borders." Yet, the range of topics and disciplines indicates that researchers take an expansive view of what borders mean.

Expanding Borders

I'm indebted to the academics for not restricting borders to defined physical spaces but seeing them as more flexible concepts. That allows me literary license. Some stories in this book, such as the Almaty airport shakedown, an unplanned one-day visit to Kenya and a briefer encounter in Shanghai, and the journey from Osh to Jalalabad in southern Kyrgyzstan, are about real encounters at borders and the challenges of getting in and out of countries. Elsewhere, as in Bangladesh, Malawi, Mongolia and The Maldives, the borders I encounter are natural—rivers, lakes, seas, and mountain ranges. Other borders are historical, racial, or socio-economic—the slave trade in East Africa, apartheid in South Africa, the importation of plantation laborers to British colonies, ethnic divisions in Nepal, Malaysia, and Pakistan. A border may even be a state of mind. People who live many miles from a physical frontier may still feel they are "on the border," because of how they live, work and trade, and because of the people and traffic that move in and out of their communities.

When borders are defined by memory, personal or collective experience or culture, you will not find them on maps. Nomadic herders do not need markers, a map or GPS to know how to reach their summer and winter pastures. Urban residents know which streets or buildings mark the boundaries of areas where they feel safe to drive or walk, and dangerous or no-go zones. The geography of the community where we live is shared knowledge, although our mental maps will differ based on our race, age, and economic status. Business commuters, school children, seniors and the homeless all live in the same city, but they experience and map it through their own lenses and experiences.

The Accidental Travel Writer

This is my third book on history, travel, and culture. As in the first two, *Postcards from Stanland: Journeys in Central Asia* (Ohio University Press, 2016) and *Monsoon Postcards: Indian Ocean Journeys* (Ohio University Press, 2019), it's a series of narratives—long postcards, if you like—about people and places, their histories and cultures. During a 30-year career as a college professor, I never completely bought into an academic culture where peer-reviewed journal articles are the coin of the realm, where you sometimes have to excavate thick layers of theory, literature reviews, methodology and research questions to figure out what someone discovered in their research. I was happier when I shared what I earned with a wider, non-academic audience, in newspaper and magazine features, radio and television documentaries, and books. I do my research as thoroughly as my academic colleagues, but I don't present it in the same way. Instead of formulating research hypotheses, I ask questions; instead of presenting findings, I just write about what I found.

I credit my writing style to my earlier career as a journalist, working in newspapers and television news in the north of England. As a reporter, I learned how to do interviews (sometimes with people who did not want to talk to me), research records, analyze documents, observe a scene. And then to write the story quickly because I was always on a deadline. In books and articles, my narrative style has evolved, with more description and background analysis, but at heart, I am still a storyteller.

Since the mid-1990s, I've been fortunate to travel widely in Central, South and Southeast Asia and, more recently, in Southern Africa. I've worked as a teacher, trainer, researcher and consultant for international development organizations, including UNESCO and USAID contractors and, most recently, UNICEF. I've completed two Fulbright Fellowships, in Kyrgyzstan and Kazakhstan, and a US Embassy fellowship in Russia's Southern Urals region. Sometimes, the job paid quite well; sometimes I worked for less than I'd earn tossing burgers (assuming I knew how to toss burgers). The benefit is that my work has taken me to places I might never have visited if I had not been hired to do a job.

Sometimes, after I finish my assignment, my wife, Stephanie Hysmith, joins me and we travel for a few weeks. She is a great companion, who does not mind figuring out which bus to take and is happy to eat at roadside restaurants and stay in modest guest houses. Like me, she is fascinated by other cultures. She's a sociable person, ready to strike up a conversation with almost anyone. As a socio-linguist, she's always ready to try out a new language, or at least learn enough of it to read a menu and shop. She is undaunted by unfamiliar alphabets and scripts; during a two-week stay in Georgia, I got by with my Russian, but she was determined to learn the Georgian alphabet and the vowel sounds. It made for some long meals because, before we ordered, she had to sound out the names of dishes, and then look them up in the dictionary. Stephanie will join me several times in the chapters that follow—in Tanzania, Nepal, Malaysia, and Georgia. And, at a temple in Bangkok, she'll have her humerus fracture fixed by a muscular massage therapist who knows just one English phrase, "No pain, no gain."

Of course, I would love to be a full-time travel writer. I would select interesting destinations, conduct background research, line up interviews, and then get on the plane. Except for a few stars, most travel writers find it difficult to make a living from what they do, unless they are writing travel guides or those thinly disguised advertising blurbs on "Three Days of Divine Shopping and Dining in Dubai" for airline magazines. That's not my kind of travel writing and fortunately, I don't have to do it because someone else is picking up the tab for my travel. In that sense, I am an accidental travel writer.

16

In front of the statue of another business traveler,
Genghis Khan, in Mongolia's capital, Ulaanbaatar.

I don't need to be at a scenic overlook or a historic site to find something of interest. One advantage of being new to a place is that the everyday—the things so familiar to those who live there that they do not think about them—are often worth recording. I find topics even in the most ordinary places—an airport departure lounge, a food court, a roadside restaurant, a government office. Every road trip offers a moving window display of landscape features, crops, livestock, houses, churches, temples, mosques, schools, factories, military bases, vehicles. I note what people are selling on the roadside, the fruits and vegetables on the markets, the restaurant menu, the indecipherable instructions for the TV remote in my hotel room. What people wear. What they eat. How they talk to each other. The questions they ask me. The questions I ask them.

I like to wander around, with no particular destination, and strike up conversations. Despite the language barrier, I find most people willing to communicate, perhaps because I smile a lot and show I'm interested and not afraid of them. It is often the commonplace that is most fascinating and revealing of culture. Don't read my writing to learn about the Taj Mahal or Victoria

17

Falls. If you're interested in what a South Asian slum looks and feels like, what you'll see as you travel across Malawi, Nepal or the delta region of Bangladesh, or what's on the menu in a student cafeteria in the Urals region of Russia, I hope you'll read on.

Memory is short. What I see or hear will disappear in an instant if I don't record it. I always have a notebook, or at least something to write on, in my hand, and occasionally (when I know I will be talking with someone at length) an audio recorder. I take photographs, not only to illustrate my stories but to serve as memory-joggers. I write down what I learn because that's the only way I can connect the dots later. I've found that first impressions are often the most vivid. Even in a place filled with new sights, sounds and smells, what is interesting and unexpected on first encounter is more familiar the next time around, and less worthy of recording.

Postcards from the Borderlands opens with an unexpected one-day visit to Kenya, then moves south—to that improbably shaped, colonially created sliver of a country, Malawi, to the road from Dar es Salaam to Arusha in Tanzania, and to Johannesburg, South Africa's commercial capital and the magnet for thousands of migrants from all over the continent. In South Asia, I focus on Bengal and how the border lines hastily drawn for the partition of British India in 1947 created long-lasting conflicts along political, economic, and religious lines. In Bangladesh, my travels help me understand how rivers sustain agriculture and provide highways for commerce yet form borders that divide this densely-populated country. Landlocked Nepal, wedged between India and China, is a country where geography and ethnic divisions have made national unity fragile. In Southeast Asia, I escape Bangkok for the highlands of Thailand, that border China and Myanmar, and travel to the colonial cities, hill stations and island beaches of Malaysia. In the scattered, low-lying archipelago of The Maldives, a country on the front lines of climate change, I skip the resorts for the crowded capital of Malé. In Pakistan's commercial capital, Karachi, I am on high security alert but still find plenty to write about in this sprawling, historic port city. On the steppe in sparsely populated Mongolia, borders mean little; in Central Asia's Fergana Valley, the crazy-quilt Soviet-era borders remain a source of national and ethnic conflict. From Georgia's ancient capital, Tbilisi, long a crossroads between Europe and Asia, I travel to Russia for a fleeting Dr. Zhivago fantasy on the Trans-Siberian Railway and cross the continental divide in the Southern Urals. Now that's a *real* border. You can stand with one foot in Europe, one in Asia. And I have the photo to prove it.

Chapter 2

In Transit: No Time
For The Lion Park

★ ★ ★

Kenya Airways customer service counter, Nairobi Airport, 6:00 a.m.

"Good morning. I've just arrived on the delayed flight from Antananarivo in Madagascar and need to rebook …"

"Welcome to Kenya, sir. I hope you have a wonderful stay in our country."

"No, you don't understand. I'm not planning to stay. I need to get home to the US. Can you rebook me on a flight later this morning?"

"The lion park is near the airport. Only ten US dollars by taxi. Many tourists visit it. Maybe you will have time too?"

"I don't think so. Can you rebook me? Other passengers got new itineraries in Antananarivo but the rest of us were told to get them here."

"I'm sorry, sir, you will need to wait."

"Isn't this the customer service counter?"

"Yes, it is."

"But you can't help me?"

"No, sir. We have to wait for the supervisor to unlock the computers."

"When will the supervisor be here?"

"Very soon, I hope. Please wait with the other passengers."

I joined a group of weary, disconsolate travelers, some of whom

I recognized from the line at Antananarivo's Ivato airport. I had spent the previous two weeks in Madagascar, trying to wrap up a two-year social research study that my university team had undertaken for UNICEF. For reasons outside our control, the project had gone badly, and I was leaving with too many issues unresolved. I was looking forward to being home. The last thing I needed was a flight delay.

I had arrived at the airport in mid-afternoon to be told that the Kenya Airways flight to Nairobi had been delayed. The passengers were bussed back into the city, where we hung out at a hotel before returning to the airport at midnight. The flight eventually left at 4:00 a.m. Everyone missed their connections to Europe, Asia and North America. A few were given new itineraries and boarding passes but most of us were told we would receive ours on arrival in Nairobi.

8:00 a.m.

"Where is the supervisor?"

"He is not here."

"Yes, I can see that. When will he be here?"

"Very soon, I hope. He rang to say he is finishing his breakfast."

"Any chance we can get some breakfast? You've got some angry, hungry passengers over there." For a moment, I imagined a group trip to the lion park and wondered who would eat who.

"I am sorry, sir. There is no food available in the transit area. Please wait."

8:25 a.m.

"Sir, this is George, our customer service supervisor."

"Nice to meet you, George. Can you rebook me?"

"Please give me your passport and itinerary and I will enter the details into the system."

"You mean it's not already in the system? I thought that's what airline computer systems were designed to do—store information."

"We will see. Your passport and itinerary, please."

8:30 a.m.

"Sir, your details are now in the system."

"So can you rebook me?"

"You need another flight?"

"Yes. Don't you understand? Your flight from Antananarivo was delayed, and I missed the connection to Paris and then on to Atlanta."

"Please give me your credit card."

"Why do you need it?"

"So you can pay for the flight."

"I'm not paying for it. It's your airline's fault I'm stranded here. You need to find me another flight."

"I will have to talk to the sales office about it."

"Please do so."

George fumbled in his pocket and pulled out a tattered slip of paper with several phone numbers. He dialed the desk phone. After a few moments he replaced the receiver, pulled out another slip of paper and called on his mobile.

"They are not answering. Maybe it is too early, and no one is there."

"What time does the sales office open?"

"In the morning."

"At what time in the morning?"

"Maybe by 10:00. It depends."

"I'll come back to the desk at 10:00, then?"

"Yes, sir, please do. And welcome to Kenya. May I recommend the lion park …"

10:00 a.m.

"Is George here?"

"No, he has left for the day."

"He's left? Where did he go?"

"He went home. His shift is over."

"He told me to come back at 10:00 and he would call the sales office to rebook me."

"I will be happy to help you, sir. My name is Gladys. Let me welcome you to Kenya. Please give me your passport and itinerary so that I can enter the details into the system."

"But George already did that."

"We each have our own system for entering data. I will take care of it."

Gladys pounded the keyboard for a few minutes while I pondered the digital disaster that was the Kenya Airways reservation system. Gladys called the sales office. No answer.

"While we're waiting for the sales office, can you check available flights for me?"

Gladys pounded a few more keys, then frowned. "You could have taken the 8:00 a.m. flight to London and then connected to Atlanta on Delta."

"I was here at this desk at 8:00 a.m. and was told I could not be rebooked."

"I am sorry for the inconvenience. The next flight is not until tonight at 10:30 p.m. The Paris flight you missed last night."

"I didn't miss it. Your airline did."

"Whatever you say sir."

10:45 a.m.

Gladys has reached the sales office which issues a new itinerary. "Can you print it for me?"

"We need to wait for the manager to approve it."

"You've got to be joking."

"No, sir. Only the manager can approve a rebooked itinerary."

"Where is the manager?"

Gladys conferred with her colleagues. "He is in a meeting."

"When will the meeting be over?"

"Soon, we hope."

11:30 a.m.

"Is the manager out of the meeting?"

"Not yet, sir. Please wait."

"We've all been here for 5½ hours. No food. No water. And no help. Please tell the manager he's going to have a riot on his hands if he doesn't deal with the situation. Can you call or text him?"

"We will try."

Noon.

"The manager has approved your new itinerary, sir. Here it is with a voucher for a hotel for the day. You will need to be back by 8:00 p.m."

For once, the anticipation I usually feel when I'm about to cross a border was missing. With my transit visa in hand, I trudged wearily through immigration and waited almost an hour for the hotel bus. The hotel was in a shopping mall on a busy highway. Nothing to do. Certainly no lions. I had a meal and a nap and waited in the lobby for the bus back to the airport. It got stuck in traffic and I wondered if I might miss my Paris flight. As I crossed the border from Kenya back into the soulless landscape of Transitpassengerland, the cheerful officer asked me if I had enjoyed my visit to Nairobi. "I hope you had time to visit the lion park," he said.

Chapter 3

Malawi: Land of Lakes

★ ★ ★

South Africa's only Ally

I moved my bag so that the heavy-set man in the business suit could take a seat. It was 8:00 a.m. at Johannesburg's O.R. Tambo Airport, and the waiting area for short-haul flights to destinations in southern and central Africa was crowded. The man looked weary, as if he'd made too many such flights. "Windhoek—delayed at least an hour." He shrugged. "I'll miss my meeting. Where are you flying?"

"Lilongwe," I replied, then added, "Malawi," assuming I needed to provide context. The man smiled. "I was there a few times in the 1980s. Never did much business. But Malawi was our only ally in the region."

"Oh, really?" He must have sensed my ignorance, and that my accent was not South African. He continued. "Yes, we built the place. All the government buildings. They wouldn't have a capital without us."

He made the comment matter-of-factly. I did not sense any nostalgia for the apartheid era, or remorse about his country's foreign aid policy. It was simply something that had happened a long time ago.

It is a paradox of history that South Africa's apartheid regime, sanctioned and shunned by the international community, had a friend in Malawi, a landlocked sliver of a country wedged between Zambia, Mozambique, and Tanzania. Its long-time authoritarian president, Hastings Banda, was politically conservative, suspicious and fearful of the socialist regimes of other countries in the region. In other former colonies, whites left after losing their jobs, land, and businesses. Banda wanted to avoid a brain drain; after independence in 1964, many whites stayed on in managerial positions in government and business. Malawi was the only country in Africa to maintain diplomatic ties with South Africa during the apartheid era; South African president B.J. Vorster visited in 1970, and Banda went to South Africa the next year. Although Banda claimed that ties would lead to better understanding between the peoples of Malawi and South Africa, it was all about aid, trade, and politics. South Africans occupied senior management positions in leading companies and helped train the security forces. Banda's position infuriated other African leaders who demanded that Malawi be expelled from the Organization of African Unity (OAU). Banda responded by calling his fellow leaders hypocrites for preaching unity and equality while oppressing their own peoples and maintaining secret trade links with South Africa.

Like leaders of other new African nations, Banda had come to power as a man of the people and then decided that no one else was capable of taking the country forward. He drove opposition leaders into hiding or exile and silenced the foreign and domestic press. In 1971, he had himself declared president for life. Controlling the government, economy and media, Banda became synonymous with the country. The phrase "Malawi is a one-man-Banda" was coined.

In 1968, Banda had announced plans to move the seat of government from the colonial capital of Zomba in the southern highlands to Lilongwe, a former fishing village in the central region that had grown to become a trading and transportation hub. The decision not only signaled a break with the colonial past but sent a powerful "one nation" message to a country where regional and tribal loyalties remain strong.

Moving a capital is an expensive business, particularly for a poor agricultural country with almost no mineral wealth and a growing foreign debt. South Africa stepped in with grants and loans to help build Lilongwe's so-called New City with its broad boulevards and manicured gardens. The government buildings stand on sloping ground (rather grandiosely named Capital Hill) north of the business district. Lilongwe officially became the capital in 1975 but there wasn't enough money available to move all government offices and some ministries remained in Zomba; the parliament did not move until 1998.

Banda did not live long enough to lord it over the first session of parliament. In the Cold War era, Malawi was a useful Western ally in a region dominated by socialist-leaning regimes in Mozambique, Tanzania, and Zambia. With the collapse of the Soviet Union, the political calculus changed, with the West now insisting on free market and democratic reforms as a condition for aid. In a 1993 referendum, two thirds of voters approved the end of the one-party system and a transition to multiparty democracy. In the 1994 election where voting was largely along ethnic and regional lines, Banda's Malawi Congress Party (MCP) was defeated. He died in South Africa three years later.

My airport acquaintance was exaggerating when he asserted that "we built the place." Other Western donors contributed to the new capital and its infrastructure but South Africa had a significant economic and political role in Malawi for more than 20 years. Poor countries have limited options and Banda, like other leaders, was simply taking aid where he could find it. When Malawi's legislators took their seats in a new parliament building in Lilongwe in 2010, they had the Chinese to thank for building the place.

What Happened to the National Airline?

In 2013, I got a call from Debbie Mesce at Population Reference Bureau, a USAID contractor in Washington, DC. Debbie's job was to work with journalists in Africa, Asia, and Latin America to improve their reporting on population issues. That also meant working with the universities and training institutes that prepare journalists for the profession. Debbie wanted to know if I was interested in designing and leading two workshops for the Malawi Institute of Journalism (MIJ) to train their teachers and

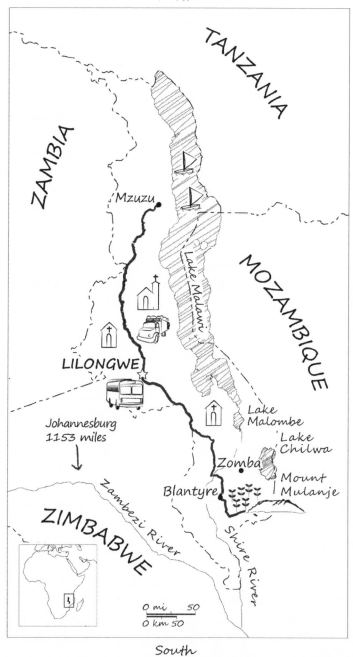

North

TANZANIA

ZAMBIA

MOZAMBIQUE

Mzuzu

Lake Malawi

LILONGWE

Johannesburg
1153 miles

Lake
Malombe

Lake
Chilwa

Zomba

Mount
Mulanje

Blantyre

Zambezi River

Shire River

ZIMBABWE

0 mi   50
0 km 50

South

develop classes on research and reporting on population and development issues.

Malawi. I'd never been there. I knew it was a former British colony and had a large lake, but not much more. I did not hesitate. "When do you need me there?" I asked. The timing for the first workshop was ideal. I was already scheduled to be in Johannesburg for three weeks in August as a member of a team conducting a workshop for UNICEF staff at the University of the Witwatersrand. I needed a few days after the workshop to wrap up business and then I could take the three-hour flight to Lilongwe.

Easier said than done. I tried to book the flight online but was stymied when I hit the "Book Flight Now" button on the Air Malawi website and nothing happened. When I contacted my liaison at MIJ, I learned that not only was the Air Malawi website down, but so was the whole airline. It had stopped flying a few months earlier because it could not pay its bills. There was talk that Ethiopian Airlines would take over, but no one knew what would happen. Fortunately, South African Airways had a daily flight to Lilongwe. When we landed, I half expected to see a row of grounded Air Malawi planes gathering dust on the tarmac but the only other aircraft were small private planes and an Ethiopian Airlines Boeing 737. "What happened to the Air Malawi planes?" I asked the taxi driver. "No one knows," he said. "They were flown to Johannesburg for maintenance, and never came back."

Lilongwe's airport, also built by South Africa in the 1970s, reminded me of Soviet-era airports in Central Asia with their faded signs, excessive use of plastic wall paneling and rough wooden tables. It was also just as slow getting through passport control. There were seven passport desks—for Assisted Passengers, Malawi Passports, Returning Residents, Other Passports, Diplomatic and International Organizations, SADC (Southern African Development Community) and African Union. With two flights arriving within a 30-minute period, long lines formed for the Malawi and Other Passports desks. After an hour of waiting, some of us broke ranks and pushed into Diplomatic and International Organizations. Still, it took at least five minutes to process each passenger—thumb and fingerprints for both hands, a photo and questions.

If he felt that the loss of the national airline was a blow to national prestige, my taxi driver didn't show it. Instead, he grumbled about the cost of petrol (about US $7 a gallon), and that fewer tourists were coming to Malawi (perhaps because it was difficult to get there). He had expected to make money the previous week when African heads of state and government delegations assembled in Lilongwe for the SADC summit hosted by President Joyce Banda, but most had been picked up in official cars. Not even low-level foreign bureaucrats, journalists and diplomatic hangers-on wanted to pay for taxis. How was he going to make the payments on his Nissan?

The future of Air Malawi was, so to speak, up in the air for a few months. Then, as had been rumored, Ethiopian Airlines stepped in to operate the airline, rebranded as Malawian Airlines, under a management contract. Ethiopian owns 49 percent of the company, so I guess Malawi can still claim it has a national airline.

Bantus and Slave Traders

With a territory of about 45,000 square miles, Malawi is a little smaller than the US State of Pennsylvania. It's 530 miles north to south but only 160 miles east to west at its widest point. In the north, a narrow wedge of land separates Tanzania and Zambia; in the south, the Shire Valley is squeezed between the Mozambique provinces of Tete and Zambezia. The southern section of the Great Rift Valley forms a deep trough in which the most prominent geographical feature, Lake Malawi, extends for more than two thirds of the length of the country. On the lake's western shore, the cliffs rise steeply to high plateaus.

For thousands of years, groups have crossed and recrossed the region, pushed by population or land pressures or conflict. From the fourteenth to the eighteenth centuries, waves of Bantu-speaking peoples migrated to the highlands and lake area; in the south the Chewa people (also known as the Maravi) established a powerful kingdom that extended into present-day Zambia and Mozambique. In the nineteenth century, Zulu groups migrated northwards, while the Yao from western Mozambique invaded the southern highlands. Arab slave traders from ports along the Indian Ocean coast pushed westward, enlisting the

Yao and other local tribes. The slaves were sold to wholesalers at trading centers on the west coast of Lake Malawi and shipped across the lake in *dhows*. From there, they were marched across Mozambique to the coast and transported to the slave market in Zanzibar. Many died from disease, dehydration or exhaustion on the long land and sea passages.

Although the Portuguese established trading links with tribes from the mid-sixteenth century, few ventured into the interior. It was not until the mid-nineteenth century that British explorers, bearing Bibles and trade goods, ventured up the Shire River, a tributary of the Zambezi, to the Lake Malawi region. As in other regions of Africa, religion and commerce went hand in hand.

"Dr. Livingstone, I Presume?"

All right, all right. Henry Morton Stanley's much-quoted greeting to the explorer in November 1871 did not take place in what today is Malawi, but further north near a town on the banks of Lake Tanganyika. David Livingstone had travelled there from Lake Malawi. At the time, there were no territorial borders, so at least I can claim that Livingstone was in the general vicinity when the famous phrase was uttered.

As a medical missionary, Livingstone believed that the best hope for spreading the gospel was to map and navigate Africa's river system and establish trade and religious missions in the interior. Other European explorers who traveled with soldiers and hired porters were regarded as invaders or mistaken for slave raiders. Livingstone traveled light with a few companions and porters, bartering for supplies along the way, and establishing relationships with local chiefs. In 1858, he led an expedition to explore the Zambezi River Basin. The passage upstream was blocked by the gorge and rapids of Cahora Bassa, so Livingstone changed his plans and with a few companions navigated the Shire River, a tributary of the Zambezi, into what today is southern Malawi. The expedition explored the two southernmost lakes—Chilwa and Malombe—before reaching the large lake which Livingstone named Lake Nyassa, a word probably derived from *nyanja*, which means lake in the language of the Chewa people. Livingstone learned of the slave raids by the

Yao and other tribes and became determined to draw attention to the traffic. His second expedition to the Shire River in 1861 ended with a two-month exploration of the western shore of Lake Nyassa.

Livingstone set out on his final expedition in 1866. Although still intent on establishing missions and trading posts and drawing attention to the slave trade, he was also seeking the holy grail of African explorers—the source of the River Nile. When reports reached Zanzibar in 1867 that he had been killed by slave traders, an expedition was dispatched to the Lake Nyassa region. Local chiefs reported that Livingstone had been seen traveling north. The *New York Herald* commissioned the journalist Stanley to lead a second expedition. When the men met, they were reportedly lost for words, and resorted to the formal behavior expected of British gentlemen, even when they were evidently the only white men for hundreds of miles around. To Stanley's question, "Dr. Livingstone, I presume," the explorer reportedly responded, "Yes—I feel thankful that I am here to welcome you." There is debate about the accuracy of the exchange because Stanley later tore the pages which recorded the encounter out of his diary. It probably does not matter what was said because the famous phrase is firmly entrenched in collective historical memory.

Livingstone refused Stanley's pleas to return to England with him and died two years later from malaria and dysentery. His fame and widely-publicized expeditions stirred interest in the region in British missionary circles. In 1875, Scottish missionaries built a mission at Cape Maclear on Lake Nyassa, which they named Livingstonia. To the south, in the Shire Highlands, other Scottish missionaries established a mission that they named Blantyre after Livingstone's birthplace, a mill town on the River Clyde, southeast of Glasgow. After several missionaries at Cape Maclear died of malaria, Livingstonia was relocated to the northern lakeshore and in 1894 to higher ground away from the lake. Meanwhile, Blantyre had grown into a thriving commercial community, and the missionaries had completed construction of the Church of St. Michael and All Angels, today a city landmark.

Traders followed the missionaries, disembarking at Indian Ocean ports, then travelling upstream on the Zambezi and Lower Shire and overland to Blantyre, or via the Upper Shire to Lake

Nyassa. The Livingstonia Central African Mission Company, established in 1878 and based in Blantyre, used small steamboats, and later Mississippi-style paddle steamers, to ferry goods and passengers to and from the coast. Within a few years, the company had dropped the word "mission" from its name and, as the African Lakes Corporation, developed a successful commercial network.

Although the maps drawn up at the Berlin Conference of 1884-1885 broadly designated "spheres of influence," the colonial powers knew that possession was nine-tenths of the law. In 1889, to ward off rival land claims from Portugal and Germany, Britain established a protectorate in the Shire highlands, and extended it two years later to include most of the western shore of Lake Nyassa; in 1907, the territory became the colony of Nyasaland. The missionaries had blazed the trail, and the traders and colonial administrators were not far behind.

The Good Friday Coup

I'm never sure whether it's a political advantage to have the same last name as a former president who is not related to you. I suppose it gives you undeserved name recognition at election time, but at the same time you may be blamed for your namesake's record in office. Either way, Joyce Banda, who served as president from 2012 to 2014, was not related to the authoritarian Hastings Banda who ruled the country for 30 years.

Joyce Banda had been elected vice president in 2009 on the ticket of the Democratic Progressive Party (DPP), led by Bingu wa Mutharika, who served as president from 2004 to 2012. Mutharika made food security his top priority and agricultural production increased, aided by government subsidies for seed and fertilizer; he undertook fiscal reforms and campaigned against corruption. However, in 2011, rising prices, unemployment and fuel shortages led to nationwide protests and at least 18 deaths. Mutharika responded by taking a page from the Hastings Banda playbook, cracking down on the press and human rights activists. He broke with his vice president, firing her from her position in the DPP when she refused to accept the nomination of his younger brother, Peter, the Foreign Minister, as the party's nominee in the 2014 election. The courts blocked attempts to dismiss her as vice president because she had been elected with Mutharika in 2009. Banda founded a new party, the People's Party. Although no longer a member of the DPP, under the constitution she remained the legal vice president.

As the country prepared for the Easter holiday in 2012, the 78-year-old president seemed in good health. His sudden collapse and death from a heart attack at his residence on April 5 threw his ministers and the DPP into a panic. Under the constitution, the vice president, the politically marginalized Joyce Banda, would succeed him. How could they prevent this and install his brother Peter instead?

If the stakes had not been so high, what followed would have had all the elements of political farce. The DPP decided not to release news of the president's death until it had ensured his brother's succession. It was announced that the president was in "critical" condition and was being flown to Johannesburg for medical treatment. At first, the South African pilot refused to fly when he discovered that his "sick" passenger was, in fact, a corpse, but consented after receiving orders from his superiors, under pressure from the South African government. The next day, Good Friday, ministers went on national TV to announce that the president was undergoing treatment and that Banda had no authority to act as president.

Banda gained the support of the head of the armed forces. Major donors, including the US and UK, had previously suspended aid because of Mutharika's erratic economic policies and human rights record; the cut-off had contributed to a collapse of Malawi's foreign currency reserves, leading to shortages of food, fuel, and medicines. The donors rallied behind Banda. About one third of the DPP's 147 MPs, seeing the way the wind was blowing, pledged their support. Banda was sworn in as president on Saturday afternoon. The Good Friday coup had failed.[2]

Cashgate and the Accidental President

On my first trip to Malawi, Joyce Banda seemed to be everywhere. Her photograph adorned the walls of offices, shops, and

2. "The Good Friday coup that wasn't," *The Economist*, May 1, 2012.

hotel reception desks. As Malawi's first woman president, and a former business owner and grassroots women's rights activist, she was well regarded in the West; in 2014, *Forbes* named her as the 40th most powerful woman in the world and the most powerful woman in Africa. At home, she projected a kinder, gentler political face than her predecessor, Mutharika, who had promised to "smoke out" his enemies, expelled the British High Commissioner, and told donors to "go to hell." By contrast, the bespectacled, respectably overweight Banda looked positively maternal and approachable. A billboard advertised: "Send an SMS and Win the Prize of Dinner with Dr. Joyce Banda."

Banda's presidency got off to a promising start. She restored relationships with major donors and, on the advice of the IMF, devalued the *kwacha*, a move that led to inflation. In a symbolic move, she sold the presidential jet and fleet of luxury cars, reportedly to pay off a government debt to a South African arms company. The undocumented transaction was soon overshadowed by "Cashgate," a wide-ranging corruption scandal. It's estimated that corrupt officials, businessmen and politicians plundered at least US $30 million from the treasury. Banda was not directly implicated; she fired ministers, had some arrested, and froze bank accounts. But Cashgate tarnished the reputation of her administration and the donors were appalled. The UK, Malawi's largest donor, the European Union and Norway suspended aid totaling more than US $150 million a year, leaving a big hole in a government budget where aid normally accounts for 30-35 percent of revenue.

In the 2014 presidential election, Banda came in a disappointing third to the DPP candidate, the former president's brother, Peter Mutharika. Although Cashgate and the devaluation of the *kwacha* hurt her prospects, for many voters, food was the main issue.[3] My workshop colleague Sandra Mapemba told me that some rural voters mistakenly associated the symbol of Hastings Banda's MCP—a black cockerel—with Joyce Banda. In speeches and posters, the party of the cock had crowed that it would eat up the maize, the symbol of the DPP. Rural voters said they were

---

3. "Malawi's new president: An end to uncertainty (but only that)," *The Economist,* June 2, 2014.

hungry and wanted to keep their maize. Joyce Banda was out.

Land of Lakes but not Enough Food

Malawi's greatest natural resource and major tourist attraction is also a barrier to development. Lake Malawi (formerly Lake Nyassa), the third largest lake in Africa, together with two smaller lakes, Chilwa and Malombe, constitutes 20 percent of the country's total land area. This puts Malawi in a league with some low-lying coastal nations; indeed, it's the world leader of landlocked nations for water as a percentage of total territory. That's good news for the fishing industry, as long as the stocks of *chambo*, a staple source of protein in the diet, last. The more serious problem is the number of people trying to get by on the other 80 percent of the land area. Malawi has an estimated population of more than 19 million, one million more than its neighbor, Zambia, which is six times its size.

Because about 85 percent of Malawi's population live in rural areas, the pressure on land and resources is intense. Agriculture accounts for 80 percent of exports but contributes only one third of GDP. Most of the population are subsistence farmers, growing maize, beans, rice, cassava, and peanuts for their families, and selling their surplus locally at harvest time. Although agriculture accounts for most of Malawi's foreign exchange earnings, most exports come from commercial farms. Demand for Malawi's leading export, tobacco, has been declining, and other commodities—sugar, tea, coffee, and cotton—have not made up for the shortfall.

In a continent of high fertility rates, Malawi is near the top of the league with many rural families having five or six children. Gender inequality, cultural practices, high illiteracy rates and limited access to family planning all contribute to the increase of population. At the current annual growth rate of 2.75 percent, the population is expected to reach 29 million by 2030 and 45 million by 2050. Rapid population growth has long concerned the government and foreign donors. How can development be sustainable when demand for food, water, electricity, health services, jobs and education is increasing every year? The country's only safety valve is migration. Thousands of Malawians work outside the country—the largest number in South Africa—as laborers, gardeners, cleaners, cooks, and maids, sending remittances home.

Debbie told me that Population Reference Bureau was concerned about media coverage of population and related issues, such as health, education, and the environment. Malawi's print and electronic media tend to focus on politics, sports, and entertainment. When demographic or social issues are covered, research is often inadequate, and the reporting sensationalized. Because MIJ (which everyone calls "mij," pronounced like the small insect) was the leading training organization for journalists, the goal of my workshops was to integrate research and reporting on population issues into the curriculum. This involved critically examining sources and statistics, not taking what the government or international and development organizations said at face value, asking the right questions of the right people, and making abstract concepts meaningful to the audience.

The Supermarket Survey

Malawi's perennial shortage of foreign exchange makes it difficult to pay for imports of fuel, manufactured goods, and some food items. The airport taxi driver's gripe about the cost of petrol is a common complaint, and fuel prices and shortages hamper transportation and economic output. The government has been slow to address infrastructure—building roads, providing electricity to rural areas, and improving telecommunications. All these are barriers to foreign investment. Despite being an agricultural exporter, Malawi cannot feed its population year-round. Every year, in the so-called "hunger season" (from January to March), when the surplus from harvests has gone, food aid from foreign donors is needed.

The internationally accepted ways of measuring the economic health of a country—Gross Domestic Product (GDP) or Gross National Income (GNI) per person, factoring in Purchasing Power Parity (PPP), and so on—only tell you so much. I've found that wandering around a supermarket or convenience store and seeing what's on the shelves is a useful guide. My not-so-statistical sample was conducted at the Foodzone Hyperstore Bakery and Butchery near the Crossroads Hotel in Lilongwe, the petrol station near the roundabout on the country's main north-south road, and the City Supermarket, on the other side of the roundabout; I did not have time to check the 7-Eleven, which closed at 9:00 p.m. because of lack of business.

The stores offered a limited assortment of bulk foods, including sacks of maize, meat, fruit and vegetables, soups, spices, and canned goods. The most prominently displayed items were cookies, candies, and juice blends. Food is only part of the inventory, even in the smallest stores. At least half the shelves are taken up by non-food items from cooking pots and light bulbs to clothes, children's toys and even—in the Foodzone Hyperstore (large in name only—it was about the size of a large convenience store)—bicycles. Items come and go as supplies arrive. On the evening when I checked, the only fish in the City Supermarket was mackerel from Mozambique. The popular Lake Malawi *chambo* was not available. In what proved to be a vain search for my favorite soda, ginger beer, I checked the "Everything from the UK" store next door which encouraged customers to "localize their UK shopping." No ginger beer. And, to be honest, not much from the UK either, despite pound sterling signs on the packaging. I flipped over a portable barbecue and plastic storage containers to see that they were "Made in China." Considering that China is now one of Malawi's largest foreign donors, building hospitals, schools, the parliament and even the football stadium in Lilongwe, I figured it was appropriate that Chinese companies would gain market share in the retail sector, even if they had to ship their products via the UK to make the sale.

Incredible Miracles and Supernatural Breakthroughs

It was Sunday morning in Lilongwe, and I had the day off. I decided to wander around the Old City, with its hole-in-the-wall shops, markets, and bus stations. Compared with other days of the week, the traffic was light, few people were out on the streets and most businesses were shuttered. I found one café open. "Where is everyone?" I asked the waiter. "They should all be in church," he replied solemnly, as if he was committing a sin by serving me a cappuccino.

According to the census, two out of three Malawians claim to be Christian. About 20 percent of these are Catholic, with the rest scattered among the mainstream Protestant groups (Anglicans, Baptists, Lutherans, Methodists, and Presbyterians) and smaller indigenous denominations. Muslims, who make up about one quarter of the population, are concentrated in the north and around Lake Malawi. They include descendants of the Swahili-Arab slave traders, and the Yao people who were enlisted to help in the slave trade. Some businesses are owned by Indian immigrants, so there's the occasional Hindu temple among the churches and mosques.

Malawi's national newspapers feature stories about religion every day, although most concern business matters—the doings of dioceses and synods and the comings and goings of priests, pastors, and bishops—and social programs, rather than religious doctrine. On my second visit, after Joyce Banda's 2014 election defeat, the major story was the church wedding of the 74-year-old president, Peter Mutharika, to his longtime partner Gertrude Maseko, 20 years his junior. *The Nation* ran a two-page color spread of wedding pictures. A *Sunday Times* editorial congratulated the newlyweds. "The first family will provide a good example to all Malawians to respect their marriages since respectable families make a dignified society." No comment on the couple's previous, unsanctified relationship.

Christianity in Malawi has a revivalist fringe. In storefront churches, roadside shacks with rough painted crosses, the music is loud and the sermons fiery—religion at its rawest, and perhaps most inspiring. Welcome to the "Mountain Fire Church of Miracles," the "Faith in God Church—Home of the Incredible Miracle" and the "Winners Church—The Home of the Supernatural Breakthrough." The Centre for Social Research (CSR) at the University of Malawi sent its post-graduate students to Sunday services around the country to collect data. They came up with a probably conservative estimate of at least 110 denominations. The indigenous ones have inspirational names such as the All for Jesus Church, Enlightened Christian Gathering,

Forward in Faith Church, Glory Zone Ministry, Step to Jesus Church and the Evangelistic New Exodus Church of God and Mission, which I assume is a breakaway from the original New Exodus Church of God and Mission. At least a dozen, such as the Charismatic Redeemed Ministries International, the Glorious Ministry International Church and Peace with God Worldwide International, have the word "international" in their titles but no website, suggesting that they are still stuck in storefronts and have yet to reach more than a few hundred souls.

Christian doctrine is mixed with traditional beliefs drawn from animism and witchcraft. Illnesses are sometimes ascribed to spells and curses, and traditional remedies are prescribed—herbal medicines administered by a healer, often accompanied by chants and dances. Ancestors play an important role, protecting a family or tribe, blessing them with a good harvest or cursing them with sickness or poverty.

Religion permeates every area of life, including the retail sector. Many of the small, hole-in-the-wall businesses along the highways sport religious slogans: "God is Wonderful Restaurant and Takeaway," the "Praise God Shop," the "God is Good Shop." These offset the more secular and whimsical business names— the "Whatever Restaurant and Takeaway" (presumably featuring whatever is on the menu today), "Al Pacino's Bar and Restaurant," the "No Fear Shop," the "No Black Out Barber Shop" (an allusion to the frequent and unpredictable power cuts), the politically progressive "Good Governance Coffin Services" and the baffling "Difficult to Understand Shopping Centre."

In Malawi, divine power is not only spiritual. It is measured in volts and amps. The sign on an auto repair shop informed customers exactly who was responsible for keeping vehicles on the road. "Thank You Jesus, Battery Charge."

The Key to Lilongwe

I knew I might have a problem when I first opened the safe in my room at the Crossroads Hotel in Lilongwe and the four AA batteries powering the unit fell out, a couple rolling under the bed. The broken plastic cover to the battery compartment had

40

been taped, but it was a dodgy fix; I had to keep reattaching it, using valuable inches of Scotch tape that I had brought for the workshop. One night the batteries fell out inside the safe and it remained locked, my passport, credit cards and cash inside. The next morning the duty manager and his assistant arrived, jangling along the corridor with bunches of keys. After 10 minutes, they admitted defeat and went back for more keys. None of them worked so they called the maintenance man. He banged on the safe and concluded that more keys were needed. He made two trips, bringing—as far as I could tell—all the 100-plus room safe keys for the hotel. I was about to despair (he was down to the last half dozen) when one of them worked. The crowd (by this time, he had been joined by the duty manager, his assistant, and several housekeeping staff) applauded loudly, and he beamed in triumph. An investigation concluded that the safe in room 71 was, in fact, the safe for room 54; someone had switched them, but there was no record. There was also no master key and no number on the safe. If there had been, we might all have saved a lot of time.

I've learned over many years of travel to keep smiling and go with the flow. That's assuming there *is* a flow. The Crossroads is officially rated as a four-star hotel, yet one morning there was no hot water, and the next morning no water at all. A couple of days later, I was about to shampoo my hair when the water shut off, saving me from appearing at breakfast with a head of lather. There were power cuts, although the hotel generator usually kicked in after a few minutes. The restaurant menu warned that some "items may not be available because of lack of supply." The most reliable things were the lovely weather (high 70s to low 80s, sunny and dry), the locally brewed Carlsberg beer (I learned to say, with studied nonchalance, "Give me a green") and, rather surprisingly, the Wi-Fi.

Lilongwe, which sprawls over the lowland area between Lake Malawi and the Zambian border, is the fastest-growing urban area in the country. The 2018 census put its population at close to one million, up by one third in the past decade. On the day before the workshop, I hung out at the N1 café (slogan—Eat, Drink, Free WiFi, Be Happy) on Robert Mugabe Crescent, just off the central square in the New City, watching the world go by. Young men wandered around, selling used clothes, bananas, bicycle tires and car mobile phone chargers. A few street vendors spread out tarpaulins with fruits and vegetables. Three soldiers with semiautomatic rifles squatted under a tree, smoking and chatting with passersby. They were not guarding a bank or public building, so their assignment wasn't clear. Back at the N1, I was waiting for the copy shop to complete my course packets. At most places, running off 20 copies of a 75-page packet and putting on spiral binders is a 30-minute job. In Lilongwe's business district, it took 3 ½ hours, although staff members periodically wandered over to my table to assure me that the job was going along very well indeed.

At least I wasn't at the bank, where Sandra and Debbie were waiting in line to withdraw cash for the participants' travel and per diem. I had called about half an hour after they dropped me off. "We're number 250 in line, and they just started serving customer 195," Debbie gloomily reported. Banking transactions are time-consuming because of the number of steps and signatures required for each deposit and withdrawal. At the end of the month, when people receive salaries and pay bills, the lines are long. Even counting money takes time. The most common denomination is the 1,000 *kwacha* bill, worth about US $2.50. If there are 2,000 or 5,000 *kwacha* bills, I haven't seen them. If you withdraw $100, that's 40 bills to count. When Debbie and Sandra arrived to pick me up, their briefcase was literally stuffed with wads of banknotes.

The Bus to Blantyre

"Mobile number for next of kin?" asked the sales agent at the bus company office in Lilongwe. "I don't understand," I said, thinking I had misheard the question. "Next—of—kin—mobile—number," the agent repeated slowly and loudly enough for the street vendors outside the office to hear. "Oh, that's my wife, Stephanie, in the United States, her number is …" The agent interrupted. "No, you didn't understand. Next of kin in Malawi," she said, her pen poised to record the information on the passenger list. I was obviously presenting a challenge to the AXA bus line passenger database, not to mention holding up the ticket line. I quickly weighed my options. A quickie marriage of convenience to one of those street vendors, then a faster divorce after obtaining her mobile number? No, Stephanie would not appreciate it, even if she understood the practical reality. I decided to stand firm. I handed over the 7,000 *kwacha* (US $18). "Just give me the ticket, please," I said politely but firmly. The agent grumbled, scribbled my name on her sheet and the ticket, and handed it over.

Asking passengers for next-of-kin contact information does not exactly instill confidence in a bus company's safety record, but I was never able to learn whether this was a legal requirement or company policy. What I was told was that AXA and another company, National, ran the fastest, most comfortable buses on the 250-mile route between Lilongwe and Blantyre, the commercial capital in the south. And that they had the best safety records. I don't want to speculate what personal questions the other companies ask. Still, the 4 ½ hour AXA trip the next morning began with instructions to all passengers to fasten their seat belts. Then the bus attendant came on the PA system. "We thank the Lord for the gift of life. Thank you for choosing AXA." The driver started the engine. "Thank you Jesus, battery charge," I mumbled to myself.

For those who have traveled in sub-Saharan Africa, the view from the bus on the two-lane highway would be familiar—a dry, flat landscape of scrub grass and small trees, broken by cultivated fields, with goats and cattle wandering dangerously close to the road and groups of men squatting under trees. We passed roadside stalls covered with sheets or tarpaulins for shade, selling fruits, vegetables, household goods and auto parts, and piles of bricks and crushed stone for construction. For commercial freight, "pile it high" is the rule; overloaded, top-heavy trucks leant dangerously to one side but fortunately, there are few curves in the road. The minibuses that make the short-haul trips between towns were packed with passengers and luggage. Young men rode bicycles or pushed them, with large bundles of firewood tied to the frame. Women carried baskets and tubs on their heads, their babies and small children tightly wrapped in bundles on their backs. Older children in uniforms walked to and from school. Malawi's main north-south highway seemed to draw all human activities onto its narrow ribbon.

Most villages consisted of small round huts of mud bricks with thatched roofs and a store built of brick or concrete. Commercial businesses, such as supermarkets and convenience stores, offered a range of products and services—the Abitu Resthouse and Hangover Clinic, Maj Hal Investments Food and Cosmetics Paradise, Yankho Fashion and Pest Control. Government billboards promoted growth, health, and civic responsibility—"Malawi—Your Investment Destination," "Wash Your Hands With Soap After Using a Latrine," "Pay Parking Fees to Improve City Roads."

Of course, much of the retail sector does not have (or need) signs. Almost everything is sold along the highways: building materials (lumber, thatching material, rough bricks fired in small kilns), tires and auto parts, living room furniture, baskets, brooms, pots and pans, firewood (from eucalyptus trees), live chickens, goats, maize, grains and seasonal fruits and vegetables—in August, bananas, tangerines, tomatoes, cassava, sweet potatoes and potatoes. The staple food is white-kernel maize, ground and cooked into white cakes called *nsima*, with a tomato-based sauce providing flavor. It's a basic food found throughout southern Africa and eaten by people of all races; in South Africa, *pap* (maize porridge) is a breakfast favorite for Afrikaners. The government is concerned that the country is over-dependent on maize and that a poor harvest will result in food shortages. It wants farmers to diversify and grow more rice and "Irish potatoes." Having Malawians change their eating habits is a challenge because *nsima* is eaten every day but the potato appears to be making inroads. Chips (fries) are on the menu at most restaurants, often in lead position, as in "Chips and chicken" and "Chips and curry."

The bus passengers who were not sleeping were watching an eclectic series of music videos on the monitor. The slickly produced ones with rap artists and scantily clothed women were from Nollywood (Nigeria's movie industry). They alternated with locally produced videos of fully clothed church choirs swaying to the religious beat in tropical locations with cutaways of ministers in white suits preaching up a storm and scenes pirated from Hollywood religious epics. The contrast—in both the amount of

44

exposed skin and social message—was striking. Homely-looking women in matching purple outfits in synchronized routines. Then sultry temptresses wrapping their body parts around rap artists or, in one video, raising automobile hoods, stretching and sweating over the engine blocks, and suggestively wielding wrenches and socket sets. Oh, excuse me, Miss, after you've finished salivating over those pumping cylinders, would you mind checking the radiator level?

Early Closing in Blantyre

I spent three pleasant days in Blantyre, preparing for the workshop, and meeting with editors and reporters and MIJ staff at the Polytechnic of Malawi campus. In colonial times, the city was separated into two sections. Most of the dirty stuff (industry and warehouses) was in Blantyre, while the Europeans who managed the enterprises lived in a separate, upscale quarter called Limbe. For half a century, the boundary between Blantyre and Limbe has been blurring; today it is a single metropolitan area, stretching for about 10 miles, with a population of almost one million.

Blantyre remains a commercial hub, but its factories and slaughterhouses have been pushed out to the fringes, leaving the downtown area for banks, shops, hotels, and markets. Many urban businesses—especially the supermarkets, clothing and electronics stores—are owned by Indians or other Asians. One colleague told me that Nigerians are the up-and-coming entrepreneurs. "They can offer lower prices because of collective buying," he said. "Meanwhile, each Malawian wants his own business and does not want to cooperate. They all end up on the same flight to Johannesburg shopping for their own stores." Perhaps they would do better business by opening for more hours. Although Blantyre is the commercial capital, most businesses close at 5:00 or 6:00 p.m. from Monday to Saturday and all day on Sunday. It was a challenge to find a restaurant open in the evenings.

Photocopying services were no better than in Lilongwe. MIJ recommended a copy shop for the workshop packets, but Debbie and I pulled the job because it was taking too long (an endless series of missed pages and paper jams). The second copy shop was open for business but none of its machines was working (which made me wonder why it was open at all). Eventually we found one with a working copy machine and feed tray, but the job still took almost four hours. Fortunately, we did not need editing services from an establishment that advertised "tonner cartilages."

Mount Mulanje

On Sunday afternoon, we drove southeast towards the Mozambique border. The Shire Highlands are Malawi's premier tea-growing region and, on both sides of the road from Blantyre, neat rows of vivid green tea bushes cover the low hills. Tea picking is labor intensive, with workers paid by the weight of leaves in their baskets at the end of a shift. The leaves are transported to factories where they are trimmed, dried, and packed in bags and boxes, mostly for export.

The workshop was held in the town of Mulanje, in the shadow of the Mulanje Massif, a high plateau area with peaks rising to more than 7,000 feet, including Chambe Peak, whose west face is the longest rock climb in Africa. It's surrounded by escarpments and near-vertical cliffs of bare rock, from which streams cascade into waterfalls. Much of the Massif consists of rolling grassland, intersected by deep forested ravines. It's popular with hikers and trekkers, with shelters and huts on the trails. The weather is notoriously unpredictable; even in the dry season, hikers face rain and cold winds and risk wandering off the trail in the mist. Between May and August, periods of low cloud and drizzle can last for days and temperatures drop below freezing.

We checked into the Hapuwani Village Lodge, a small resort hotel that offered splendid views of the Massif without any of its dangers and inconveniences. The lodge was a new facility and had spared no expense to help guests figure out the assorted remote control devices in the rooms. One read, "Dear Guest—The remote control to your air conditioner is in Chinese. You may find this convenient for you." I suppose you need to know both English and Chinese to efficiently use the AC. The hotel was still waiting for a diesel generator to be delivered to provide back-up power. However, everyone in Malawi is accustomed to power cuts; when the lights went out and the video projector went dark, almost no one commented. Power was almost always restored by early evening when Debbie and I headed over to the small bar for a couple of "greens," then ate at the small restaurant where *chambo* was available most days. "Is it grilled?" I asked the server the first night. She looked puzzled, probably because of my accent, so I repeated the question. "Yes, killed and grilled," she replied.

Onward Christian Soldiers

The evening before the workshop began, Debbie and I walked through the garden behind the hotel into the neat rows of tea bushes. The scenery was spectacular—fields of lush green plants, with the sheer slopes of the Massif rising to the south, the sun setting in the west. On the edge of the plantation, a group of teenagers, dressed like Soviet young pioneers or scouts in white shirts with orange kerchiefs, was marching up and down the dirt yard in front of the Seventh Day Adventist Church to a tape loop of "Onward Christian Soldiers." The youth leader barked orders through a microphone, presumably about pace, posture and spreading the gospel. Spotting two potential *mazungu* (white person) converts looking on, he hurried over to invite us to join the parade or participate in a service. We had a pleasant chat, told him that his troop of Christian soldiers looked smart and well drilled, and said we had a tea plantation to explore.

The scene made me think about Livingstone, the nineteenth century missionaries and the lasting impact religion has made on almost every aspect of life in Malawi. The next morning, the workshop opened with a prayer, the sole Muslim in the group gamely mumbling along. And when one of the participants hit the bar at the end of the day and ordered a glass of sweet South African red, he joked that he was drinking "church wine."

Five days later at breakfast, MIJ instructor Gabriel Nyirenda looked me straight in the eye and asked the question I sensed he had wanted to ask all week: "Are you a believer?" I was not surprised by the question. I had told the participants they could ask me anything they wanted, but they had been polite enough to stay away from politics and religion during the week. With the workshop now over, Gabriel had his opening.

*Onward Christian soldiers—marching as to war in the tea
plantations below Mount Mulanje.*

I could have answered Gabriel's question by talking about
my disillusionment with organized religion, but we were not
there to debate doctrine, and I did not want to make this smart,
sincere young man feel uncomfortable. I said something about a
general belief in a moral power in the universe (a quick-and-easy
Deism), offered that most Buddhists I'd met seemed to have a
pretty good outlook on life, and then asked him about his faith.
Gabriel is from Mzuzu, the main city in the north of Malawi,
and, like his parents and many of his friends, is a Catholic. He
said he had friends from other denominations—Presbyterians,
Anglicans, Assemblies of God, Pentecostal. At one time, he said,
politicians in Malawi had tried to use religion to divide the
people, but they had been discredited. Most of the time, he said,
the religious groups co-existed peacefully.

Hail to the Chiefs

After we had exhausted the topic of religion, I asked Gabriel
about another traditional power bloc in Malawi—the tribes.

When the British arrived, they made alliances with the chiefs, allowing them limited authority in their traditional homelands while providing them with income and status in the colony. The largest tribal group is the Chewa (whose language is used all over the country), followed by the Yao in the south and the Tumbuku (Gabriel's tribe) in the north, but there are many others, each with its own traditions and language. What developed was a kind of parallel governance system, with the civil administration and courts operating alongside the chiefs and traditional justice. You can't call the police or file a civil case in court for every misdemeanor, so the chiefs have the authority to dispense justice, fining villagers a chicken or a goat, depending on the severity of the offence. The chiefs are now on the government payroll with a guaranteed salary and are subject to official scrutiny; I had read several newspaper stories about chiefs being hauled into court for skimming and scamming or using their office to sell sub-chief posts (and taking a cut on the new sub-chief's salary).

I'd jokingly asked Edward Chitsulo of *The Nation*, a wise and witty senior journalist and one of the founders of MIJ, how I could become a chief. "Oh, you are already a chief to us," he answered diplomatically. "No," I said, "I mean a real chief or at least a sub-chief." Edward said he'd check the going rate in *kwacha*.

Chapter 4

The Road from Dar

★ ★ ★

The view from the top deck of the SS Universe Explorer on a sunny morning in early March took my breath away. Dar es Salaam's harbor was full of single and double-mast *dhows*, the traditional trading vessels of the Arabian Sea and East African coast. With their sails billowing in the breeze, their long thin hulls seemed to slice through the gentle waves. The smaller *dhows* carried merchandise and passengers to villages and islands along the coast. The larger vessels were likely bound for ports up and down the coast of Tanzania and Kenya, and for the archipelago of Zanzibar, 100 miles to the north.

My wife, Stephanie, and I were halfway through the University of Pittsburgh's Semester at Sea program, a round-the-world voyage that took us (and more than 600 students, faculty and staff) to the Bahamas, Cuba, Brazil, South Africa, Tanzania, India, Japan, South Korea and Alaska (visits to Vietnam and China were cancelled because of the SARS epidemic). I was assigned to accompany a busload of 70 students to Arusha in northern Tanzania, where they would join a group of parents for a five-day safari in the Ngorongoro Crater and the Serengeti.

Dar es Salaam (usually abbreviated as Dar) was not on the original itinerary. The Universe Explorer was scheduled to dock at Mombasa, Kenya's main commercial port, but the destination was changed after terrorists blew up an Israeli-owned hotel in November 2002, killing 13 people and injuring 80. Western governments advised their citizens not to travel in Kenya, so the ship had to change course. Its Swedish captain, Anders Andersson, ruled out a nighttime arrival at Dar. The route into the port, he informed us, passed several islands and the Msimbazi river estuary, making navigation tricky. We picked up a pilot early in the morning and docked at the commercial cargo terminal, alongside grubby freighters registered in Liberia and Panama. Unlike our previous ports of call—Nassau, Havana, Salvador (Brazil) and Cape Town—Dar did not have a cruise ship terminal. It was not a tourist destination.

The East African Slave Trade

For almost two centuries, the dominant economic power in East Africa was a small island state. The Arab merchants of the Zanzibar archipelago grew wealthy trading ivory from the mainland and spices—cloves, nutmeg, cinnamon, and black pepper—grown on the islands. Their *dhows* sailed along the coast, north to the Horn of Africa and the Arabian peninsula, and east to India. They brought Islam and the Swahili (which means "of the coast") language, which spread into the interior. Traders enlisted tribes such as the Yao to capture slaves and march them to the coast. Historians estimate that during the nineteenth century slaves made up at least two thirds of Zanzibar's population; on its mainland plantations, as many as nine out of ten laborers were slaves.

In 1865, Zanzibar's Sultan Majid bin Said began building a new city in a natural harbor on the coast. He named it Dar es Salaam, which in Arabic means "house of peace." Today, the name sounds hypocritical, given the Sultan's appalling record for human trafficking, although the port never became a hub in the slave trade. In 1873, under the threat of a British naval blockade, Majid's successor signed a treaty that abolished the slave trade in the sultan's territories, closed all slave markets and protected liberated slaves.

At the Berlin Conference, Britain and Germany divided East Africa into spheres of influence—the British in present-day Kenya and Uganda, the Germans in Tanganyika and Zanzibar. In 1887, the German East Africa Company established a trading station at Dar and made the town the administrative and commercial center of the colony. Colonial geopolitics meant little to the peoples of the region, most of whom lived in small villages. The political borders of Kenya and Tanganyika were illusory for the nomadic Maasai, who grazed their herds of cattle across vast stretches of grassland. From time to time, German census-takers showed up and attempted to count the Maasai. They reckoned, probably correctly, that if they and their cattle were counted they would also be taxed, so they wandered off into the bush until the officials gave up and headed back to Dar.

In 1905, the German colonial government launched an ambitious project to develop the economy by building the Central Line (*Mittellandbahn*) railroad. From Dar, the line ran almost 800 miles west, reaching Lake Tanganyika in 1914, just before the outbreak of World War One. The railroad spurred agricultural and economic development, turning Dar into a major port and industrial center. Defeat in World War One ended German control, and Tanganyika and Zanzibar were ceded to Britain under a League of Nations mandate. Dar continued to grow, with migrants from British India arriving to work on the plantations and in commerce.

Tanzania—the combined State of Tanganyika and Zanzibar—became independent in 1961, and for the next decade and a half experimented with socialism under its first leader, Julius Nyerere, whose political ideology was an eclectic mix of Marxism and Biblical teachings. Nyerere, celebrated as one of the leaders of the pan-African movement, was more successful on the world stage than at home, where state control strangled growth, agricultural output declined, and state enterprises were robbed by their managers. The socialist state deteriorated into a one-party, authoritarian regime. After Nyerere left office in 1985, successive governments privatized state enterprises and liberalized the economy. Yet Tanzania remains one of the poorest countries in the world, with most of its population engaged in subsistence farming. Nation-building is a huge challenge in a country with almost 170 tribes or ethnic groups. In 1996, in an attempt to unite the country, Tanzania moved its capital from Dar to the inland city of Dodoma.

North

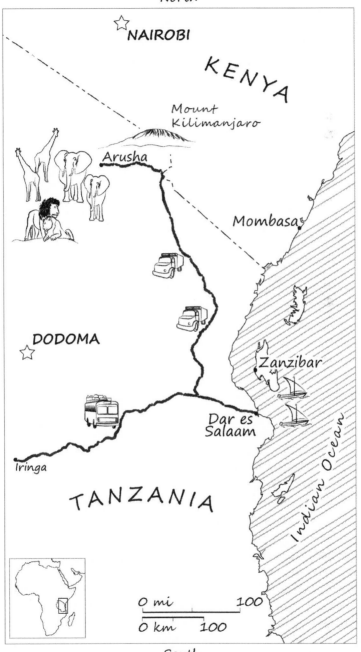

NAIROBI

KENYA

Mount
Kilimanjaro

Arusha

Mombasa

DODOMA

Zanzibar

Dar es
Salaam

Iringa

TANZANIA

Indian Ocean

0 mi   100

0 km   100

South

The Road to Arusha

Dar, with a population of more than six million, is Tanzania's largest city (and the seventh largest in Africa), a center of education, arts and culture and the major driver of the economy. Its population is an ethnic mix, with Arabs, Indians, Pakistanis, and Europeans prominent in the commercial sector. It has a predictable high-rise downtown skyline, but most of the sprawling, noisy and colorful city is distinctly low-rise—markets, roadsides lined with stores, bars, restaurants, auto repair shops, and small lumber yards turning out household furniture and, ominously, coffins.

The road to Arusha—a crossroads city on the main route to Nairobi and the jumping-off point for most safaris—runs northwest from Dar through sandy brush country. It's heavily traveled, with trucks from Kenya and Uganda heading for the coast. Although the surface is well maintained, it is a two-lane most of the way; despite frequent speed bumps, crashes are common. The bus drivers seem to have developed an elaborate system of hand signals to warn each other of dangers ahead—one sign for a speed trap, another for a goat crossing. The danger is increased by the number of people on the road, on foot or on bicycle, carrying produce, firewood, building materials, farm tools. Accidents involving pedestrians are common at night, even in the towns where many streets are unlit. For women, the go-anywhere-hold-anything five-gallon plastic bucket (in blue, red, yellow or black) seems to have replaced the traditional basket or pitcher as the vessel of choice to carry on their heads.

In East Africa, most people travel long distances in a minibus, a shared public taxi with a fixed route. The generic term in English-speaking African countries, even for minibuses that operate on urban routes, is "bush taxi"; in former French colonies, it's a literal translation, the *taxi-brousse*. Similar species exist in most developing countries. In Turkey, it's called a *dolmus*, in Bangladesh, a *coaster*, in the Philippines, a *jeepney*, in South America, a *colectivo*, in Central Asia, a *marshrutka*. In Tanzania, it's called a *dala dala*, the name reportedly derived from the slang term for five Tanzanian shillings ("dala" for dollar), which was the bus fare in the 1970s and 1980s when these vehicles started operating. In Kenya, it's called a *matatu*. The name derives from a Swahili colloquialism meaning "three." One explanation is that the first minibuses used were fitted with three rows of bench seats, another that three coins were a typical fare in the 1960s. Several people told me, with a nod and a wink, that in Swahili *matatu* means "there's always room for three more." My colleague Andrew Carlson, who served in the Peace Corps in Tanzania, remembers his astonishment at how drivers filled their vehicles beyond any sensible load capacity. On one trip from his station in the Iringa region to Dar, he hitched a ride on the back of a pickup truck that passed a *dala dala*. "It was piled high with stuff. People had luggage inside, and the luggage rack was stacked with water barrels and sacks of corn. And, amazingly, on top of all that stuff on the rack they had tied a goat. It was just standing up there, swaying back and forth."

Most rural families in Tanzania survive on what they grow—maize (corn), beans, sweet potatoes, bananas—and have a few goats, cattle, and chickens. Because of the tropical climate, farmers plant two crops a year; as we traveled northwest, fields were being burned in preparation for planting and the rains, due to start at the end of March and to last until May. Most cash crops—tea, coffee, cashew nuts and sisal (which looks like a giant yucca plant or an upside down pineapple)—are grown at higher altitudes on commercial farms and have a single growing season.

For about the first 30 miles beyond Dar, most houses were built of block with tin roofs. As we travelled inland, traditional materials became more common—mud bricks and straw, with roofs thatched from coconut leaves. Except for commercial businesses, few houses had electricity or running water. We passed through a string of small villages, each with a store, a bar and a beauty salon, often decorated with hand-painted images of African-American cult heroes such as Muhammad Ali and Michael Jordan. The small towns had truckers' hotels, guesthouses, and bars, boasting hand-painted signs with improbable names such as the Camp David Resort and the Manchester Executive Bar.

Arusha, at the foot of the mountain range that forms the northern border of Tanzania, was once a small commercial center for an agricultural region. Today, it is a multi-ethnic city of half a million. It is a diplomatic hub, with the headquarters of the East

African Community, an intergovernmental agency; it was the site for negotiations to end civil wars in Rwanda, Burundi, and South Sudan and for almost 20 years hosted the International Criminal Tribunal for Rwanda. It's a major tourist destination, the staging point for safaris and climbers ascending Mount Kilimanjaro, at 19,341 feet the highest peak on the African continent and the highest free-standing mountain (not part of a range) in the world. At Arusha, the main road turns north to Nairobi. To the west, the blacktop soon runs out. Safari guides take delight in telling tourists there are three types of roads in Tanzania—the good, the bad and the ugly. Get ready for the bumps and ruts.

Chapter 5

The Borders of Johannesburg

★ ★ ★

"Two adult tickets, please." I passed two 100 *rand* bills under the glass window of the ticket booth at Johannesburg's Apartheid Museum. I handed one ticket to Stephanie. "Mine looks different from yours," she said. We examined them. Stephanie had been issued a "White" ticket, mine was a "Non-White" ticket. "You go in separate entrances," the man in the ticket booth explained.

"Apartheid" is an Afrikaans word meaning "separateness," or "the state of being apart," literally "apart-hood" (from the Afrikaans "-heid"). Our moment of confusion offered a brief but safe glimpse of what the "state of being apart" meant for South Africans for half a century. The museum issues "White" and "Non-White" tickets on a random basis. Of course, there's no gun-toting museum guard with a snarling dog to make sure you're using the correct one, but the designation is a potent symbol of how daily life was for people of all races. Your ticket takes you to separate exhibits on identity documents, based on your randomly assigned racial status. Then the "White" and "Non-White" paths converge. The history, ideology and social impact of apartheid, and the domestic and global resistance to it, are documented in images, media, artifacts and oral history interviews. It is a nuanced history because apartheid was a complex, many-faceted form of racial segregation. For example, one exhibit explains that almost every year some people were able to legally petition to change their racial status.

No museum, however well designed and curated, can really take you back in time to experience the brutality of an authoritarian system and a policy of divide-and-rule in its most severe form. But if you do not rush through the exhibits, if you take the time to stop and reflect, the Apartheid Museum, opened in 2001, comes as close as a museum can. On my first visit, I left after several hours feeling deeply unsettled. I knew more than when I had entered but realized there was so much more I did not know. In later visits to Johannesburg, I returned three more times. As I talked with South African colleagues, I began to think about borders that still exist. As a legal system, apartheid was officially abolished in 1991 but its impact is still felt in many areas of society, the economy and daily life.

The Soweto Tourist Trail

It tells you something about how South Africa has changed since the end of apartheid that the sprawling townships of Soweto outside Johannesburg are now on the tourist bus routes. Soweto (derived from the acronym for Southwestern Townships) came to world attention on June 16, 1976 when mass protests erupted over the government's policy of enforcing Afrikaans as the only language of instruction in schools. Police opened fire on 10,000 secondary school students marching from a high school to a stadium in Orlando West. Official reports claimed 23 people were killed, but most historians put the death toll at 176 or higher. Among them was 12-year-old Hector Pieterson, his death marked in an iconic photograph of friends carrying his body. The protests, shootings and arrests continued. Worldwide reaction to the crackdown increased pressure for economic sanctions against South Africa and led some African countries to provide a safe haven for African National Congress cadres engaged in armed resistance. Although many more protests occurred over the next 15 years, some historians regard the Soweto massacre as the beginning of the end for apartheid.

In 1976, Soweto was an urban slum. Blacks lived in small block and brick houses or in one or two-room shacks with leaky metal roofs—hot in summer, draughty in winter. Many did not have electricity or gas; families cooked and heated with wood and children did their homework by oil lamps. Soweto had a large coal-fired power station that belched smoke over the townships, but the electricity went east to Johannesburg's businesses, factories and white, middle-class suburbs. Every day, blacks made the long journey to work—to mines, factories and offices, and to the suburbs to work as cooks, cleaners and gardeners. Because of pass laws, they were not allowed to stay in the city at night without official permission. Crowded living conditions in Soweto bred crime, domestic violence, and disease.

Soweto today is economically and socially mixed. Most of the shacks have gone, replaced by public housing. There are middle-class districts with ranch-style homes, well-tended lawns, hotels, and bed-and-breakfasts. Soweto has parks, shopping malls and two massive sports stadiums—Soccer City and Orlando Stadium—built for the 2010 World Cup. Near Orlando Stadium is one of Soweto's mega-churches; with its sweeping architecture and multi-story parking lot, it looks like a transplant from Atlanta or Dallas. New roads have replaced the dirt and potholed streets, and a major four-lane highway runs east-west through the townships. There are business and industrial parks with aspirational names such as the "Soweto Empowerment Zone." There is even a Soweto Country Club, where on a sunny Sunday morning the golfers were out in force.

The landscape of the townships is still scarred by a century of gold mining with strip-mined hillsides and tipples. There are open patches of scrubland with goats grazing, and too much trash, but overall Soweto has enjoyed an economic and social revival. People actually move *to* Soweto from other districts of Johannesburg because the housing is affordable, and municipal services have improved. The crime rate has dropped to close to the average for the city. That's an encouraging trend, especially when put in context. Johannesburg was once one of the most dangerous cities in the world, with a high rate of murder and violent crime. According to a 2019 survey, it no longer makes the top 50 list of "most violent" cities in the world. Statistically, that may have something to do with an increase in violence in cities in countries such as Mexico and Brazil, but even so Johannesburg has made progress. Two other South African cities, Cape Town and Nelson Mandela Bay, rank at 11th and 12th in the world, and Durban comes in at 47th.[4] However, Johannesburg still has more burglaries, car thefts and muggings than most cities. Almost every resident I met had either been a victim of crime or knew someone—a family member or friend—who had. Even in the hottest days of summer, you keep the car doors locked and the windows closed when you stop at an intersection.

My Soweto tour was courtesy of my colleague and friend Andrew Carlson, who teaches at a university in Minnesota. His dissertation research was on the economic impact of the 2010 World Cup on Soweto, especially on small businesses, and he knows his way around. That's helpful, because although most streets are now paved, they don't all have names. In some Soweto townships, the roads fan out from a central point like spokes on a wheel; in others, there is no intelligible road plan.

Although there are malls, most business in Soweto is small scale, run out of hole-in-the-wall shops with hand-painted signs. The typical developing world row of businesses—a small grocery store next to a storefront church, then a fish and chip shop, a construction materials yard, the "Zodwa and Naughty School of Cooking," a liquor store, a mobile phone stall, a funeral parlor, a beauty parlor and a tire repair shop. You can buy food, earn salvation, get take-out, buy lumber, learn to cook, get drunk, buy airtime, get fitted for a casket, get a perm, and have a puncture fixed on the same street, although maybe not in that chronological order. The "tuck shop" (a term familiar to British readers, especially those who endured boarding school) is a small counter or stall selling snacks, candy, and soft drinks, but perhaps also (under the counter) cigarettes and beer. I was taken aback by the number of funeral parlors and their aggressive marketing: "21st Century Funerals—Tombstones at Incredibly Low Prices," "Pay R5 [50 cents] a month, get R2000 [US $200] funeral cover."

Most of the drinking is done in the shebeens, the neighborhood bars. The word is of Irish origin, derived from síbín, meaning illicit whiskey. Shebeens, usually managed by women,

---

4. "South Africa's 3 most violent cities to live in," *Businesstech*, April 2, 2019.

operated from basements, attics, sheds, garages and living rooms in Ireland, Scotland, England, Canada, and the English-speaking Caribbean, but became an institution in Southern Africa, especially Malawi, Namibia, Zimbabwe, and South Africa. In the apartheid era, when alcohol sales were strictly controlled, home-brewed beer was an important part of the informal economy. Shebeens were the only public drinking establishments open to blacks who were banned from pubs, bars and restaurants reserved for whites. In many African societies, the role of alcohol brewing has been traditionally assigned to women, so shebeens were operated by the so-called Shebeen Queens, who sold home-brewed and distilled alcohol. The shebeens provided a place for people to meet, listen to music, dance, and discuss social and political issues. Although owners and patrons faced periodic police raids and arrests, shebeens remained important social centers throughout the apartheid era. The Apartheid Museum displays photos of township residents arrested, both for breaches of the pass laws and for illegal home brewing. Today, shebeens are legal and are an integral part of South African urban culture

Most tourists on the typical Soweto-in-three-hours minibus tour go to Walter Sisulu Square, named for a prominent African National Congress (ANC) leader, in Kliptown. It's an architectural statement in grey concrete with a funnel-like memorial commemorating the signing of the 1955 Freedom Charter, a statement of the core principles of the ANC and its political allies. The Charter was officially adopted on Sunday, June 26 at a gathering of about 3,000 people, known as the Congress of the People. It was read in full, the crowd roaring its approval of each section. When the police broke up the meeting on the second day, ANC activist Nelson Mandela, whose movements had been restricted, slipped away by disguising himself as a milkman.

As a statement of human rights, the Charter is a remarkably forward-looking document in regard to the rights of women and children. But it is also a document of its time, a post-war period when most South Africans were still working on farms. Among its provisions: "The state will help the peasants with implements, seed, tractors and dams to save the soil. People shall not be robbed of their cattle and forced labour and farm prisons shall be abolished." In places, it veers towards the utopian: "Rents and prices shall be lowered, food plentiful and no one shall go hungry."

Outside the memorial, vendors hawk wooden masks, T-shirts, Soweto baseball caps and other souvenirs. There are more vendors on the spruced-up Vilakazi Street, which boasts the home of the Mandelas (now a museum), the Mandela Family Restaurant, two other large restaurants, a live snake show, and Soweto TV, a community station. The only item I bought was not officially for sale. It was a glazed brick that was holding down one end of a clothing rack. It bore the name Vereeniging, the town south of Johannesburg where the peace treaty ending the Anglo-Boer War was signed in 1902. I bought it for my friend Ed Newman, an avid brick collector, and paid 20 rand (US $2), mostly to compensate the vendor for the time he needed to find another brick. I had given away some books, so I figured I could take the weight in my suitcase.

Urban art—the twin cooling towers of Orlando Power Station in Soweto. Anyone for bungee-jumping?

The twin cooling towers of the Orlando Power Station are one of the most impressive sights in Soweto. The coal-fired plant was commissioned after World War II to help meet Johannesburg's growing electricity needs and served the city—although not the residents of Soweto—for half a century until it closed in 1998. Artists were commissioned to paint murals depicting the social and cultural life of the townships on the towers, and they offer a welcome splash of color in a landscape that is for some months various shades of brown. The towers have been featured in action sequences in movies and TV series. For a fee, you can bungee jump from the walkway between them, or down into one of them.

The Soweto of 1976 is now literally history, preserved in books and archives, in the remarkable photographs and oral testimonies of the Apartheid Museum, and in the memories of older residents. Yet the economic and social conditions that gave rise to the protests against the apartheid regime persist. A black middle and upper-middle class has emerged but the gap between the wealthy and the poor is as wide as ever. Many are disappointed that politicians have not fulfilled the promises made in the heady days of the early 1990s.

Driving Lessons

My tour of Soweto came on my fourth trip to Johannesburg in 2014. I had spent a few days in the city in 2012 at a conference. I returned in March 2013 to work with colleagues at the University of the Witwatersrand School of Public Health to plan the first of three annual workshops on communication for development for UNICEF staff from offices around the world. Andrew was on the faculty team for the workshops.

Most of the flights I take are to Asia, either east via Europe or west across the Pacific. They're all much longer than I want them to be. Psychologically, I expect a flight south to be shorter, but it usually isn't. Indeed, the longest direct flight I've ever taken is from Atlanta to Johannesburg, an interminable 16 hours. And when I emerge, bleary-eyed, from O.R. Tambo Airport, I face another travel challenge—driving a rental car on busy highways to my hotel.

In South Africa, they drive on the left. That's not new to me—I did it for a decade in Britain before I moved to the US—but after many decades of driving on the right, it does not come naturally. For the first few miles from the airport, when I click what I think are the turn signals, I start the windshield wipers.

On my planning trip in March 2013, my colleague and friend Nicola Christofides picked me up at the airport and then devoted a couple of hours a day to, as she put it, "teaching me to drive" in her car. I protested mildly that I already knew how to drive, but it helped. On my later trips for the UNICEF staff workshops, I was the designated driver for our faculty team. Nicola's "driving lessons" paid off.

The City of Gold

Although residential segregation by race has officially ended, Johannesburg remains a divided city, with stark socio-economic contrasts. There are green and leafy upper-middle class Anglo suburbs, with parks, golf courses, churches, and schools. Their curving roads with slight inclines have quaintly English and Scottish names such as Carse O'Gowrie or mix English and Afrikaans as in Glencoe Weg. A few names sound downright silly; say "FredenHarry Road" with a London accent and you'll see what I mean. Many houses are surrounded by walls topped with spikes or barbed wire, security cameras and a sign, sometimes featuring a snarling dog, warning intruders that setting off an alarm will trigger an "armed response." Most blacks who work in the suburbs, as cooks, maids and gardeners, do the daily commute from their townships, just as they did under apartheid but without having to show a pass.

Johannesburg is still, at least figuratively, the "city of gold," an economic magnet for migrants from poorer African nations such as Nigeria, Mozambique, Angola, Zimbabwe, Zambia, Malawi, and the Democratic Republic of Congo. From Malawi's capital, Lilongwe, the bus journey to Johannesburg takes just nine hours and costs less than US $30, allowing migrant workers to travel home for holidays, weddings, and funerals. For many, the entry point is the crowded and crime-ridden inner city district of Hillbrow, where multiple families live together in apartments with broken windows and dodgy wiring and plumbing. Yet a few blocks away is the bustling, gentrified inner city area of Braamfontein, with its upscale restaurants, shops, art galleries and office blocks.

In the 1990s, corporations started moving their offices out of the downtown area to the northern suburb of Sandton. It's now the city's financial center, with the Johannesburg Stock Exchange, high-rise commercial and residential buildings, upscale shopping malls, luxury hotels, the Sandton Convention Centre, parks and a polo club; real estate agents tout its "Manhattan-style living." The M1 highway forms the border between affluent Sandton and Alexandra township, one of the poorest urban areas in the country. Alexandra is a grim legacy of apartheid-era urban planning. It was laid out as an almost perfect square, with streets on a grid pattern. In the 1960s, the government planned to demolish all family housing and replace it with single-sex hostels. The plan faced massive resistance, and only two hostels were completed. Because of its proximity to the city, Alexandra's population grew rapidly, exacerbating the housing shortage, but successive urban redevelopment plans have done little to alleviate crowding and improve services. Soweto has been transformed by urban redevelopment; Alexandra has not.

The deep Ditch

To gain a sense of how Soweto used to be—and how many people in South Africa still live—you have to travel out of Johannesburg to one of the informal settlements where economic migrants from African countries and other South African provinces eke out a living.

Journalism professor Anton Harber, founder and former editor of Johannesburg's *Mail & Guardian*, a weekly with a reputation for its investigative reporting, describes driving north past the shopping malls and gated communities to an urban-rural borderland of golf courses, nurseries, kennels, wedding venues and roadside restaurants. On the northern outskirts of the city, the built landscape changes abruptly as he crosses a socio-economic border:

> "You have come face to face with the hard reality of South African poverty: a dense forest of shacks, crowds of unemployed people milling on the streets, and attempts by some at small-scale commerce in makeshift shops. Men cluster in groups, throwing dice or playing cards. The place has the dull metal glow of aging zinc housing, the chaos of unpaved

roads, the noise of a life lived in packed public areas, the smoke of smoldering braziers and the stench of sewage spilling into the streets. It is stark and bare in the unrelieved dull dryness of a Highveld winter. This is Diepsloot."[5]

The name in Afrikaans means deep ditch, an ironically apt description for the financial hole in which many residents find themselves. Diepsloot was established as a transit camp for refugees in 1995 but grew quickly from a handful of shacks to become a sprawling settlement. Most estimates put its population at about 200,000 but no one has an accurate count because people arrive and leave every day. There are long-term residents but for many migrants, it's the first stop on a longer journey, as they try to move up the ladder from the informal economy to regular jobs and better housing.

The government has built houses and provides subsidies to residents who construct their own homes. Nevertheless, most families live in small shacks, assembled from scrap metal, wood, plastic and cardboard; some lack access to running water, electricity, and sanitation. Migrants come from Zimbabwe, Malawi, Nigeria, Mozambique ,and the Democratic Republic of Congo, with most local businesses owned and operated by Ethiopians, Somalis, Indians, and Pakistanis. With so many people living in poverty and crowded conditions, the crime rate is high, and violence periodically breaks out between ethnic groups, some of it directed at business and retail shop owners. The local authorities estimate that half the population is unemployed. The school dropout rate is high, as families move in and out of the settlement.

And that may be the main difference from Soweto in 1976. Economic and living conditions in the deep ditch are poor, and the crime rate high, but at least families have the freedom to move on in search of opportunities.

Borders in Sports

Andrew and I were sitting on the bleachers of the football stadium at the University of the Witwatersrand, watching under the

---

5. Anton Harber, *Diepsloot* (Jeppestown, South Africa: Jonathan Ball, 2011), p. 2.

floodlights as the home team, Bidvest Wits (the "Clever Boys," sponsored by the Bidvest banking corporation), dispatched a lackluster Bloemfontein Celtic side by a 3-0 margin. Neither was likely to challenge the two major Soweto teams—Kaizer Chiefs and Orlando Pirates—or SuperSport United, which was tipped by the Johannesburg *Star* to win the league, but they were decent middle-of-the table teams.

Sport in South Africa still reflects racial divisions. For whites, rugby is the most popular sport, attracting huge crowds. Football (soccer) is followed mostly by blacks, although some coaches and players are white. There were probably a few other whites at the Friday night match, but Andrew and I were the only ones in our section of the stand. Two Wits players were white. One was a lanky central defender, Matthew Booth, who has played for the national team. Each time he touched the ball, the crowd shouted "Booooo." Indeed, it was a friendly, noisy occasion. The singing was almost constant, punctuated by the low monotone sounds of the ubiquitous *vuvuzela* horns, the plastic sports version of a traditional instrument used to summon villagers to community gatherings. Some fans sported *makarapas*, the decorated miner's helmet that is unique to South African football. Vendors moved through the crowd, though none seemed to be selling the beer that some people were drinking. We asked where we could get a beer and were directed towards a group of policemen standing at one corner of the stadium. On the other side of the high metal fence, a local entrepreneur had set up shop. You passed your 20 *rand* (US $2) through the fence and got a plastic cup of Castle lager. We're pretty sure that the police were providing security, and probably also getting commission on the concession.

Allemand Right to Elsburg

"Yee-haw, Elsburg. Let's hear it from you." Dance caller Teper Blundell, sporting butt-tight jeans, a plaid shirt with a neatly knotted scarf and a black cowboy hat, strutted across the stage at the church hall trying to energize a crowd more interested in eating and drinking than dancing. He tried again. "Come on, Elsburg. You can do better than that. Yeeeee-haw." This time, the

67

crowd responded with a louder and slightly out-of-sync chorus of yee-haws. Welcome to the barn dance, Johannesburg style.

I didn't know what to expect when I drove out to the southeastern suburbs on a Friday night. I had done an Internet search for contra and square dances in the city, but all that showed up was a website for Teper and his wife and dance partner Siobhan, and a list of social events where they were calling. I opted for the barn dance at the Dutch Reformed Church in Elsburg. Siobhan forwarded my message to the organizer, Hendrina. She wrote back to say that admission was 90 *rand*, and that there was one place left. It turned out that the food, not the size of the church hall, was the limiting factor. This was dance and dinner—or, to put it in priority order, dinner and dance. "We never do anything without food," Hendrina informed me. "You're at table number 3 with Teper, Siobhan, Pastor André, his wife and some of the regulars. I hope you like our shepherd's pie."

In Elsburg, I was in another world—Afrikaner territory. The Afrikaners are descendants of the original Dutch settlers. From the 1830s, under pressure from Britain, the competing colonial power, they moved northward from the Cape, defeating the tribes and seizing their lands. In the Anglo-Boer War at the beginning of the twentieth century, they were defeated by the British who took the land, the gold, the diamonds, and pretty much anything else worth taking. After the war South Africa was legally unified, with the Afrikaner Nationalist Party (NP) coming to power after World War II. NP leaders argued that South Africa was not a single nation but was made up of four distinct racial groups: white, black, coloured (mixed race) and Indian. It created black-only townships and so-called "homelands" for ethnic groups, prohibited mixed marriages, and segregated schools, universities, hospitals, public transportation, and recreation areas such as parks and beaches.

The NP's apartheid system was the result of several factors: economics (the need for cheap black labor in industry and agriculture), social control (fear of being overwhelmed by other racial groups) and a sense of racial superiority. The Dutch Reformed Church provided a theological veneer for apartheid. I hadn't thought much about the religious rationale for racial superiority, but the Apartheid Museum traces how this developed in popular Afrikaner thought. Major events such as the 1838 Battle of Blood River (so-called because the river ran red with blood) when a small force of Boers circled their wagons and routed a Zulu army, reinforced notions of divine mandate for racial domination. The Dutch Reformed Church's pro-apartheid position led to its expulsion from the World Alliance of Reformed Churches. In 1986, sensing the way the social and political winds were blowing, it opened its doors to all races.

I guessed that some older members of the crowd had supported apartheid, or at least tacitly accepted the system. "This is a pretty conservative group," Teper told me. Maybe so, but perhaps more bewildered by changing social norms than prejudiced. Pastor André Scheepers told me that the church had black and coloured members, although they usually didn't come to barn dances. In a society that has changed rapidly, the Afrikaners struggle to maintain their culture and institutions. The pastor gave the blessing and made announcements in Afrikaans, but the introductions (including a welcome to "our friend from West Virginia") were in English.

The evening felt like a church social but with one difference—the booze. Groups arrived with coolers of beer and wine. In the foyer, next to the barn dance art installation—a saddle and stirrups, leather belt and cowboy hat, garnished with very clean straw—was a table with shots of sherry. You had a shot before you walked in, another one on the way to the bathroom, and a third to give you the courage to go out on the dance floor. I hadn't brought a bottle, so Pastor André reached into his cooler and put two bottles of Amstel in front of me. At the next table, they were drinking whiskey.

With all the drink and food—pork and beans, shepherd's pie, bean casserole, pumpkin and apple pie and ice cream—it's a wonder there was any dancing at all. The younger and middle-aged members of the crowd stumbled out between courses for simple circle, square and short line dances, including a slightly modified Virginia Reel, interspersed with country line dances. All the music was recorded. "We can't afford a live band," said Teper.

Most of the crowd sat at their tables, preferring to eat, drink, chat and try to look as if they had just moseyed into town after a long cattle drive, rather than having taken the Germiston exit off N17. The décor and fashion—many were dressed in jeans, fancy leather belts, boots, cowboy hats and plaid shirts with silver stars—showed that a barn dance meant cowboys and cowgirls, cowboy food, straw bales, saddles, and yee-haws. It actually made some historical sense. The northward trek from the Cape brought Afrikaner farmers to the High Veld, the plateau region of grassland and scrub bushes that begins at the Drakensberg Escarpment east of Johannesburg and slopes gently west. More than 4,000 feet above sea level, it resembles the High Plains of Montana or Wyoming. This is cattle country, where Afrikaner cowboys drove their herds, cooked pork and beans on campfires and slept out under the stars. Then they started moving from their ranches to ranch-style homes in Elsburg and other suburbs and working in IT and customer service. But these suburban cowboys can still muster a pretty good yee-haw.

Breaking Down Borders

If a country's progress is to be measured by how it breaks down borders between racial and socio-economic groups, South Africa has a lot of work still to do. Official segregation and pass laws have ended but, despite the promises of ANC politicians, the economic situation for many has changed little since the early 1990s. Some feel that the hopes and dreams that came with the end of apartheid have been, if not lost, severely compromised. Although tensions between blacks and whites, particularly Afrikaners, remain, most recent attacks, such as those in Diepsloot, have targeted immigrants from other African countries. In typical populist anti-immigrant rhetoric, they are accused of taking away jobs from native South Africans, driving up rents and burdening overstretched medical and social services. In March 2020, after South Africa declared the coronavirus pandemic a national disaster, the government ordered the closing of most border crossings. In the case of Zimbabwe, it went one step further, building a six-foot high fence 12 miles on either side of the main crossing at Beitbridge. Border closures, said the Public Works Minister, Patricia de Lille, are not effective "if the fences at the border are not secure, which in many places, they are not."[6] At the time, Zimbabwe had no reported cases of the virus, so it was clear the government was using the public health crisis to clamp down on both legal and illegal migration.

Hundreds of thousands of Zimbabweans, facing political violence and economic hardship in their own country, live and work in South Africa, but, like migrants from other African countries, face discrimination. The classic 2012 "Diversity" TV commercial from Nando's Chicken, the popular fast food chain, lampooned xenophobia, pointing out that almost all South Africans were immigrants:

Announcer: You know what's wrong with South Africa? All you foreigners.

[Africans with suitcases stand up in tall grass and begin running.]

You must all go back to where you came from.

[Line outside tent with Immigrations sign.]

You Cameroonians, Congolese, Pakistanis, Somalis, Ghanaians and Kenyans.

[Figures disappear in white puffs of smoke.]

You Nigerians.

[More white puffs.]

And you Europeans.

[Young white couple in car disappear in puffs.]

Let's not forget all you Indians and Chinese.

[More white puffs.]

Even you Afrikaners.

[Man wearing bush hat driving a *bakkie* (a pickup truck) with a dog in the cab disappears in puff of smoke.]

---

6. BBC World News, March 19, 2020

[Khoisan bushman dressed in loin cloth with bow and quiver of arrows speaks.]

Caption: I'm not going anywhere. You ⋆$&!@#⋆ found us here.

Real South Africans love diversity. That is why we have introduced two more items …

The South African Broadcasting Corporation (SABC) and a satellite channel refused to air the ad, claiming it trivialized xenophobia and could incite attacks on foreigners. Nando's responded that the ad was "aimed at addressing a social ill" and that it was seeking "to have South Africans take a stand against these prejudices by encouraging them to embrace the diverse inhabitants of our land."

Chapter 6

India-Bangladesh:
The World's craziest Border

★ ★ ★

It could be a screenplay for a Bollywood movie or for a soapy
TV series about the early days of the British Raj, where the main
characters spend their time lounging around in pastel-pink palaces
and wandering through well-manicured gardens, plotting against
the Mughal Emperor or the British East India Company, while
trying to figure out which of their relatives has betrayed them or
made off with the family jewels. The characters, male and female,
are expensively dressed, dripping with gold and silver. They are
attended by small armies of servants who open and close massive
doors, wave large feather fans and bow as they enter with trays
of food, and deliver letters with elaborate wax seals.

In this scene, the Maharaja of Cooch Behar, a princely State
in Bengal, is receiving his neighbor, the Faujdar[7] of Rangpur,
who shows up with the usual retinue of retainers and elephants,
all of which need feeding. As traditional rulers go, they are in
the minor leagues. The Faujdar owes his allegiance to the Mughal Emperor in Delhi; the Maharaja to the British who are
protecting his state from the aggressive Bhutanese kings to the
north. Because the Mughals and the British left local rulers to

---

7. In the Mughal Empire, the *faujdar* was a military commander with administrative, judicial and tax collection duties.

73

run their own domestic affairs, the two princes have control over their own territories.

"How about a game of chess?" the Maharaja asks his guest.

"Yes, that will pass the time agreeably," the Faujdar says. "But what will be our wagers?"

The Maharaja calls on a servant to bring a map of the two states. "Let us use our lands," he proposes. They agree on a sliding scale. If one player takes the other's pawn, he wins a rice paddy in the other's kingdom; a bishop or a castle brings several houses and fields; checkmate, a village.

And so, over several years and many chess games, with scribes diligently recording lands won and lost, the map of the region became dotted with enclaves or *chitmahals*, small pockets of Cooch Behar territory within the boundaries of Rangpur, and vice versa. In its etymology, the word *chitmahal* intriguingly suggests that debts were owed, and that the currency was land. *Chit* is a Hindi and later Anglo-Indian word for a note recording a sum owed. In India, a *mahal* can be a palace (as in the Taj Mahal) but the derivation is from the Arabic *mahalla* which means district or neighborhood, and the word passed into both the Hindi and Bengali languages.

Unfortunately, there is no historical record of high-stakes chess games between the Maharaja of Cooch Behar and the Faujdar of Rangpur or of other princely sporting events on which bets were placed. The story is repeated in several articles about the *chitmahals*, but without evidence. A more plausible explanation by Brendan Whyte of the University of Melbourne (Australia), is that the *chitmahals* are the result of a series of messy peace treaties signed in 1711-13 between Cooch Behar and the Mughal Empire. Cooch Behar ceded some estates and villages, where Mughal nobles ruled and collected taxes from the population.[8]

In total, there were 162 *chitmahals*, ranging in size from ten square miles to less than an acre. As long as the region was subject

---

8. Whyte, B. R. (2002). "Waiting for the Esquimo: an historical and documentary study of the Cooch Behar enclaves of India and Bangladesh." Research paper: School of Anthropology, Geography and Environmental Studies, University of Melbourne.

to the Mughal Empire, and later British India, it did not matter which local potentate ruled over a village or a few fields. It was only when British India was partitioned that the *chitmahals* left thousands on the wrong side of the border, essentially making them stateless. Muslim-majority Rangpur became part of East Pakistan. The Maharaja of Cooch Behar dithered for a couple of years before opting to join India in 1949. Suddenly the borders were closed and the residents of the *chitmahals* found themselves surrounded by a foreign country.

And that's how things stayed until a historic land swap agreement in 2015. India had 111 enclaves within Bangladesh's Rangpur Division with a population of about 38,000. Within them were 21 Bangladeshi counter-enclaves, an island of Bangladeshi land, surrounded by Indian territory, within mainland Bangladesh. On the Indian side were 51 Bangladeshi enclaves, with a population of about 15,000, all but four within the Cooch Behar district of West Bengal; within them were three Indian counter-enclaves. No wonder *The Economist* described the zigzagging lines between India and Bangladesh as "the world's craziest border."[9]

I became interested in the enclaves in summer 2016, a couple of months before I travelled to the northeast State of Assam for an Indian government-funded program to teach a two-week seminar on communication for development to junior faculty and doctoral research students. This was going to be my ninth trip to India. I first visited in 2003 with Stephanie; Chennai (Madras) was the next port of call after Dar es Salaam on the Semester at Sea voyage. Over the next decade, I made trips for workshops, teaching and consulting. Most assignments took me to the capital, Delhi, and to Hyderabad in south-central India, with shorter visits to the States of Odisha and Gujarat. The visit to Tezpur University in Assam would be my first to northeast India, the so-called "chicken neck," precariously attached to the rest of the country by a narrow strip of land between Bangladesh and Nepal, the Siliguri Corridor. I was also interested in the region because I expected to make my first trip to Bangladesh

---

9. "Why India and Bangladesh have the world's craziest border," *The Economist,*
   July 25, 2015

for a UNICEF project a few months later.

To prepare myself, I did what I do every time I am about to travel to a country or region I've never visited. I pore over the maps. The border between India and Bangladesh looked like nothing I had ever seen before, zigzagging for hundreds of miles. And what were those blobs along the border? Even on a detailed map, only the largest of the *chitmahals* showed up. The borders were confusing, yet fascinating.

The Fifth-longest Land Border in the World

Bangladesh's border with India is more than 2,500 miles long, making it the fifth-longest land border between two countries in the world. It's almost half as long as the 5,558-mile US–Canada border, the longest, and more than 300 miles longer than two of Russia's borders—with China and Mongolia.

The statistic is a surprising one, even to most Bangladeshis I know, because the country is one of the smallest in Asia, about the size of Iowa or Illinois. Apart from its short southern border with Myanmar, Bangladesh (formerly East Pakistan) is completely surrounded by its larger neighbor. From the Bay of Bengal, the border meanders north for 1,378 miles, with the Indian State of West Bengal to the west. At its furthest northwest point, it forms the southern edge of the Siliguri Corridor, the strategically vital stretch of land that connects mainland India to its northeastern states; at its narrowest point, Bangladesh is separated from Nepal by only 17 miles. The Indian States of Assam and Meghalaya form the northern border with Bangladesh; to the east, the border jogs around three sides of the former princely State of Tripura before heading south again with the State of Mizoram separating it from northern Myanmar. Until 2015, it would have been even longer if the boundaries around the enclaves had been included.

Why is Bangladesh such a strange shape, with a border that zigs, zags and occasionally turns back on itself? The answer, as with many cartographic puzzles, lies in decisions that were hastily made by a colonial power.

In 1905, six years after Prime Minister Lord Salisbury was "engaged in drawing lines upon maps where no white man's

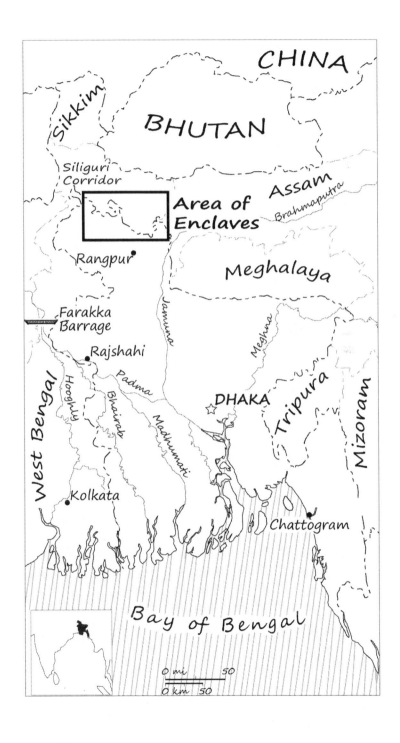

CHINA

Sikkim

BHUTAN

Siliguri
Corridor

Assam

Area of
Enclaves

Brahmaputra

Rangpur

Meghalaya

Farakka
Barrage

Jamuna

Rajshahi

Meghna

Hooghly

Padma

Bhairab

Madhumati

DHAKA

Tripura

Mizoram

West Bengal

Kolkata

Chattogram

Bay of Bengal

0 mi   50

0 km   50

foot ever trod" in Africa, the Viceroy in India, Lord Curzon, from his office in the capital, Calcutta, was engaged in his own territorial shenanigans by splitting the province of Bengal into two parts. The official reason given was administrative efficiency: the province was simply too large in area to govern effectively. However, the border lines revealed a policy of divide-and-rule because they created two religious-majority provinces—Hindu West Bengal and Muslim East Bengal. Bengalis of both faiths, who felt more united by language and culture than divided by religion, protested. Five years later, the partition was scrapped. The British left Calcutta in a huff, moving their capital to Delhi.

In 1947, Curzon's plan was realized with the decision to partition British India and its almost 400 million people into Hindu-majority India and Muslim-majority Pakistan. Cyril Radcliffe, a lawyer with no experience in India, was tasked with heading a commission to draw the borders and was given just five weeks to do it. The main challenge was in two large provinces—Punjab in the west and Bengal in the east—which had roughly the same numbers of Hindus and Muslims. Radcliffe had to figure out how to divide them, but his advisors could not agree, the maps were out of date and the census figures inaccurate. No neat lines could be drawn to divide communities that had lived side by side, mostly peacefully, for centuries.

The so-called Radcliffe Line was announced on August 17, 1947, a few days after independence; in some places, it ran through villages, and even through the middle of houses. Roughly 12 million people found themselves on the wrong side of the line and tried to move; between half a million and one million were killed in the ensuing religious violence. Radcliffe burned all his notes before leaving India. At home, he was knighted for his achievements, but he realized the consequences of the commission's decisions and never returned to India or Pakistan. "There will be 80 million people with a grievance looking for me," he said. "I do not want them to find me."[10]

The decision to divide British India along religious lines set the stage for almost three quarters of a century of conflict between India and Pakistan, and communal violence between Hindus and

---

10. Quoted in "Cyril Radcliffe: The man who drew the partition line," BBC News, August 1, 2017.

Muslims. The country of Pakistan—its two parts separated by 1,400 miles of India—was never viable, politically, economically or culturally. After years of sporadic resistance, the Bengalis of East Pakistan fought a bitter nine-month liberation war in 1971 to earn independence as Bangladesh.

It's surely unfair to hold one lawyer solely responsible for decades of conflict. Radcliffe was given an impossible mission with a short timeline and limited resources. The British were in a hurry to leave; neither they, nor the new leaders of India and Pakistan, fully considered what had to happen to ensure a less painful transition. The fundamental error was to create borders along religious lines, ignoring geography, history, language and culture. Would the future have been different if, as some political leaders had demanded, Bengal, with its mixed Hindu and Muslim population, had become an independent state? Because of the lines drawn in 1947, we will never know.

Stateless in the *Chitmahals*

For a few years after partition, residents of the *chitmahals* were able to move fairly freely within their new countries—to go to work or school, the market or health clinic. After 1952, as relations between India and Pakistan deteriorated, border controls made travel more difficult. To obtain a passport and visa, a *chitmahal* resident had to go to Delhi or Dhaka, but the only way to do so was to make an illegal border crossing. As both countries expanded roads, railroads and electricity supply to rural areas, the improvements stopped at the boundaries of the *chitmahals*. They lacked schools, health centers, police stations and courts; with no law enforcement or judicial system, residents were easy prey for gangs and violent crimes went unreported and unpunished.

The first attempt to eliminate the *chitmahals* was made in 1958, when India and Pakistan agreed to an exchange "without any consideration of territorial loss or gain." Less than a decade after partition, and after fighting for control of Kashmir, some Indian leaders were loath to give up any land to a hostile neighbor and filed lawsuits to block the deal. India's Supreme Court ruled that a constitutional amendment was required to make the transfer. The issue remained unresolved as relations between the two countries worsened. In 1971, after Bangladesh became independent, India, which had at first secretly, then openly, supported the resistance movement, seemed more open to a deal.

The Land Boundary Agreement, signed in 1974, was supposed to resolve all border disputes, including the *chitmahals*. Bangladesh's parliament immediately ratified the agreement, but it took India 41 more years to do so. The ruling Congress Party, sensitive to criticism that it was soft on illegal immigration from Bangladesh, was not ready to give ammunition to its main rival, the Hindu nationalist Bharatiya Janata Party (BJP), by handing over territory to a Muslim state. Ironically, it was the BJP's victory under Narendra Modi in the 2014 elections that paved the way for the transfer. The BJP introduced the constitutional amendment to resolve the dispute once and for all. On June 6, 2015, Modi flew to Dhaka to meet Bangladesh's prime minister, Sheikh Hasina, and sign the land swap and other agreements, including investments in the energy sector and bus routes across the border.

Under the agreement, the *chitmahals* became part of the country that surrounded them; in terms of land area, Bangladesh got the better deal, gaining 17,161 acres (26.8 square miles), while India gained 7,110 acres (11 square miles). The agreement excluded the largest Bangladeshi *chitmahal* in India, the ten square mile area of Dahagram-Angarpota in West Bengal. At its closest point, it was less than 600 feet from the border, so a narrow land bridge, called the Tin Bigha Corridor, was leased in perpetuity to Bangladesh. From Dahagram-Angarpota, the *chitmahals* descended in size and population. The smallest, Natatoka, an Indian *chitmahal*, was about one quarter of an acre. India also had sovereignty over the world's only counter-counter enclave, a ¾ acre patch surrounded by a Bangladeshi village, which in turn was surrounded by an Indian village within a district in Bangladesh proper.

Residents of the *chitmahals* were given the option of choosing either Indian or Bangladeshi nationality. The Indian press claimed that thousands wanted to leave Bangladesh for a better life, but that the authorities, fearing a mass exodus would look bad, put pressure on them to stay. Whatever the truth of the claim, the fact that less than one thousand moved to India suggests that many people did not want to abandon the land their families had farmed for generations. A sense of place and community was more important to them than religion or nationality.

The land agreement raised new questions about who owns what. For decades, *chitmahal* residents, who did not want to risk an illegal border crossing to reach the nearest land registry, bought and sold land informally; few had valid documents to prove their ownership and some feared losing land they had inherited or bought. Some former *chitmahal* residents at resettlement camps in India said they were unable to sell their land in Bangladesh because they could not obtain the official stamps from government agencies and were not allowed to travel back to finalize sales. Most who moved across the border, both Hindu and Muslim, did so because they believed the economic prospects in India would be better, but author Robin Hemley, who visited the resettlement camps, found that some were frustrated. "[T]he bloom of Indian citizenship had faded for many, as virtually all ... remained in the temporary camps. With their land unsold in Bangladesh, they had little money at hand, nowhere to go, and few ways to earn money." Some wanted to return to Bangladesh.[11]

The 2015 agreement not only made "the world's craziest border" a little saner but dramatically reduced the number of territorial enclaves on the world map from more than 200 to less than 50. Most are in Western Europe and on the fringes of the former Soviet Union, including eight in Central Asia's Fergana Valley (see Chapter 15). A true enclave is one that cannot be reached without passing through the territory of the single state that surrounds it. There are only three enclaved sovereign States—San Marino and Vatican City, surrounded by Italy, and Lesotho, by South Africa. Other small, landlocked countries such as Andorra, Luxembourg, Liechtenstein, and Swaziland do not count because they have borders with more than one country. Germany and Italy each have an enclave surrounded by Swiss territory; Baarle-Hertog is a collection of Belgian enclaves in The Netherlands; Spain's Lllivia enclave is surrounded by France and its Ceuta and Melilla outposts in North Africa by Morocco. Russia's Kaliningrad Oblast counts as a semi-enclave because it is

---

11. Robin Hemley, "The Great Land Swap," Pacific Standard, November 27, 2018.

bordered by two countries—Poland to the south and Lithuania to the east and north.

Smuggling across the Padma

South of the *chitmahals*, the border between the State of West Bengal and Rangpur Division zigzags through a fertile agricultural region. This was once the major tobacco growing area of Bangladesh, but in recent years farmers have switched to other crops—corn, potatoes, and mustard seed. The border veers west along the northern edge of Bangladesh's Rajshahi Division before it meets the Ganges River, three quarters of the way through its 1,600 mile course from the Himalayas to the Bay of Bengal. For 70 miles, the Ganges, which is called the Padma in Bangladesh, forms the border between the two countries. After it enters Bangladesh proper, it joins two other great river systems, the Jamuna (Brahmaputra) and the Meghna. The channels and distributaries of the three rivers empty into the Bay of Bengal in a delta region the size of the US State of West Virginia.

Rajshahi, the fifth largest city in Bangladesh with a population of about 750,000, straggles along the north bank of the Padma, with West Bengal to the south. Once famous for its silk industry, Rajshahi is a regional administrative, commercial and agricultural processing center, with universities and hospitals. Compared with the two largest cities, Dhaka and Chattogram (Chittagong), it is relatively free of pollution and traffic jams, with parks, gardens, and some stylish British colonial buildings.

As my flight from Dhaka arced over the river for its final descent, the Padma's shifting course was plain to see. The river had eaten away chunks of the shoreline on both sides. Low sand bars and narrow islands rose above the water, some sprouting rough grass and shrubs. During spring floods and monsoon season, these islands will disappear, only to re-emerge, in different shapes, sizes and positions, during the dry season.

The Padma's vagaries make precise calculations impossible. "How far to the southern shore?" I asked one boatman. He shrugged. It depended on the season, the Himalayan snow melt, and even the current state of relations between India and Bangladesh. Ten miles upstream from the point where the river becomes the border is India's Farakka Barrage, built in 1974 to control its flow. The dam diverts water to the Hooghly River which flows south to Kolkata. It was built to stop Kolkata's port from silting up, reducing the need for mechanical dredging; however, the water flow has never been adequate to the task. The barrage also serves as a reservoir for drinking water and supplies a thermal power station. Although the two countries concluded a water sharing agreement in 1996, Bangladesh often complains that it gets too much water—or too little. Too much water causes downstream flooding and eats away at the shoreline; too little deprives farmers of the water to irrigate their crops.

On a sunny, breezy day in early February, looking across the Padma, the south shore of West Bengal was a distant, hazy blur. It was a Saturday and in a park built on an artificial headland, families strolled among the food and novelty stalls and children played games under the trees. A small flotilla of brightly colored boats ferried passengers to one of the fragile islands in the channel where they built sandcastles and took selfies. From the park, I walked east along the footpath on the levee that protects Rajshahi from the Padma's vagaries. Or at least it protects the city proper.

Fishing boats moored on foreshore of Padma (Ganges) River at Rajshahi.

Thousands of people live on the narrow strip of sandy, marshy land on the river side of the levee. Although some are in rough, bamboo-framed shacks with mud-daubed walls and metal roofs, other have built substantial two and three-story brick or block houses. Goats and chickens peck in the dirt for food scraps; cattle are tethered in sheds. Women and children fill water cans from a community pump. In small courtyards, bamboo sticks with dried cattle dung, used for cooking fires, dry in the sunshine.

In winter, these informal settlements are perhaps one hundred yards from the river's edge. When the snows melt or the monsoon rains come, the river rises, flooding many dwellings. These people are squatters, who built their homes on the wrong side of the levee on what is technically government land. The authorities could evict them and bulldoze their homes but that would not only create resistance but a larger problem: where would they go? In a city that faces a shortage of affordable housing, there's no good alternative.

Vulnerable sections of the levee are strengthened with concrete blocks. When the river rises, it loosens the blocks, allowing the water to run into the foundations of the levee. During the dry season, sand bags are used to plug the gaps, but residents complain that no permanent repairs have been made and they fear that their homes will be washed away when the rains return.[12] It's estimated that over the last half century the city of Rajshahi has lost more than 250 square miles of land—about the size of the city of Chicago—to erosion by the Padma.

From the levee I walked out to the grass-covered sand dunes. The river had gouged out huge sections, loosening the sand and rocks, so I trod carefully, clinging onto tufts of grass on the slopes. Sheep and goats, some tethered, some herded by young boys, grazed on top of the dunes. A few fishing boats were moored at the water's edge and others pulled up on the mud bank. The Padma provides ample supplies of the popular freshwater *hilsha*, a meaty, bony fish served fried, grilled, and in curries, and *catla*, the South Asian carp.

---

12. "Rajshahi city protection embankment vulnerable," *Bangladesh Post*, February 1, 2020.

Fishermen on the Padma. Hilsha, a meaty, bony fish served fried, grilled, and in curries, is a staple in the diet.

Further east, at another riverside park, I pointed to a line of boats with radio aerials. "That's the border patrol," said my companion, the local UNICEF officer. "They're trying to stop smuggling from India." I asked her what was smuggled. "Cattle are the major contraband," she said. "The Hindus can't eat beef, so there's money to be made bringing cattle across the river." I asked what else was smuggled. It was a diverse list—saris, matches, medicines, and drugs including fentanyl, the notorious heroin additive. Much is sold on Rajshahi's central bazaar, where Indian-made goods (legally and illegally imported) dominate. In January 2020, Bangladesh's border guard agency reported the confiscation of US $11.7 million of contraband, including narcotics, liquor, jewelry cosmetics, clothes, sculptures, firearms, trucks, pickups, autorickshaws and motorcycles.[13]

It seemed to me that the border patrol boat crews faced an impossible task in policing the Padma. The river is a major highway for internal commerce. Small cargo boats and *nouka*, the

---

13. "11 Bangladeshis killed by BSF in one month: BGB," *The Independent* (Bangladesh), February 6, 2020

traditional Bangladeshi craft with a high prow, powered by a diesel engine or by poles, carry fruit, vegetables, animals, rice, fuel and oil barrels, building materials and passengers between river towns and villages. It's difficult to know which *nouka* or fishing boats are traveling up and down the river, and which are trying to smuggle goods across from West Bengal.

India's Border Wall

There might be less smuggling if it was easier to trade legally with India. Although the border with West Bengal runs for 1,378 miles—by far the longest with any Indian state—it has only four authorized road border crossings with customs and immigration posts. Along most of the land border, India is constructing a 10-foot high fence of concrete and barbed wire to stop smuggling and illegal immigration; in places, the fence is electrified. Bangladeshi and foreign media accuse India's Border Security Force (BSF) of a "shoot-to-kill" policy in which innocent, unarmed farmers and fishermen, not smugglers or illegal migrants, are the main victims.

The border shootings came to worldwide attention in January 2011. Muhammad Nur Islam, a worker whose family migrated to India when he was six, had arranged a marriage for his 15-year-old daughter, Felani, in his birth village in Bangladesh. They attempted to scale the barbed wire fence with a ladder; Islam crossed first but Felani's clothes became entangled in the wire. Her screams alerted BSF troops who started shooting. Felani's body hung from the fence for five hours before the BSF took her down, tied her hands and feet to a bamboo pole and carried her away. Her body was handed over the next day and buried at the family home in India. A picture of her body, first published in a Kolkata newspaper, was widely circulated in international media. India issued a feeble apology; a BSF special court dismissed a charge against the guard who killed Felani, holding that the evidence against him was inconclusive.

Felani's death was not an isolated incident. Human Rights Watch estimates that in the decade preceding the shooting, the BSF killed almost 1,000 Bangladeshis, on average one every four days. To put the number in historical context, *The Economist* noted that the death toll "dwarfs the number killed attempting to cross the inner

German border during the Cold War."[14] For several years after Felani's killings, the number of deaths dropped. Indian government officials repeatedly promised that the BSF would arrest smugglers and illegal migrants, not shoot on sight. "A forgotten promise," said Bangladesh's *Daily Star*, reporting that there were 43 killings in 2019, triple the number of the previous year and the highest in four years. "The Indian government is not sending the message to its trigger-happy border force," said Dhaka University international relations professor C.R. Abrar. "Imagine what would happen if a single such death happened along the India–Pakistan border."[15]

India's Mexico?

Most smuggled goods go into Bangladesh. Most people go the other way. Migration, both legal and illegal, to India has a complex and highly politicized history. In the years after partition, most who left East Pakistan did so out of fears of religious persecution; they included both Hindus and Christians, the latter moving to tribal areas of Assam (now the State of Meghalaya) which has a significant Christian population. From the mid-1950s, most were economic migrants, unable to make a living on the land. During the 1971 Liberation War, about 10 million refugees fled to India. Although many returned, some decided to stay, buying land or finding work in urban areas. The war devastated Bangladesh's economy and left many in poverty, so migration continued, particularly north to Assam. About one third of its population of 32 million are Bengali Muslims. Some are the descendants of laborers imported by the British to work on the tea plantations. Even the Liberation War refugees who stayed on have been in India for two or three generations; their children and grandchildren have known no other country.

How many illegal migrants from Bangladesh live in India, both in the surrounding states and across the country? For years, BJP politicians have been trotting out the round number of 20

---

14. "Felani's last steps: India's shoot-to-kill policy claims one more innocent," *The Economist,* February 3, 2011.

15. "A forgotten promise," *The Daily Star,* January 24, 2020

million, without much evidence for it. It is more a question of perception. If you want to believe your country is being flooded by illegals who take away jobs, drive up rents, become a burden on social and medical services and don't share your religion, you will be open to the doom-and-gloom messages from nationalist politicians. You will likely support the border fence and the BSF's unwritten shoot-to-kill policy. To some Indians, Bangladesh represents "poor immigrants." It's India's Mexico.

Figuring out who is legal is a complex process, particularly among a population where literacy rates are low, and people lack documents to prove residency or land ownership. It's as dodgy a statistical exercise as any that aims to measure illegal activities, such as crime or the informal economy. That's because people engaged in illegal activities do not usually inform the authorities about what they are doing. Criminals do not show up at police stations to report their crimes. Market vendors and hole-in-the wall retailers do not report sales to the tax authorities. Day laborers do not file income tax returns. Similarly, illegal immigrants fly under the radar. No one shows up at an Indian government office and says, "*Namaste,* my name is Mohammad Ali Rahman. I just crossed the border from Bangladesh illegally because I want to work and raise my family in your wonderful country. Please report my arrival to the appropriate agencies." Illegal migrants simply disappear into majority-Muslim districts, especially urban areas where they have relatives or know people from their own village; they find jobs in the informal economy and pay for faked papers. Good luck counting them.

Who's a Citizen in Assam?

In the early 1980s, the student-led Assam Movement brought to a head long-standing grievances over the growing economic power and political clout of Bengali Muslims, legal and illegal. The Assamese, supported by indigenous groups, claimed that years of uncontrolled immigration was making them a minority in their own homeland and that they faced the loss of their lands, livelihoods, language, and culture. In 1983, in the so-called "Nellie massacre" in 14 villages in the Nagaon district, Assamese killed more than 2,000 suspected illegal immigrants, including women and children. In August 1985, the central government and the Assam groups signed the Assam Accord, under which migrants who had entered illegally after March 24, 1971, the day the Bangladesh Liberation War began, would be declared foreigners and deported.

Easier said than done. There was little motivation for the Congress Party, which had long ruled the state and took a secular approach to politics, to boot out the Muslims who supported it in elections. Tensions continued, as new arrivals competed for low-wage jobs as construction workers, domestics, rickshaw pullers, and vegetable sellers. In 2012, at least 77 died and 400,000 fled their homes following violence in western Assam between indigenous Bodos and Bengali Muslims. Eventually, India's Supreme Court stepped in, ordering that the National Register of Citizens (NRC) that was prepared for the state in 1951 should be updated to identify genuine citizens.

Modi's BJP won the 2014 national election with the usual campaign promises to reform and expand the economy, alleviate poverty, tackle environmental issues, improve education and health care systems, stamp out corruption, and make India a stronger player on the world stage. During its first term in power, the BJP played down its Hindu nationalist agenda. The party's landslide election victory in May 2019 emboldened those who saw it as their mission to culturally redefine India, which has a secular constitution, as a predominantly Hindu nation. Its legal weapon against Muslim immigrants was the NRC. "Infiltrators are like termites in the soil of Bengal," BJP President (and later Home Affairs Minister) Amit Shah said during election rallies in West Bengal in 2019. "A BJP government will pick up infiltrators one by one and throw them into the Bay of Bengal."[16]

Roughly 80 percent of India's population of 1.3 billion self-identify as Hindus, even if some don't show up at the temple any more often than US citizens who identify as Christians go to church. The percentage masks the real numbers. India has about 200 million Muslims, making it the country with the largest

---

16. "Amit Shah vows to throw illegal immigrants into Bay of Bengal," Reuters, April 12, 2019.

Muslim minority population in the world. There are almost as many Muslims in India as in Pakistan which (after Indonesia) has the world's largest Muslim population. Calling India a "Hindu nation" is a powerful slogan but sends the message to roughly 15 percent of the population that they are second-class citizens.

The BJP came to power in Assam in 2016, winning a majority in the state assembly, and set about implementing the Supreme Court order to update the NRC in the state. To be added to the NRC list, a resident has to prove that she or he arrived before March 24, 1971, the date the Liberation War began. In a region with high illiteracy rates, some people lack documents to prove their residency. By mid-2018, more than 32 million Assam residents had applied to be listed on the NRC. Some were summoned at short notice to appear at hearings to substantiate their claims, or as witnesses for neighbors who had applied. "People are confused," one social worker told *The Indian Express.* "Most are illiterate and have not travelled outside their village or district." Some had to sell livestock or jewelry to pay for transportation to hearings held hundreds of miles from their homes.[17]

The NRC left out nearly four million people in Assam, effectively depriving them of citizenship. Both the Assam and central governments say they can appeal, but many fear they will be deported. The problem for the BJP is that those four million include not only Bengali Muslims but Hindus, a strong voter base for the party. The BJP backed off, claiming that the NRC was "error ridden" and announcing it will be updated. To date, Assam is the only state where the NRC has been conducted. On Bangladesh's western border, one third of West Bengal's population of more than 91 million are Muslim and most likely include many who arrived after March 24, 1971. Its chief minister, the firebrand Mamata Banerjee, a bitter opponent of the BJP, has described the NRC as discriminatory and has adamantly refused to go along with the count.

The BJP needed to come up with a mechanism to achieve its goal of deporting Muslim illegal migrants while protecting

---

17. "Assam districts panic, notices at night for NRC hearings 300 km away," *Indian Express*, August 5, 2019.

Hindus. It found it in the Citizenship Amendment Act (CAA), passed by India's parliament in December 2019. The CAA amends a 64-year-old law that prohibits illegal migrants from becoming citizens. It offers amnesty to non-Muslim illegal immigrants from three neighboring Muslim-majority countries—Pakistan, Afghanistan and Bangladesh. Modi says that the new law is "for those who have faced years of persecution and have no place to go except India." He tweeted that the law reflects, "India's centuries old culture of acceptance, harmony, compassion and brotherhood."[18]

Political opponents and the protestors who came out onto the streets of Delhi and other cities in late 2019 condemned the law as part of a Hindu nationalist agenda to marginalize Muslims. They pointed to Kashmir, India's only Muslim-majority state, where a few months earlier the central government had revoked the state's special status, sent in the army to quell protests, shut down the Internet and imprisoned local political leaders, activists and journalists. Rahul Gandhi, Modi's opponent in the 2019 election, described the CAA and the NRC as "weapons of mass polarization unleashed by fascists." Assamese leaders who support the NRC viewed the CAA as a betrayal by the BJP. They want all illegal Bengali migrants, Muslim and Hindu alike, deported.

Under the CAA, illegal Hindu migrants from Bangladesh will be able to stay and have a path to citizenship. Although some may have been victims of religious persecution in Bangladesh, many migrated for economic reasons. Yet religion is the defining criterion. The Hindus can stay. The Muslims face deportation to Bangladesh, a country most of them have never known.

Violence on the Streets of Delhi

On Thanksgiving Day 2019, as Americans tucked into the turkey and trimmings, I was enjoying a plainer meal of *dahl*, *paneer*, *roti* and rice at the guesthouse on the campus of Jamia Millia Islamia University (JMI) in South Delhi, where I was conducting a workshop for university faculty sponsored by UNICEF's India office.

---

18. "Citizenship Amendment Act: Fresh violence erupts in Delhi," BBC News, December 17, 2019.

JMI, founded in 1920, is one of India's oldest and most prestigious universities, an institution committed to tolerance and inclusivity. According to one of its founders, Zakir Hussain, its mission was to "lay the foundation of the thinking that true religious education will promote patriotism and national integration among Indian Muslims, who will be proud to take part in the future progress of India." JMI, founded to educate Muslims, is a diverse institution, with students from all religions, regions and castes.

Two weeks after I left Delhi, the campus and the streets around it erupted in violence as students protested against the NRC and CAA. Rocks and bottles were thrown and buses set on fire. Police responded with tear gas, rubber bullets and, by some accounts, live ammunition. They broke down the gates of the campus and attacked and arrested students in the library and bathrooms. Protests were held in other cities, with Muslims joined by Hindus and people of other faiths. In north Delhi in February 2020, the protests spiraled into communal violence, with Hindu mobs attacking Muslim neighborhoods and torching homes and businesses. More than 40 people, mostly Muslims, were killed and hundreds injured. Journalists and eyewitnesses reported that the police, who report to the BJP central government, not the Delhi city authorities, sometimes failed to intervene to stop the loss of life and property and, on occasion, supplied the mobs with sticks and bricks.

The violence might have continued for months, had it not been for the onset of coronavirus in early 2020 and the Modi government's decision to impose a national lockdown. In India's cities, hundreds of thousands of day laborers were left stranded without work, unable to return to their home villages where at least they would have had food and shelter. India's gradual economic recovery is likely to spark more Hindu nationalist rhetoric and anti-Muslim violence as people compete for a limited number of jobs. For Modi and the BJP, there is a political calculation to make: is it worth pursuing the anti-immigrant agenda in the face of opposition from states such as West Bengal and disapproval from the international community? And there will be a series of legal challenges. It took more than 40 years for India to sort out its border dispute with Bangladesh over the *chitmahals*. Figuring out who's a citizen could take even longer.

Chapter 7

Bangladesh: River Borders

★ ★ ★

"What's the best way to travel from Khulna to Barishal?" I asked my UNICEF colleague Yasmin Khan at her office in Bangladesh's capital, Dhaka. "I don't mean the fastest or the cheapest way. The most *interesting* way?"

Yasmin smiled. For the last three years, I had been working on a project to introduce curriculum on communication for development at universities, and train faculty members in social research. This was my eighth visit to Bangladesh, and I had traveled to almost every region of the country. Yasmin and I had taken several long road trips together, and she knew that I was always looking for a good travel experience.

Before she could answer, I pitched my idea. "How about The Rocket?" I had read about the legendary paddlewheel steamer that for decades was the fastest way to travel between ports in the southern delta region. The four Rocket steamers in service were long ago outpaced by faster vessels, but the trip was still recommended for travelers who were not in a hurry. I was in no hurry. After a symposium at the university in Khulna, the main city in southwest Bangladesh, I had two days to reach the river port of Barishal in the central delta. I would book a first-class cabin on The Rocket for the overnight journey. I would sit on deck sipping tea (no alcohol served), reading, watching life on the rivers and enjoying the sunset and sunrise.

Yasmin sounded doubtful. She said that on a recent river

journey from Dhaka to visit relatives in Barishal, her passenger boat had run into heavy fog, delaying her arrival by several hours. It was wintertime (late January), the water levels were low, and The Rocket could not steam all the way up the Rupsha River to Khulna. Instead, it was scheduled to depart from Morrelganj, a two-hour drive to the south. I did not give up. I called the Bangladesh Inland Water Transport Corporation for advice. The answer was not reassuring. "We cannot guarantee departure," said the agent. "Perhaps you should travel by road."

The Rocket would have to remain in my travel dreams, not in my travel plans. I contacted the UNICEF field office in Khulna to arrange for a car and driver. "How long will the trip take?" I asked. "I'm not sure," said the administrative officer. "It depends on whether any of the bridges are under repair. You have a lot of rivers to cross." I instantly resolved to count them. It's one of the arithmetic exercises that keeps me engaged in travel. How many miles from one place to another? How many hours will the trip take? How many seats on the plane or the bus? How many rivers to cross?

Land of Rivers

For a small country, close in size to its near neighbor, Nepal, or about the size of Illinois or Iowa, Bangladesh has a lot of rivers, around 700 according to most estimates. Roughly 10 percent of its total area is water, a high proportion considering that it has no large lakes. In other words, most of that water is moving. When the Himalayan snows melt in the spring and the monsoon rains come in the summer, as much as one third of Bangladesh's land area may be under water. The rivers are constantly shifting course, creating new channels or distributaries, making accurate mapping a frustrating exercise. Even describing them is a challenge, because the names of some rivers change several times along their courses.

For Bangladesh's rural population, the rivers are interwoven with every aspect of their lives. They sustain agriculture—rice paddies, fields of corn, mango orchards, fish and shrimp farms, herds of cattle, and flocks of ducks. They are the main highways for commerce, with *nouka* carrying fruit, vegetables, livestock, and building materials. In many places, you need to travel by river to reach the school, the health clinic, or the government office.

The rivers are also borders, dividing the country. Most flow south towards the Bay of Bengal, creating barriers to east-west travel and commerce. In many places, people rely on ferries—from simple *nouka* poled by boatmen that carry passengers, bicycles, motorbikes and cargo to diesel-powered vehicle ferries. Ferry traffic depends on navigability; on a foggy winter day, in rough weather or in the dry season, east-west commerce may be delayed or halted.

The Bangladesh Inland Water Transport Corporation lists 22 major river ports and 448 secondary ports in the waterways network. It's estimated that more than half the total freight traffic in the country moves by water, and that boats carry about 50 million passengers a year. Keeping the traffic moving is a challenge because of seasonal variations in water level. During the rainy season, passenger steamers—called "launches" in Bangladesh—and cargo vessels can navigate more than 3,700 miles of rivers; in the dry season, it's less than 2,500.[19] Every year, the national and local governments allocate contracts for dredging to keep channels open and to repair and maintain the *ghats*, the ferry and cargo terminals.

From the early 1980s, as the economy began to recover after the 1971 Liberation War, Bangladesh embarked on an ambitious project of bridge-building to connect districts and communities by road and rail. It's an expensive, long-term program, because there are just so many rivers to cross. Some districts, reachable only by boat, remain isolated and underdeveloped, without paved roads or electricity. Although some rivers are easily bridged, crossing the major rivers requires huge investments.

Bridging the Padma

It is the most challenging and expensive construction project in the country's history—the bridge across the Padma (Ganges)

---

19. Robert Shuvro Guda, "Developing inland waterways," *The Financial Express*, February 18, 2018.

North

CHINA

Brahmaputra

INDIA

Jamuna

Padma

Kushtia

Madhumati

Hooghly

Bhairab

Meghna

DHAKA

Gopalganj

Khulna

Rupsha

Barishal

Mongla

Patuakhali

Chattogram

Payra

Bay of Bengal

0 mi   100

0 km   100

South

linking the southwest to northern and eastern regions of Bangladesh. At 3.84 miles, it will be even longer than the 3½ mile Bangabandhu Bridge that spans the Jamuna, the name given to the Brahmaputra in Bangladesh. For centuries, the Jamuna divided the country vertically into two nearly equal halves. When the bridge, named for the hero of the independence movement, Sheikh Mujibur Rahman, known popularly as Bangabandhu (Friend of Bengal), was opened in 1998, it was the 11th longest bridge in the world. It carries a two-lane roadway, a dual-gauge railroad line, a natural gas pipeline and power and telecommunications lines, and has helped transform the economy.

Like the Bangabandhu Bridge, the Padma Bridge project has been dogged by delays and spiraling costs. In June 2012, the World Bank cancelled a US $1.2 billion loan over corruption allegations. Two years later, the government, proceeding without the loan, began construction. It will carry a four-lane highway on the upper level and a single track railway on the lower level and is expected to boost national GDP by as much as 1.2 percent. The economic stimulus will be welcome because by early 2020 the cost estimate had risen to US $3.6 billion. That's almost a billion dollars a mile.

At airports, shopping malls and commercial centers, the companies that supply the concrete and steel for the Padma Bridge have bought space for glossy posters and video displays advertising how their products meet international construction standards and are building the future of the country. The message is clear: if the concrete and rebar are good enough for the Padma Bridge, they are certainly good enough to build your apartment complex.

To describe the Padma as simply a river—a feature in physical geography like a mountain or a desert—is a gross understatement. Padma, the Sanskrit word for lotus flower, is mentioned in Hindu mythology as another name for Lakshmi, the goddess of wealth, fortune, power, luxury, beauty, and fertility. For millions of people in India and Bangladesh, its waters are the source of life, sustaining fishing and agriculture and providing a highway for commerce. When the Himalayan snows melt, they wash earth from the mountain slopes into the river. Downstream in Bangladesh floodwaters submerge farmland and leave thousands of people trapped on levees and narrow spits of land. Yet when the muddy waters subside they leave behind rich, alluvial soil that makes the river basin one of the most fertile regions in Asia. The Padma is fearsome in its natural power, seemingly changing its course at will. It is both worshipped and cursed, loved and feared. Lakshmi the goddess brings wealth, but she is also a temperamental mother, restless and whimsical.

Along its 1,600 mile course, the river gathers tributaries, many of them already great rivers with their own tributaries. By the time the Ganges reaches the India-Bangladesh border and becomes the Padma, it starts to release its raw energy by branching out into channels or distributaries. Like wayward children, some wander off for a few miles before returning to their mother. Others leave home, never to return. They make their own way across the plains and become major rivers in their own right, plotting their course to the Bay of Bengal. The Padma is not merely a river, but a river system with many component parts—tributaries, channels, distributaries and *chars*, the river islands.

Bangladesh's third river system, the Meghna, also brings together rivers flowing out of India's northeast. The combined waters of the Padma and Jamuna join the Meghna south of Dhaka to form the Lower Meghna. At its widest point, the Lower Meghna is almost eight miles across, land and river merging into one hazy landscape. A maze of channels and distributaries combine into the great Gangetic Delta. The delta is ground zero for climate change, with floods and cyclones blowing up from the Bay of Bengal to submerge low-lying islands and pushing brackish water inland.

Before it joins the Jamuna, the Padma has already cast out distributaries. The Hooghly (Bhagirathi) flows south to Kolkata and on to the Bay of Bengal, its flow artificially swelled by the discharge from the Farakka Barrage. Further east, just north of the city of Kushtia, the Madhumati leaves the Padma and flows 190 miles southeast before turning south across the swampy Sundarbans region, changing its name several times along the way. The river port of Khulna was founded at the confluence of the Madhumati and another Padma distributary, the 100-mile long Bhairab. At Khulna, the river becomes the Rupsha, flowing south to Mongla, the country's second largest deep seawater port.

Cooling in Khulna

Khulna is the third largest city in Bangladesh, but a distant third. Dhaka has a population of around 12 million, with another eight million in the metropolitan area, the port city of Chattogram (formerly Chittagong), four million. Khulna's population is a little over one million. It's a bustling place, crowded with trucks, buses, autorickshaws, and cars. It's just not as frantic as Dhaka or Chattogram.

For centuries, the Khulna region was known for its production of jute, the natural fiber used to make twine, rope, matting and gunny sacks for rice, wheat and grains, and the city became the center for processing and exporting jute. Khulna still has some operating jute mills, but the industry has been in decline for years; today, commercially farmed shrimp is the major export. The city is a manufacturing center, with factories processing agricultural products and small workshops turning out metal and wood products.

The Rupsha was once a major commercial waterway, with ocean vessels sailing up from the Bay of Bengal to dock at the port. Although fisheries, docks and factories still line the banks, Khulna has declined in importance as a port because the river bed has silted up, making it impossible for large vessels to navigate the channel. Trade has shifted downstream to Mongla, which is connected to the city by a new highway and bridge across the Rupsha. Khulna is still an important transportation hub, where containers are transferred to trucks and rail cars for distribution around the country, and goods, mostly textiles which account for 80 percent of the country's export trade, are assembled for shipment. It's the administrative capital of Khulna Division (province), with universities and hospitals.

From the west bank of the Rupsha, the city spreads west, north and south, expiring in a ring of small villages and rice paddies. It's still relatively compact, without the urban sprawl of the capital. And the main streets, while busy, are not nearly as dangerous as those of Dhaka where you often feel as if you're taking your life in your hands when you step off the sidewalk. That's because, per capita, there are fewer cars on the road. The buses, which career around madly with their horns blaring, are the main hazard. But the dominant species in this urban landscape is the autorickshaw.

I do not claim to be an expert on urban transportation, but you don't need to be one to observe that different species of autorickshaw thrive in different environments. The most common Dhaka species is a small three-wheeler, powered by Compressed Natural Gas, and referred to by passengers and transportation experts alike by the abbreviation CNG. It is usually green, or greenish, in color, and is distinguished by the metal grilles protecting the driver and passengers. When you get into the back bench seat (which can accommodate three Bangladeshis or two well-fed Westerners), the driver bolts the door shut so that, when you are stalled in traffic (as you inevitably will be), no one can reach in and snatch a purse, bag or mobile phone.

The dominant species in southwestern Bangladesh is a larger vehicle, with two bench seats facing each other (space for six Bangladeshis) and a wider front seat for passengers to sit on each side of the driver. It's an open vehicle; there's no need for protective grilles when the traffic is moving. In rural areas, the capacity is increased with standing passengers hanging onto the metal frame on each side. This autorickshaw comes in various colors—green, yellow, blue and black—and is powered by a battery. It is slower than the CNG but has less environmental impact. On the streets of Khulna, I walked by workshops where autorickshaw frames are assembled, and showrooms where new models are displayed. I had a notion to do some window shopping and see if the salesman could quote me the I-will-have-to-talk-to-my-manager price.

If you don't travel by autorickshaw, you go by bicycle rickshaw or bicycle. Pedal power is the main means of short-haul commerce in Khulna, with the ubiquitous "van," a tricycle with a short flat bed and a long chain to the back wheels. As far as I could tell, all had bells but no gears. There's a modestly upscale version powered by a small battery, but most rely purely on leg power. They haul everything imaginable—bricks, bags of cement, bamboo scaffolding, firewood, sacks of rice, bales of hay, baskets of coconuts, fruits and vegetables, large blue oil and rainwater barrels, living room suites. I saw one van carrying a refrigerator with the driver's helper sitting at the back of the bed, balancing the glass tray on his knees to prevent it from shattering when the driver had to swerve to avoid a collision with a bus.

Autorickshaws, a dominant species in the urban landscape, at riverfront market in Barishal.

Tricycle "van" with shredded paper for recycling.

In Khulna, almost every block has a couple of tea stalls—small shacks with bamboo or lumber supporting the metal roof, and a couple of rough-hewn tables and benches. The proprietor boils the water on a small gas stove or a fire. There's no running water, so a van driver fills large aluminum flasks from the nearest supply and delivers to the stalls. For a larger establishment that serves food, fresh chicken are available, also by van delivery. You pick your chicken, the driver weighs it, and kills it on the spot. A little blood on the sidewalk, but it's very fresh. This is the supply chain, farm-to-table Bangladesh style.

Too Many Rivers to Cross (and Count)

With my dream of a leisurely river cruise on The Rocket postponed, I resigned myself to travelling from Khulna to Barishal by road and counting bridges. It's just under 100 miles on a circuitous route that loops north through the district of Gopalganj. There's a shorter, more direct route (70 miles) but it includes a ferry crossing and can take an hour more. Although there was relatively little traffic most of the way, the trip took 3 ½ hours. It would have taken even longer had it not been for the flamboyant maneuvers of my driver, Abdul, as he dodged trucks, buses, autorickshaws and slow-moving vans. I don't speak more than a few words of Bengali, so I had to resort to hand flapping to make him slow down.

Three miles out of Khulna, the mile-long bridge over the Rupsha links the city with the port of Mongla, a 90-minute (35-mile) drive to the south, and to western districts. The bridge is an impressive structure, its large spans carrying the divided highway high over the river. It's named for a famous religious builder, the fifteenth century Muslim administrator Khan Jahan Ali, who is reputed to have built the nearby Mosque City of Bagerhat, now a UNESCO World Heritage Site. The bridge is also, I learned later, the best spot to view Khulna's annual boat race, the *Nouka Baich*, in which village teams compete for prizes and pride. For centuries in Bengal, farmers and fishermen—and the carpenters who designed and built the *nouka*—took a few days off work after the fall harvest to come together for a *baich* to demonstrate their skills and provide entertainment for the community. Think of it as a South Asian equivalent of the Highland games, or the horse races of nomads on the steppe of Central Asia or Mongolia. Khulna's *Nouka Baich*, held in October, is one of the largest and most colorful in the country, and draws thousands of spectators to the river bank and bridge.

A few miles after the Khan Jahan Ali bridge, at a roundabout where a billboard promoted the "Mongla Power Pac Economic Zone," we turned off the Mongla road and headed northeast. The tree-lined two-lane highway ran along an embankment above the irrigation canals, rice paddies, and fish and shrimp ponds. In between the paddies, narrow levees, lined with banana trees and coconut palms, led to small huts with metal and thatch roofs, rough shelters for farmers from the summer sun and monsoon rains. In places, the roadside was lined with felled trees, ready to be transported to small sawmills and fashioned into building lumber and furniture. There were speed bumps at the outskirts of most villages, but no warning signs. Abdul either knew the road very well, or had special bump-detecting mental powers, because he slowed down for all of them, before accelerating rapidly again.

I had begun the trip with the firm intention of counting bridges. After an hour or so, as we crossed the umpteenth one, I just gave up. I devoted my energies to gritting my teeth and gripping the door handle as Abdul executed his dangerous maneuvers.

A few miles outside the city of Gopalganj, Abdul stopped at a barrier across the road and paid a 20 *taka* (25 cent) toll. "Sheikh Hasina—home district," he informed me matter-of-factly. The road surface immediately improved. The district of Gopalganj in Dhaka Division is famous as the birthplace of the independence hero Sheikh Mujibur Rahman and his daughter, the current prime minister, Sheikh Hasina. There's a museum and mausoleum in his home town, Tungipura, which is where Sheikh Hasina symbolically launches her election campaigns. Our route did not take us through Tungipura, but a few miles further on, after crossing the Kaliganga River, the city of Gopalganj, the administrative and commercial center of the district, literally burst into view. A modern urban landscape sprouted above the bamboo stands and mango orchards—gleaming white apartment blocks, office complexes, a new science and technology university. It offered a vivid contrast to the rice paddies and straggling villages that had lined the road so far. At the last census in 2011, Gopalganj was just a mid-sized provincial town with a population of around 50,000. It has grown substantially since then. The government has invested heavily to make the chief city of Sheikh Hasina's home district a regional showpiece.

On the eastern outskirts of Gopalganj, we turned off the main road to Dhaka and headed southeast on the last leg of the journey. The road curved along a narrow embankment above the rice paddies. Even if I had not already given up counting bridges, I would have done so now, because we crossed a stream or small river every two or three miles. Down in the waterways, fishermen cast their nets, and men dressed in *lungi*, the traditional loin cloth, poled their *nouka*. We passed schools painted in bright colors—pink, blue, green and red. Paddy, the stacks of rice stalks used for cattle fodder, were piled at the roadside. The villages seemed to cling to the highway for safety; most houses and businesses were built on stilts standing in ponds, with only the top floor at road level. Finally, we looped south again, crossed two more rivers, the Sikarpur and the Arial Khan, and reached the northern outskirts of Barishal.

The Barrels of Barishal

"What was in them?" I was looking at a stack of blue metal barrels stacked on a short wooden jetty on the riverside at Barishal. They looked greasy so I guessed they had contained a petroleum product. "Oil," the young man standing beside me confirmed. "They bring them up from the coast."

Although Bangladesh has major reserves of natural gas, it imports most of its petroleum products through the seaports of Chattogram and Mongla, where they are transferred to the inland waterway system to reach refineries and distributors. Large tanker ships sail up the Lower Meghna to the Dhaka area. At Barishal, as in other regions, the oil arrives in drums stacked on barges. From the dock, the drums are loaded onto trucks, vans and handcarts for final delivery. Empty barrels are piled up on the dock, ready to be shipped south again. There are no cranes or winches in operation with all loading and unloading done by laborers. As I watched, they carried baskets of bricks and sacks of cement on their heads from barges.

Barishal, on the west bank of the Kirtankhola, a distributary of the Lower Meghna, is the commercial gateway to the southwest delta. It's been whimsically described as the "Venice of Bengal" or "Venice of the East," although if you're just counting waterways, almost any large town in southwestern Bangladesh is a Venice. The Kirtankhola is not deep enough for the ocean-going cargo ships that steam up the Lower Meghna but can handle smaller freighters and barges that ply between the towns of the delta region, carrying bricks, building materials, and bulk agricultural produce.

Commercial barges drawn up on the litter-strewn beach at Barishal; the barge in the foreground is being loaded with flattened cardboard to be recycled.

On a Saturday afternoon in late January, Barishal's commercial dock was buzzing with activity. Calling it a "dock" may be an overstatement. The brightly colored barges were drawn up on the muddy, litter-strewn beach, with gangplanks connecting them to wooden jetties uncertainly anchored in the banks. Vans, handcarts and small trucks waited in the dirt loading zone for their freight. At first glance, it looked pretty chaotic. There was no uniformed port official controlling traffic. And certainly no security checks; I had just wandered in from the main road that runs along the dockside. But everyone seemed to know what they were doing and where they were going. The commercial port was working perfectly well without technology or bureaucracy. Just as it had functioned for many centuries.

Just keep on pushing, please. All dock labor is manual.

The port dates from the Mughal period when it was called Gird-e-Bandar (The Great Port), and was known for its trade in salt, spices, and woods. During British rule, its name was changed to Barisal Bandar. From the 1880s, it became an important center for the passenger steamers that were the main means of internal transport in Bengal, with connections to Dhaka, Chittagong, Calcutta and smaller ports. Today, Barishal, with a population of 350,000, is second only to Dhaka for the volume of passenger traffic. In 2003, the government began a programme, completed 10 years later, to rebuild and expand the passenger terminal (*ghat*) and jetties.

At the Barishal ghat: three-deck launches for long-distance travel and cross-river nouka.

"Dhaka, Dhaka, Dhaka," the ticket agent buttonholed me at the entrance to the passenger *ghat*. "Green Line, depart in one hour." I explained that I wasn't traveling anywhere, that I just wanted to walk along the jetty where the launches and smaller short-haul ferries were moored. He waved me through the barrier, and I clattered down the metal ramp to the waterfront. Passengers from Dhaka were disembarking from one launch; four others were moored, ready to head north to the capital or south to other ports in the delta. For many years, it was an overnight 10-12 hour trip between Dhaka and Barishal; passengers who could afford to booked first and second-class cabins, while others travelled in steerage. Then the Green Line shipping company upset the market by introducing service on two faster launches, halving the travel time to five hours with two daily departures in each direction. Some travelers still prefer the slow overnight trip from Dhaka, where they leave behind the dense traffic and pollution, relax on deck with a cup of tea, and float south under the night sky. Others opt for speed, an air-conditioned lounge, an airline-style snack box and action movies on the TV monitors.

The four- and five-deck launches dwarf smaller short-haul ferries, with one or two decks. Most of them do double duty, carrying both passengers and cargo. As I strolled along the jetty, crew members were loading sacks of rice, onions, potatoes, chilis and coconuts into the holds; a small truck pulled up and the driver and his helper carried large bundles of paper onto one boat. In communities throughout the delta region, some of which lack road access, shopkeepers rely on these boats to keep their shelves stocked.

Sacks of rice, onions, potatoes, chilis and coconuts are loaded onto a launch serving towns in delta region.

There's a newish road bridge across the Kirtankhola, but most rivers and channels are not bridged. On the other side of the passenger ferry terminal is what I'll call the shared taxi station. Here, flat-bottomed *nouka,* powered by outboard motors or poled by boatmen, provide short-haul service to villages up and down the Kirtankhola.

Nouka line up to carry passengers to towns and villages on the Kirtankhola River.

Each takes a dozen or more passengers, fewer if there's bulk cargo—sacks of fruit and vegetables, water flasks, a motorcycle, a cow or a couple of goats. There's also a catamaran version—two *nouka* with a wooden platform—that is large enough to carry a couple of vehicles. Even before they reach the beach and the short concrete slipway, passengers leap off and run up the short slope to the bazaar to hail an autorickshaw.

Like a shared taxi, a *nouka* departs when it's full, or when the boatman figures he has enough fares to make the trip worth making. No *nouka* advertises its destination. You just know that Faisal goes to one village, Mamun to another, and that Amit will make sure your children get to school on time.

Across the Pigeon River

I had been mildly disappointed that my road trip from Khulna to Barishal did not include a ferry crossing because I wanted to have a sense of how travel used to be in the delta region before they built more bridges than I could count. I was rewarded three days later with a road trip to Patuakhali, an agricultural and fishing district on the Bay of Bengal. Patuakhali is less than 30 miles due south of Barishal, but the trip takes at least 90 minutes. And a lot longer if you're stuck in traffic waiting for the ferry across the Payra.

Like the Kirtankhola, the Payra (the Bangla word for pigeon) is a distributary of the Meghna, breaking off from the main channel northeast of Barishal and then meandering to the Bay of Bengal. It's at this point, where the river meets the sea, that Bangladesh's third deep-water seaport is under construction. The port of Payra, together with the already operating port at Mongla to the west, will help relieve the maritime traffic snarl at Chattogram, the country's oldest port, where container ships sometimes anchor for weeks in the Bay of Bengal while they wait for a berth.

The bridge under construction across the Payra will link the port and the Patuakhali district to Barishal and points north. It's another massive civil engineering project—almost one mile long and supported by 31 pillars, sunk into the riverbed. Approach roads are being constructed on both sides. Like most major infrastructure projects, this one, started in July 2016, was running behind schedule and over budget. The bridge is being constructed by a Chinese company with local labor. Contracts for most road and bridge projects in Bangladesh go to Chinese and South Korean construction companies (the Turkish firms specialize in residential development). Until it is opened, the only way across the Payra is by ferry.

If the great Bengali poet Rabindranath Tagore had traveled this way at the turn of the twentieth century, I'm sure he would have penned a few verses in honor of the broad, meandering Payra with the evening sun reflecting off the water and the fishermen casting their nets from *nouka*. If he were to come back from the dead and visit the Payra today, he would be at a loss for words. There's not much romance to be found in Leberkhali (lemon in Bangla), the ferry terminal on the north bank. When the two-lane highway from Barishal ends, trucks, buses, cars, autorickshaws and motorbikes jolt over a dirt construction site under one of the bridge pillars; the road, such as it is, is lined on both sides with rough shacks with metal roofs, housing small shops, tea stalls and metal fabrication workshops. It's a bone-rattling ride in the dry season; in the monsoon season, vehicles stall in the mud. When the traffic is heavy, the line for the ferry stretches back for half a mile on each side of the river; it can be a one or two-hour wait for the 10-minute crossing.

After our vehicle edged onto the ferry, I got out to take photos. The ferry is a commercial outlet, with food stalls set up on one side of the vessel. It's also a hangout for beggars. "Should I give her a few *taka*?" I asked one of my companions. "Give to one, and she will bring three more," he warned, almost philosophically. I moved to the front of the boat, where motorcycle riders had gathered, ready to make a quick getaway when we docked. The ferry carries all human, vehicle and cargo traffic across the Payra, including farm animals. One farmer offered to sell me his cow (or, at least, that's what I thought he was saying).

The bridge and port, and the road improvements built to serve them, will open up a relatively isolated region of the delta, and boost the economy. The local university, a former agricultural college, sees it fulfilling a destiny to which its name—Patuakhali Science and Technology University—aspires. It's a new public university on a rural campus, with research programs in agriculture and fisheries. The Vice Chancellor spoke enthusiastically with me about the expected economic boom the bridge and port will bring to a poor region where most people depend on rice farming, fruit growing and fishing.

He didn't mention the environmental impact. The port of Payra will have terminals for containers, general cargo, sand and aggregate, and grain. It will have an airport, fishing harbor and dry dock. But it will also have terminals for coal, oil and liquefied natural gas. An oil refinery and three large coal-fired power plants are under construction. As Bangladesh struggles with the impact of climate change, progressive government policies, such as its regulations to ban plastic bags, stand in stark contrast to its need to generate more electrical power, mostly from coal-fired plants, to boost industrial output and supply power to rural areas.

When I visited the university, I was told that most industrial plants in Patuakhali operate for only part of the day. The line from the main grid to the city was under repair, and power was turned off for up to 12 hours a day. The lights came on around 7:00 in the evening and went off at 7:00 in the morning. At the university, a diesel-guzzling generator provided back-up power, but at a high cost. As in most developing countries, the balance between economic growth and environmental impact is a difficult one. An adequate power supply is essential to bringing people out of poverty in urban and rural areas, but it comes with a long-term cost.

Chapter 8

In Transit: Shanghaied

* * *

"Where's the check-in counter for Shanghai Airlines?" I button-holed a Malaysian Airlines agent at Kuala Lumpur International Airport. "I don't think they have one," she offered. "I think China Eastern handles their check-in. Sorry, I'm not sure."

I had arrived at the airport in plenty of time because I had a nagging suspicion about the first leg of my return flight to the US. My travel agent had e-mailed a few days earlier that the early-morning flight to Shanghai was cancelled, even though it was still showing on the online schedule. I called the Shanghai Airlines office in Kuala Lumpur several times, but no one picked up. I arrived at the airport, expecting problems.

I waited an hour at the China Eastern desk before an agent appeared and started fiddling with keys and the computer keyboard. On the departure monitor, the Shanghai flight was showing as cancelled. "That's a mistake," he said. "It's still scheduled. Come back here in an hour and check in." I retreated to the restaurant to spend my last *ringgits*, relieved that the issue had been settled.

An hour later, there was no one at the China Eastern desk and the flight was still listed as cancelled. "You have to rebook," the Malaysian Airlines representative at the next counter confirmed. "China Eastern has no more flights tonight so the representative will not be back. You should try calling them."

No one from China Eastern or Shanghai Airlines was answering the phone at 2:00 a.m., so I returned to talk to the Malaysian

Airlines agent. "We can get you on our delayed flight to Shanghai, leaving at 5:00 a.m.," he said. "Can I see your China visa?"

"I don't have one," I said. "Do I need one if I'm changing to another international flight?"

"You don't need one if you have a confirmed itinerary from Shanghai. The problem is that you missed your flight to Tokyo, so you no longer have a confirmed itinerary."

It was a classic Catch-22. No confirmed itinerary. No visa. The agent could have refused to rebook me on the Malaysian flight, but he realized that the problem was not of my making. "Here's your boarding card," he said. "I'm just not sure what will happen in Shanghai.".

The flight touched down midmorning at Shanghai's Pudong International Airport. The runway and terminal buildings were shrouded in thick smog. In the airport, many people were wearing face masks. Pollution levels had spiked. I was happy that a visit to Shanghai proper was not on my schedule.

Because I was not officially a transit passenger, I had to go through the immigration line. The officer didn't know what to do with this visa-less, itinerary-less passenger. "Please, you sit," he said. I was directed to a holding area while he consulted with his supervisor. They kept glancing in my direction while they called whoever it was who was authorized to decide my fate. I was just about resigned to being sent back to Kuala Lumpur, when the officer returned with my passport and released me (without a visa) into the departure area to rebook my Tokyo flight with All-Nippon Airways. This took another hour, several calls and one computer reboot. I could have just walked out into the smog of Shanghai.

I had almost as much trouble returning through immigration to board the Tokyo flight. "You have been traveling in China without a visa?" the officer asked. I explained that the only part of China I had seen was the airport departures area. He flipped through the visa pages in my passport, pausing at a page with a Kazakhstan visa in Cyrillic script. "You have come from Russia?" he asked. "No, Malaysia," I replied. He could probably tell from my expression that it was a long story and he didn't want to hear it. "Have a good flight and a happy new year," he said.

My first and only visit to China had lasted almost four hours. It felt like much longer.

Chapter 9

High Times in Nepal

★ ★ ★

Lights Out in Kathmandu

"Can you come a day earlier? There's going to be a *bandh* on Friday in Kathmandu." The Senguptas, the parents of one of my colleagues, had invited Stephanie and me for dinner, but now our hostess was calling to warn us that a one-day general strike was scheduled for the day she had chosen. It would shutter businesses and keep most traffic off the roads in the city. "It may be dangerous to travel," she said. "I'm sorry—we have to be flexible." "We'll see you Thursday," I replied.

At 7:00 p.m., we arrived by cab at their large, comfortable home in an upscale district. We enjoyed snacks and *momos*— steamed and fried dumplings, stuffed with meat or vegetables. And then the lights went out. Our hosts simply shrugged and brought out the Coleman lanterns. The other dinner courses were served. The conversation went on as normal. No one even commented on the power outage, let alone grumbled about it. When you live in Kathmandu and other cities in Nepal, outages and *bandhs* become part of your regular routine.

This was my second visit to Nepal's capital, but I was still impressed by how people coped with what was euphemistically called "power shedding," the scheduled shut-offs to specific districts. When you walked down a busy commercial street at night, all the street lights were off. Restaurants and shops with diesel generators kept the lights on, but everywhere else was in darkness, except for a few candles and battery-powered lights. Power cuts of 12-16 hours a day were common in Kathmandu, and the situation was worse in some regional cities.

If there was ever a country that you thought could rely on its topography to generate power, it is Nepal. Hundreds of fast-flowing rivers and streams from the Himalayas can be harnessed for hydroelectricity. In the 1960s and 1970s, the government, with foreign aid, embarked on a massive public works program to increase power generation, especially for rural areas. Many plants built in that period, and the electrical grid they support, need to be repaired and upgraded. The government, divided by political wrangles and facing other budget priorities, has struggled to make major investments, so the engineers just keep patching up the plants to keep them running.

Hydroelectrical capacity varies by season because most plants are "run-of-river," without a large reservoir dam from which water can be released in a controlled fashion. "Run-of-river" plants generate adequate power when the snows melt in the spring and during the summer monsoon season; in the dry season, the water—and the electricity it produces—is literally reduced to a trickle. It's a paradox. Nepal's hydroelectric capacity is greatest in the spring and summer when it least needs it (not many people use air-conditioners), and lowest in the dry winter months when demand peaks. In some months, Nepal has to import electricity from India. The lack of a reliable power supply forces hotels, restaurants, retail stores and offices to use back-up generators which consume expensive diesel fuel, reduces industrial productivity and makes it difficult for children to do their homework at night.

Along with darkened streets, one of the most common sights in Kathmandu were long lines at petrol stations. At one station, I counted more than 30 cars lined up at one side and 50 motorcycles on the other, with street vendors working the lines, plying snacks and bottles of water. One rider told me he had used his last liter to drive across the city because he had heard this station would have a delivery today. Nepal has no known oil, gas or coal deposits. It imports all its petroleum products from India, with tanker trucks making the 12-15 hour trip from the

State of Bihar to Kathmandu on twisting mountain roads. When shortages occur and the lines stretch for blocks, rumors circulate. Some claim the wholesalers are hoarding supplies, some that the national oil corporation has not paid its bills and India has cut off supplies. Whatever the cause, keeping a full tank is a challenge.

The "Hippie Trail"

Perhaps it was because Kathmandu sounded a bit like Xanadu, the summer capital of China's Yuan dynasty, described in lavish detail in *The Travels of Marco Polo* and later the inspiration for the Romantic poet Samuel Taylor Coleridge's *Kubla Khan*, reportedly composed after an opium-inspired dream. Or maybe in my own mind I combined Xanadu with Shangri-La and threw in a little *Brigadoon* to create my own romantic notion of a remote mountain kingdom. Either way, Kathmandu had always sounded like the kind of place about which I would have travel fantasies but never visit.

In my earlier days of travel, the closest I came was in 1976 when I hung out at the so-called "Pudding Shop" in the Sultanahmet district of Istanbul. Since the 1960s, the restaurant had become known not only for its traditional Turkish desserts but for its crowded bulletin board where travelers posted messages to friends and shared information about rides on the "hippie trail" through Turkey and Iran to Afghanistan, India, Nepal and points further east. "Minibus leaving for Kathmandu June 1. One seat left. $45. Bring your own tent." It was tempting, but I had a job and a mortgage back home in the UK.

I eventually made it to Kathmandu, not in a minibus but on a flight from Delhi. In 2007, I was invited to lead a UNESCO workshop on reporting on social and development issues for Nepal's national TV and radio broadcaster. In 2012, after a second UNESCO workshop on legal issues for journalists, Stephanie joined me, and we spent two weeks traveling.

Maoists in Business Suits

Nepal is a landlocked country, a little larger in land area than Greece or about the size of the US State of Iowa. Its northern

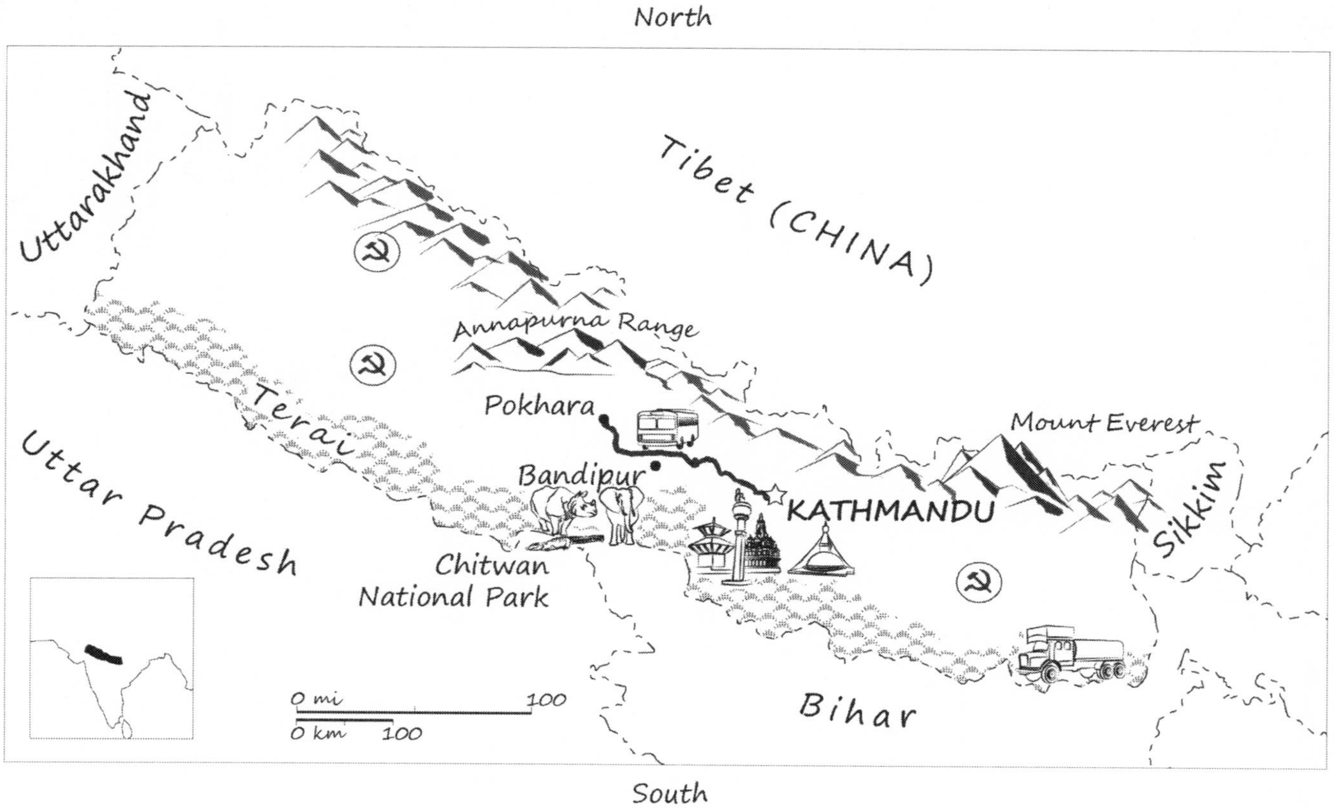

North

Uttarakhand

Tibet (CHINA)

Annapurna Range

Sikkim

Mount Everest

Pokhara

Bandipur

KATHMANDU

Bihar

Terai

Chitwan
National Park

Uttar Pradesh

South

0 mi   100
0 km   100

border with China is formed by the Himalayan range, which includes Mount Everest and eight more mountains more than 26,000 feet high. South of the Himalayas, the forested hills and valleys of the Pahad region, including the Kathmandu Valley, are heavily populated. The plains of the southern region, the Terai, crossed by low hill ranges, border the north Indian States of Bihar and Utter Pradesh and have a sub-tropical climate.

From the mid-nineteenth century, Nepal was a buffer state between the Chinese Empire and British India. Today, it remains stuck between, and dependent on, its two larger and more powerful neighbors. Because of the mountain barrier to the north, Nepal's links with India are stronger. In the Terai, the countries share a 1,000-mile land border over which (except during times of tension) people and goods move freely. Hindu and Buddhist pilgrims regularly travel across the border to religious sites and for festivals. Nepal depends on India for oil, gas and many other products, including medicines and manufactured goods. India is Nepal's largest trading partner, and most of its international exports go through the port of Kolkata. The Nepalese rupee is pegged to the Indian rupee. This gives the government of India a lot of leverage. Shut down the border crossings or limit the export of certain commodities and the feuding politicians in Kathmandu, faced by lines at gas stations and empty supermarket shelves, will soon come to their senses. Nepal's leaders are quick to say they resent India meddling in the country's internal affairs. In politics, memories are short. They have India to thank for helping broker the deal that, in 2006, ended a decade-long Maoist insurgency that claimed the lives of more than 16,000 Nepalis and paralyzed the economy.

The Maoists won most seats in the 2008 election, taking over leadership of a coalition government. Their leaders swapped their camouflage fatigues for business suits and entered the maelstrom of multi-party politics. The Maoist cadres were officially disarmed and rehabilitated; some younger fighters joined the army or police, while the older ones were given severance pay, skills training, a booklet on crop rotation and a bus ticket home to their village. However, there are still militias and armed wings of political parties around the country, and they know where they stored their Kalashnikovs and plastic explosives.

Despite the fears of Nepal's business class, the arrival of a Maoist-led government did not herald the end of capitalism-as-we-know-it. Foreign investment increased, the banking sector expanded, creaky, bureaucratic state-run public enterprises were slowly dismantled, and new hotels and restaurants opened to serve the growing number of tourists. The red flag with the hammer and sickle is still a potent political symbol, but these days most of the hammering is over deals for foreign aid and investment; farmers still use sickles, but they're being encouraged to study agricultural financing and marketing.

May Day march outside royal palace in Kathmandu.

Stephanie and I saw hundreds of red flags and banners at a May Day celebration in Kathmandu's Durbar (Palace) Square. There were a few fiery speeches from the podium—no Maoist politician would skip a May Day event—but the mood was party-like, with a live band on stage performing what sounded like Nepali techno-rap, presumably with appropriately proletarian lyrics. It was somewhat surreal to be touring the royal palace museum, which documents the wealth and achievements of Nepal's monarchs, and to look out of the palace windows on a sea of red-shirted, red-flag waving Maoist supporters. Were there any monarchists among them?

What About Those Royals?

For centuries, the country that would become Nepal was divided into rival states ruled by warrior chiefs. In the mid-eighteenth century, the Gorkha king Prithvi Narayan Shah embarked on a campaign to extend his realm and by 1769 had conquered the Kathmandu Valley, uniting the kingdoms of Kathmandu, Patan and Bhaktapur. The Gorkha armies moved east, gobbling up small kingdoms, but were stalled by the Imperial Chinese Army when they tried to invade Tibet. To the south, they tangled with the British East India Company; the Anglo-Nepalese War of 1814-1816 ended in a treaty that established Nepal's current borders.

The Shah dynasty was overthrown in 1846 in a violent palace coup. After a meeting at the palace armory turned ugly, a prominent noble, Jung Bahadur Kunwar, and his brothers killed more than 30 royal officials, military officers and palace guards, including the prime minister. Several hundred princes and chieftains loyal to the Shah monarchy were later executed. Bahadur Kunwar founded the Rana dynasty, in which the office of prime minister was made powerful and hereditary. The Shah king became a titular figure, stuck in his palace in Kathmandu and wheeled out for ceremonial occasions.

After the partition of British India in 1947, new political parties based in India allied with the Shah king Tribhuvan to overthrow the Rana regime and establish a parliamentary democracy. A decade-long power struggle ensued, with Tribhuvan and his successor, King Mahendra, accusing the politicians of corruption, failing to maintain law and order and putting party above national interest. In 1960, Mahendra scrapped the constitution, dissolved the parliament, banned political parties and established direct rule. For the next 30 years, Nepal was governed under the Panchayat system, a traditional form of party-less governance in South Asia where people elect representatives at the local, district and national levels. The system cut out the political elites, with the monarch holding the real power. The regime undertook land reform and development and infrastructure projects but at the same time curtailed civil liberties and press freedoms.

In 1990, strikes and pro-democracy protests forced King Birendra to abandon the Panchayat system and agree to become a constitutional monarch. The restoration of multiparty democracy led to a renewal of political infighting and, in 1995, the Maoist insurgency. By all accounts, Birendra accepted his reduced role with grace and worked hard to use what influence he had to serve the country. It all ended dramatically one night in 2001.

It was Friday, June 1, and most members of the royal family had gathered, as they did once a month, for a dinner party at the Narayanhity Royal Palace. In another part of the palace, the 30-year-old Crown Prince, Dipendra, was getting drunk and high on drugs. He put on his camouflage fatigues, loaded his weapons and marched into the dining room. He killed his father, his mother, Queen Aishwarya, and seven other members of the royal family, including his two younger siblings, before shooting himself in the head. He survived but fell into a coma. Because of the automatic succession law, he was declared king while lying in his hospital bed but died three days later. Birendra's brother, Prince Gyanendra, who had been out of town, was declared king.

Why did he do it? The most commonly accepted version is that Dipendra was angry with his family for opposing his plan to marry Deyvani Rani, a member of the Rana dynasty. They had fallen in love in England, where Dipendra attended Eton school and met Deyvani at the Norfolk home of his local guardian, the baronet Sir Jeremy Bagge. Deyvani had the social rank suitable for a royal marriage, but Queen Aishwarya opposed the match when she learned that one of Deyvani's grandmothers had been a concubine rather than a full-fledged member of the family. That was definitely a no-no in terms of preserving the purity of the Shah dynasty's family tree. Dipendra was willing to give up his title to marry, but Deyvani said no: she would be queen or there would be no marriage. Dipendra was devastated, and on the night of June 1, flew into a drunken rage.

Not everyone bought this version. Questions were raised about the apparent lack of security at the event and why the official investigation lasted only two weeks and did not include major forensic analysis. And why did Prince Gyanendra just happen to be out of town that evening? It was known that he had been unhappy with the country's shift to a constitutional monarchy and thought that Birendra had given up too much power.

Gyanendra came to the throne promising to defeat the Maoist insurgency, now in its fifth year. In February 2005, after political deadlock and delays in elections, he reverted to the autocratic style of his father Mahendra, suspending the constitution and assuming direct authority. Widespread protests forced him to back down and restore parliament in April 2006. A peace agreement was reached in which the Maoists agreed to lay down their arms and take part in the political process of drafting a new constitution. In May 2008, the constituent assembly declared Nepal a republic and abolished the monarchy. Gyanendra became a private citizen. Despite occasional calls for the restoration of the monarchy, the former king has stayed out of politics and, from his palace in Kathmandu, managed his business empire with interests in hotels, textiles, energy, tea plantations and auto dealerships.

Royal intrigues and massacres. You can't make this stuff up.

Old Patan

A short walk from our hotel in Kathmandu took us into the winding lanes of Patan (today, the city of Lalitpur). Once one of the three ancient kingdoms of the Kathmandu Valley, Patan has been absorbed by metropolitan Kathmandu, but has been well preserved as a historic district. Its streets are lined with three and four-story Newari houses, some dating from the eighteenth century. The houses, with elaborately carved and decorated windows, doors and pillars, almost seem to lean over into the street. Inside the low doorways are small businesses selling groceries, fabrics, saris, household goods, snacks, Hindu religious icons and mobile phone recharge cards.

Traditional Newari architecture—a wrought iron window in Patan, one of the three ancient kingdoms of the Kathmandu Valley.

Traditional Newari architecture—elaborately carved doorway in Patan.

Traditional Newari architecture—doorway in Patan.

Tucked between them are Patan's cottage industries. The area is famous for its metal work—from pots and pans and metal trunks to elaborate ornaments and decorations. Other workshops make windows, doors and furniture. There's a steady business in motorcycle repair. Machines weave wildly through the alleys, narrowly missing pedestrians, pushcarts and oncoming traffic. All the braking and bumping over unpaved sections strains the machines, but there's always a shop nearby to fix a tire or replace a busted cable.

Family outside storefront in Patan.

125

The Newars, a linguistic and cultural community of primarily Indo-Aryan and Tibeto-Burman ethnicities who practice both Hinduism and Buddhism, are the historical inhabitants of the Kathmandu Valley. Over the centuries, they became dominant in trade, industry and agriculture. The Newars are made up of castes associated with hereditary professions, such as potters, weavers, dyers, metal workers and jewelry makers. For centuries, Newari merchants handled the trade between Tibet and India, with porters and pack mules transporting merchandise over mountain trails. From the eighteenth century, the Newars spread out across Nepal and established trading towns.

The narrow streets of Patan eventually open out onto the Durbar (Palace) Square, with its temples and royal palace, listed as a UNESCO World Heritage Site. This was the center of civic and religious life in the kingdom of Patan, which vied for influence with the two other Newari kingdoms in the Kathmandu Valley—Kathmandu, across the river to the north, and Bhaktapur, to the southeast—until unification by the Gorkha king Prithvi Narayan Shah in the late eighteenth century. The palace, built in local brick with large, carved wooden windows around a series of courtyards, has been restored and is now a national historical museum.

In some cities, palace squares are cordoned off to protect the ancient monuments, separating them from the city around them. Yet all the Durbar squares are living, breathing hearts of cultural and commercial districts, with shops, restaurants and offices. Local people travel through them on their way to work or school. They worship at the temples, where goats, chickens and ducks are sacrificed. The temples are the starting places for religious festivals, with giant wooden chariots wheeled through the streets.

Stupas Galore

The skyline of the Boudhanath district, about seven miles from the center of Kathmandu, is dominated by the gigantic Boudha, one of the largest Buddhist stupas in the world. It's a UNESCO World Heritage Site and a major destination for both worshippers and tourists. As with many ancient religious sites around the world, there's considerable debate among historians and religious scholars about who built it and when it was built, with numerous references in mythology and religious writings. Suffice to say, there was probably something on this site from at least the fourth century. Since then, the Boudha has been rebuilt, enlarged and repaired, eventually yielding today's massive structure.

Boudha, one of the largest Buddhist stupas in the world and a UNESCO World Heritage Site.

The latest renovation was completed after the April 2015 earthquake which severely cracked the spire. As a result, the whole structure above the dome, and the religious relics it contained, had to be removed. The repairs, costing more than US $2 million, were funded entirely by private donations from Buddhist groups and volunteers.

The stupa is on the ancient trade route from Tibet to the Kathmandu Valley. After China invaded and annexed Tibet in 1950, many refugees who crossed into Nepal decided to settle around Boudhanath. Today, it is home to most of Kathmandu's Tibetan population, many of whom have never seen Tibet and probably never will. In other districts, you can't walk more than a hundred yards before coming across a small Hindu temple or shrine. In Boudhanath, the spiritual heart of Tibetan Buddhism in Nepal, it's stupas and monasteries.

The streets are full of Buddhist student monks (including a few transplants from New York and Paris) in their distinctive maroon robes. Far from being isolated from the real world (as Christian monks often are), they eat in the restaurants, shop in the stores and catch up on the sacred reading homework on their iPads and smart phones. Buddhism is big business in Boudhanath, with many traditional handicrafts including rugs and paintings, and the usual tourist tack. At stores where the speakers pound out a constant low-frequency chant, you can buy music to meditate by, recorded speeches by the Dalai Lama, and documentaries and action-adventure movies on Tibet and the Himalayas. To demonstrate that Buddhism is a world religion, there are also DVDs on Mayan culture, the Alaska wilderness and, more improbably, Jane Fonda's Complete Workout.

Maybe Jane isn't out of place, because Stephanie and I ate very well in Boudhanath. Indeed, we consistently underestimated portion size, and were sometimes unable to finish our evening meal. We particularly enjoyed the Tibetan dishes—the hearty *thukpa* and *thenduk* soups, *momos*, and *sha-bhalay*, a fried pastry stuffed with meat. All the yogurt dishes were excellent. In a predominantly Hindu country, the only beef in sight was that wandering along the highway medians, but the substitute was "buff," or water buffalo, which shows up in curries, soups and many other dishes. We avoided restaurants that claimed to offer Mexican, Italian, American and Continental cuisine, alongside the usual Nepali menu.

Whose Constitution Is It?

The Maoists proved much better at guerrilla warfare and election campaigning than at governing. The major challenge facing the coalition they led from 2008 was to come up with a constitution acceptable to all political and ethnic groups. There was broad agreement to move away from a centralized model to a federal system, similar to that in India, but no consensus on how this should be done or how to distribute power between the central government and the states. National politics in Nepal is notoriously fractious, with the major parties struggling to form coalition governments that all too easily fall apart; in the 11 years following the 2006 peace deal, the country had ten prime ministers. *The Economist* quoted the Nepalese political columnist C.K. Lal who described the ruling alliance in 2016 as a "fascistic formation consisting of malignant monarchists, malicious Maoists and malevolent Marxist-Leninists—each one masquerading as nationalists."[20]

Nepal, with a population of 30 million, is a diverse society with more than 100 languages (24 of them officially recognized), and social divisions between hill and lowland groups and upper and lower castes. It is still a primarily rural society, with about three quarters of the population employed in agriculture, most as subsistence farmers or farm laborers. The Maoists, who gained support during the insurgency and election campaigns by promising to redistribute land, alleviate rural poverty and protect the rights of minorities, backed proposals for states based on ethnic identity. The Nepal Congress and other parties thought this was a terrible idea. Apart from the usual platitudes about the need for a pluralistic, multi-ethnic society, they pointed out that some of the "states" proposed by the Maoists could never be economically viable. They would depend on handouts from the central government, and that would anger other states that were paying for their poorer neighbors. The negotiations and deal-making dragged on. Almost every day, the newspaper front pages featured a new map of states proposed by one political group or another. Meanwhile, ethnic groups, fearing that they would not get what they wanted, called *bandhs* that paralyzed commerce and transportation, set off bombs, kidnapped government officials and threatened journalists. The two major ethnic groups in the southern region of the Terai, the Tharu and the Madhesi, together make up more than one third of Nepal's population. According to Nepali journalist Anurag Acharya, "they have long complained about being treated unfairly by dominant hill-caste groups, taunted and politically marginalised for appearing to be

---

20. "Nepal's constitutional stand-off: Trouble in the basement," *The Economist*, January 30, 2016

'more Indian and less Nepali.'"[21]

It took a natural disaster to spur the notoriously fractious politicians into action. On April 25, 2015, a devastating earthquake with a magnitude of 7.8 struck Nepal. It was followed by a 7.3 magnitude aftershock two weeks later. The combined death toll was 8,500, with about 21,000 injuries and more than 600,000 buildings, including historic structures in the capital, damaged or destroyed. The coalition political parties finally came together and, on September 20, adopted a new constitution that divided the country into seven states.

The new constitution, noted *The Economist,* "looked like a stitch-up among the upper castes," gerrymandering the Tharu and Madhesi into states where they would be in a minority. The police and paramilitary forces cracked down ruthlessly on protests, with more than 40 people reported killed. With tacit support from India, the Tharu and Madhesi switched tactics and blockaded border crossings, cutting off vital supplies of oil, gas and other imports. The lines of trucks stretched for miles. In Kathmandu, cars and trucks sat idle on the sides of roads. Hotels and restaurants ran out of cooking gas. Pharmacies ran out of medicines.[22]

The Indian government decided not to intervene to open the border, knowing that its inaction would put pressure on the major parties. It was sympathetic to the Tharu and Madhesi but also feared that, a decade after the Maoist insurgency ended, the battle over state boundaries might tip Nepal into more conflict. The blockade lasted for six months but had the desired political effect. On January 23, 2016, the ruling coalition pushed through amendments to the constitution that went some way towards meeting the protestors' demands. Under the new rules, the Terai region would get a larger share of parliamentary seats, and marginalized groups would receive a percentage of state jobs. Some Nepalis are still not happy, saying the constitution does not grant adequate legal and civil rights to women. Some religious groups complain

21. Anurag, Acharya, "Nepal: A costly constitution," *Al Jazeera,* December 8, 2016.

22. "Mr. Oli's winter challenge: A growing fuel crisis is the outcome of Nepal's divisive constitution," *The Economist,* October 26, 2015.

that although the charter describes Nepal as a secular country, it requires the state to protect Hinduism and makes the cow, sacred to Hindus, the national animal. Others simply hope that a stable government will be able to get on with the job of improving the economy and health care systems and reducing power cuts.

Mountain Vistas?

Given the fuel shortages, Stephanie and I counted ourselves lucky that none of the buses on which we traveled ran out of petrol. They had other problems—broken seats, bald tires, the oil check light permanently on, excessive emissions and too many Bob Marley stick-on posters—but they got us where we were going. They were also cheap. We paid 300 *rupees* each (less than US $4) for a five-hour trip from Kathmandu to the crossroads town of Dumre.

The two-lane Prithvi Highway, named for the Gorkha king who conquered the Kathmandu Valley in the mid-eighteenth century, is the main route west, linking Kathmandu with Nepal's second-largest city, Pokhara, at the foot of the Annapurna Range. From the capital, the road winds up to the western ridge, then plunges down in a series of wild hairpin turns to the next valley. And so it goes—up again, down again, up and down, through a succession of deep river valleys for more than 125 miles to Pokhara. Construction of the highway began in 1967 with aid from China, and it was completed seven years later. Since then, it's been under almost constant repair. In spring when the snows melt, and in monsoon season, landslides block the road and crews have to remove boulders, mud and trees; water flowing down the mountain sides loosens the gravel and tarmac surface, making the road sink or lopping off short sections that tumble into the valleys below. For most of its length, the highway twists and turns with no passing lane; accidents are common as drivers attempt to pass trucks and buses on blind curves. Except in towns, no speed limits are posted. Vehicles dodge boulders, wandering cattle and goats, cyclists, and pedestrians. The highway is heavily congested with brightly-colored Tata and Leyland trucks wheezing up the slopes. Ironically, they sport logos that evoke speed and daring—Road Raja (king), A-One Boys, Off-Road Express.

Our so-called "long-distance" bus stopped for passengers almost anywhere; when the bus was full, with people standing or sitting in the aisles on sacks of rice, new passengers climbed up onto the roof. In towns, vendors boarded the bus. In Kathmandu, they sold bottles of water, soft drinks, snacks, T-shirts and flashlights; as we moved west, locally grown products dominated—peeled and sliced cucumbers with spicy relish, bunches of the small and tasty monkey bananas, smoked river fish on wooden skewers.

Our destination was the historic Newari town of Bandipur, high on a ridge overlooking the valley of the Marsyangdi River. From the late eighteenth century, Newaris established trading posts in the hills. Bandipur was founded at a point where overland routes from central Nepal and Tibet converged to head south, crossing the Terai to reach the railroads of British India. By the early nineteenth century, it was a stylish town with substantial houses, some with shutters and neoclassical façades. Its streets were paved with slabs of silver-colored slate. Bandipur began to lose its commercial importance in the 1950s when an airfield was opened at Pokhara. Its death knell appeared to have been sounded in 1972 when the Prithvi Highway was opened, leaving the town stranded on the ridge. Yet the bypassing of Bandipur turned out to be a blessing in disguise. Unlike other Newari towns on the highway where traditional buildings were torn down or obscured with commercial façades, its sturdily built merchant houses remained unchanged. When Nepal started attracting large numbers of tourists, they were converted into hotels, restaurants and stores, and the town prospered.

Stephanie and I left the bus in Dumre and took a shared taxi up the mountain to Bandipur. After the noise and traffic of Kathmandu, it was a welcome oasis. The main street, which is not open to motor traffic, is lined with three-story houses built from local brick, field stone and slate, with round logs supporting the floors. Slate is used for almost every building purpose—from street paving to the tables in our hotel, the Old Inn, a restored Newari house with a terrace overlooking the valley, dotted with rice paddies. We enjoyed walking around the town and enjoyed dinner in the company of other tourists. The air was clean and cool and the pace of life slow.

We decided to take one hike down into the valley to the Siddha

Cave, the largest in Nepal and the second largest in South Asia. The map from the hotel did not show where the trail began and so we wandered along the ridge for half an hour before someone directed us to the trailhead. It was a steep descent, made more hazardous by the slippery surface. Recent rains had dislodged rocks and scattered wet leaves along the trail. I went first, with Stephanie hanging onto my backpack for support. By the time we reached the cave, our toes were numb and bruised. We hired a guide and stumbled for a few hundred yards into the darkness, the guide's flashlight illuminating stalagmites and stalactites. By that point, Stephanie had had enough. "It's really dark and slippery on the rocks," she said. I went ahead with the guide. Stephanie sat on a rock and started singing, her soprano voice echoing through the cave. It was an easier, gentler descent to the Prithvi Highway, where we took a shared taxi back up the mountain. A few days later, Stephanie paid dearly for the adventure, when the nail on her big toe split and detached.

The terrace café of the Old Inn reportedly offers dramatic views of the Himalayan peaks to the north. Or, to use *Lonely Planet Guide* vernacular, a "gob-smacking vista." What the guide books don't tell you (although it may be in the small print) is that you have to be there at the right time. September and October, after the end of the monsoon season, are the best months for jaw-dropping, spirit-transforming mountain gazing. That's when Western tourists feel at one with the earth and sky, briefly consider converting to Hinduism or Buddhism (or at least reducing meat in their diet) and buy lots of art pieces that will forever need to be dusted. For those of us who show up in April and May, when the hotels have few guests and the temple guide touts are in price-cutting mode, the landscape is less dramatic. At the end of the long, dry season, the clouds are heavy with dust, creating a shimmering haze. The occasional evening shower cools the temperature by a few degrees but does not break it.

Elephants, Rhinos and Crocs

It was 6:15 a.m., and Stephanie and I were getting ready for a morning elephant ride in the jungle of Chitwan National

Park in south-central Nepal. We assumed the hotel staff would drive us to the park entrance to join other tourists. Instead, the Sapana Village Lodge literally provided door-to-door service. I looked out of the door of our room to see a *mahout* backing up his elephant to the second-floor terrace and waving at us. The elephant, catching sight of two overweight Westerners, belched and did an elephant-size dump on the flower bed.

Chitwan National Park covers an area of 360 square miles—about the size of South Dakota's Badlands—in the subtropical Terai lowlands. From the end of the nineteenth century, it became a favorite hunting area for Nepal's royal family and the ruling class. During the cool winter season, they traveled south to the forest and grasslands to stay in lodges and camps, and hunt tigers, rhinoceroses, leopards and sloth bears. From the 1950s, poor farmers from hill areas moved into the area and poaching became common. By the end of the 1960s, 70 percent of Chitwan's jungles had been cleared for agriculture, thousands of people had settled there, and the one-horned rhinoceros was on the verge of extinction.

The park was established in 1973, and its boundaries expanded four years later. The protection of wildlife came at a human cost. The Nepalese army burned down Tharu villages inside the park boundaries and forced people at gunpoint to leave their lands. The government did not provide new housing or land. The evictions fueled resentment against the government which played out over the next decades, culminating in the violent protests over the proposed state boundaries in the draft 2015 constitution.

Today, the park is home to 68 mammal species, including Bengal tigers, leopards, sloth bears, otters, foxes, badgers, hyenas, wild boars, antelope, and deer. Poaching has reduced the number of one-horned Indian rhinoceroses, and only about 2,500 still survive in the wild, but more than 400 of them are in Chitwan. More than 500 species of birds have been identified.

We did not see any tigers or bears during our excursion, but enough rhinos and other wildlife to return well satisfied. From the platform on the elephant's back (about seven feet above the ground), we had both sweeping and intimate views of the landscape—the rice paddies with the water buffalo grazing, the forest edge of the national park, small brick and family dwellings with bamboo roof joists and metal or thatch roofs, with goats tethered in sheds and chickens running free. With temperatures in early May often in the 100s, people get up early to cook, clean and tend their animals, so there were friendly waves and "Namastes" from those we passed. When we returned a couple of hours later, the sun was already high in the sky and some people (including us) were ready for a morning doze.

Across the River Rapti, we entered the forest of kapok, sal and rhino apple trees. The elephant paused here and there to lop off a few leafy branches to eat, then moved on with the *mahout* using the rope harness to direct and occasionally striking him with a stick. We saw sambar deer sheltering in the deep undergrowth, a pair of rhinos in a clearing, monkeys swinging from tree to tree and many birds. One wild peacock danced for us, the *mahout* deeming this a lucky sign. A few more grunts and dumps and then it was time to disembark (it literally feels like that) onto a platform. There are other ways of getting on and off an elephant, of course. The *mahout* stands on the trunk and has the elephant raise him up; he then basically walks up the head to his seating position. This looks like a maneuver you need to practice with a very cooperative elephant.

In the afternoon, we ventured deeper into the national park in a seven-passenger jeep, the guide standing on the runner to scan for animals. The dirt roads pass through areas of forest and grassland, crossing creeks and following the shores of lakes. Prime time for animal viewing is February and March, after controlled burns clear the grassland and the animals come out to forage on the new growth. By May the grasses are often six feet high. There could be a convention of tigers a few feet from the road and you would not see them. Still, we had some success—sambar, spotted and barking deer, a wild boar, three species of monkey, and many land and water birds including eagles and herons.

The big game count consisted of several one-horned rhinos. At a lake we saw one bathing, flipping around in the water. As I approached the shore through the undergrowth to get a better camera angle, I felt a tap on my shoulder. It was the guide. "Rhinos can run at 40 km per hour," he offered. I did a quick calculation. I can't run at 40 km per hour. The jeep was averaging 25 km per hour on the bumpy track. The rhino would win the race. No wonder the driver kept the engine running.

In the middle of the park is a crocodile breeding facility. It consists of a series of ponds, each containing one year's breed— from this year's minnows to whatever massive beasts are lurking below the surface in the other ponds. In the mid-afternoon heat, most of the crocs were beached and dozing. They're in all the rivers in this region and we saw three or four during a canoe trip the next day. They're at their most dangerous during monsoon season when the rivers flood and they show up in rice fields, backyards and hotel bars.

Admission to the national park is strictly controlled. Villagers are allowed to gather grass and forest products for eating and medicinal products. Every day, the so-called "government elephants," which are used for tourist rides, park patrols and agricultural work, cross the river to graze and return loaded with grass for fodder. Army patrols try to prevent poaching, which can carry a sentence of up to 15 years in jail. The poachers are after the big game—the wild elephants, rhinos, tigers, leopards, and bears. The illegal trade in tusk extracts and animal skins thrives in Asia, so the rewards are high. After a fall in wild animal population during the Maoist insurgency, the populations are coming back, and many Western aid agencies and corporations have funded research.

The unexpected highlight of our visit was an early-morning bird-watching walk with Mukunda, one of the naturalists from the hotel. After passing a line of much-too-serious Japanese birders, each of whom seemed to be carrying at least two cameras with long lenses and a tripod, we dove into the forest. Mukunda was expert at spotting the birds, and often he heard them before he saw them. We felt amateurish as we scanned the trees with binoculars. "Which branch? Oh, that one. Damnit, it just flew off." But we saw many birds—kingfishers, bee-eaters, mynahs, sand martins, red sunbirds, marsh hens, egrets, a purple heron, peacocks, a serpent eagle and something called the "brain fever" bird. We heard, but didn't see, the Indian cuckoo, but by the end of the hike Stephanie was doing a pretty good impression of its call. Mukunda knew all the plants—wormwood, wild turmeric, mimosa, *kusha* (the sacred grass used in Hindu ceremonies) and others that villagers use for medicines. Unfortunately, there's also lots of kudzu, which strangles and chokes native species.

We stopped to eat breakfast on the rickety terrace of the former royal lodge, abandoned since the fall of the monarchy in 2008—a string of bungalows overlooking the river with central meeting rooms. The jungle has invaded, with trees and creepers lacing over the buildings; the stucco is peeling from the brick walls, the roof thatch has been washed away by the monsoon rain, exposing the rusting metal, and the porches lean and sag. It was a scene of eerie, less-than-genteel decay. At one time, Nepal's royal family rode to the lodge on elephants. Now the only visitors are birdwatchers and monkeys.

Chapter 10

Making up Malaysia

★ ★ ★

Gun Belts on the Coat Rack, Please

I've never felt a pressing need to make a fashion statement with a pith helmet, but if I did, Kuala Lumpur's Coliseum Café would be the place to do so. When you push aside the swinging doors from Jalan Tunku Abdul Rahman, a busy downtown street, you'd be forgiven for thinking you'd stumbled onto the stage set for a glossy TV drama set in the waning days of the British Empire. The bar area looks like the kind of place Ernest Hemingway would have hung out if he'd traveled this way instead of going to Paris and Havana. Dark, wooden paneling, a worn tiled floor, high-back brown leather chairs, small wooden tables, and framed black-and-white photos and cartoons on the walls. Beside the bar a set of wooden screen doors leads into the main dining area, with white tablecloth-covered tables, swishing ceiling fans, coat racks on the walls, and elderly Chinese waiters, slightly stooped in posture after a long career of dish-carrying. All that's missing is a clientele of mustachioed British colonial officers and businessmen sweating in safari suits.

If this was a TV set, the producers would have gone over budget to give the place an authentically timeworn look, taking the shine off the woodwork and the floors, scratching the leather seating, and selecting a paint mix to give the walls a slightly blackened-by-cigar-smoke tinge. Fortunately, the century-old Coliseum Café needs no touch-ups because it is the real item. Since new owners took over in 2011, they have smartened up the place, replaced furniture and modernized the kitchen, but have been careful to retain its colonial-era ambience. Upstairs from the bar and dining room is the original hotel with 10 colonial-style rooms.

The Coliseum Café and Hotel was opened in 1921 by a group of business partners from the island of Hainan in southern China. After the Japanese occupation of the Malay Peninsula in World War II ended, it became a favorite hangout for rubber planters, tin mine owners and the British colonial brass who gathered in the bar for gin and tonics after a cricket match at the Royal Selangor Club. The café is duly famous for its char-coal-grilled sizzling steaks and Hainanese chicken chops, but the menu includes British comfort food, including fish and chips and bangers and mash; it may be the only restaurant in Southeast Asia where you can order mushy peas. "The food may not be Michelin-starred," noted owner Cheam Tat Pang, "but a lot of people will share the memories they have of this place."[23] He's right. I have no memory of what Stephanie and I ate there, but I vividly remember the place.

I did not use the dining room coat rack. It was a mild, sunny day and I didn't have a hat. I certainly didn't have a gun belt. That was not always the social norm. By the 1950s, when the mostly white clientele gathered at the café, some carried guns, and the post-cricket match conversations turned to labor problems at the plantations and mines, and attacks launched by communist guerillas from jungle bases.

It was called the "Malayan Emergency." And it lasted 12 years.

War in the Jungle

By the early twentieth century, most of the Malay Peninsula was effectively under British control. Penang Island, Malacca and Singapore formed the Straits Settlements colony. In the traditional Malay kingdoms, colonial officials served as "advisors" to

---

23. Joy Lee, "Nearly 100 years on, Coliseum Café is set to remake itself for the 21st century," *The Star*, July 13, 2013.

the rulers. The economy was based on the extraction and export of natural resources, primarily tin and rubber. To provide a labor force, the British brought in Chinese and Tamils from south India. Middle-class Chinese, like the founders of the Coliseum Café, arrived to engage in trade and business. The growth of the Chinese population created economic tensions with ethnic Malays, most of whom were subsistence farmers.

After World War II, Britain tried to revive the rubber and tin industries, but unemployment and inflation remained high. Communist-led strikes were brutally suppressed, with strikers arrested and deported. In 1946, Britain attempted to unite the peninsula into a single colony where all citizens—Malay, Chinese and Indian—had equal rights, but Malays opposed the weakening of their traditional rulers and the granting of citizenship to ethnic Chinese. The Malay Union was dissolved and replaced in 1948 by the Federation of Malaya, which restored the autonomy of the rulers under British protection. Ethnic Chinese felt betrayed and supported the demands of the Malayan Communist Party for the British to leave.

It is one of the ironies of history that many of the pro-independence fighters of the Malayan National Liberation Army (MNLA), the military wing of the Communist Party, had served in the guerilla army trained and funded by the British to fight the Japanese. They employed the tactics they had learned, including the use of explosives, firearms, and radios. Their support came primarily from rural Chinese, many of whom lived in poverty, faced racial discrimination, and were barred from voting in elections. The MNLA was led by Chin Peng, a charismatic 24-year-old trade unionist who had served as the liaison with British forces in operations against the Japanese. The MNLA said it was fighting the "Anti-British National Liberation War." The British called it the "Malayan Emergency," not only to downplay the conflict for propaganda purposes but for financial reasons. London insurance companies were legally bound to reimburse plantation and mine owners for losses during an emergency, but not for losses caused by war.

From its jungle bases, the MNLA targeted police and military posts, railroads and bridges, mines and plantations. Its leaders calculated that if they disrupted the economy, the British would find it too expensive to maintain their occupation. At first, the British did not know how to fight an enemy who moved freely in the jungle and enjoyed support from the Chinese rural population. In 1950, a new strategy was adopted to cut off the MNLA from its supporters and food supply. Platoons went out on search and destroy missions, killing livestock, spraying crops with chemical herbicides, burning houses and executing villagers accused of harboring guerillas. More than half a million rural people, most of them Chinese, were forcibly relocated from land on the fringes of jungles to "new villages," surrounded by barbed wire and police posts. Meanwhile, the British launched a hearts and minds campaign by giving medicine and food to Malays and indigenous tribes. The guerillas were driven deeper into the jungles. The strategy provided a model for future anti-insurgency operations, notably (but with much less success) by the US during the Vietnam War.

From 1955, with dwindling forces and shortages of arms and food, MNLA attacks became less frequent. In 1957, Malaya became an independent country, although one in which ethnic Chinese did not enjoy the same political, economic and legal rights as Malays. By the time the conflict officially ended in 1960, the crowd at the Coliseum Café was less worried about guerilla attacks than about lobbying the new political elite for tax breaks.

A Country of Many Parts

Malaysia fits well into my not-so-scientific category of cobbled-together countries, along with Malawi, Bangladesh and Nepal. Geographically, the country is divided into two distinct parts. Peninsula (Western) Malaysia, the far southeastern tip of mainland Asia, is about the size of England or Greece, or the US State of Louisiana. More than 75 percent of Malaysia's population of 32.4 million (2020) live in peninsula Malaysia, which accounts for most of the country's economic output. On the other side of the South China Sea, East Malaysia—the States of Sabah and Sarawak and the island of Labuan—occupy more than one quarter of the land area of Borneo, the world's third largest island (the rest is part of Indonesia). East Malaysia makes up about 60 percent of the country's land area but is less developed and has less than a quarter of the country's population.

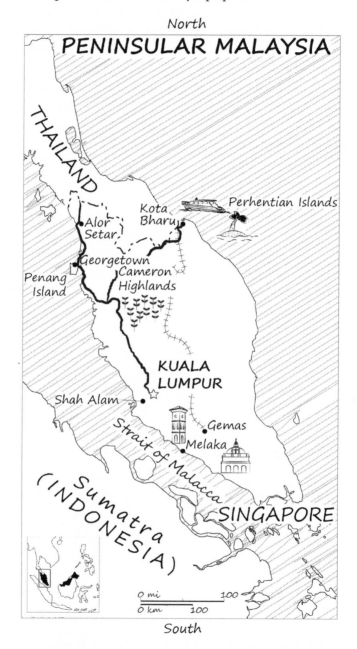

Creating a united Malaysia has been a challenge. It began in 1948, when Britain abandoned its plan for a colony in which all ethnic groups had equal rights and gave the traditional Malay rulers a leading role in the Federation of Malaya, consisting of nine states and the colonies of Penang Island and Malacca. The Federation gained independence in 1957. Six years later, the British colonies of British North Borneo (Sabah), Sarawak and Singapore joined, and the federation was renamed Malaysia. After two years of political intrigue and ethnic protests, Singapore, with its majority ethnic Chinese population, left the federation and became an independent country.

Singapore's exit is symptomatic of the intense inter-ethnic politics that has marked the country's history. For more than six decades, the United Malays National Organisation (UMNO) has dominated the political landscape. The party is pledged to protecting the interests of the Bumiputera (derived from the Sanskrit *bhumiputra*, meaning "son of the earth"), the term used to describe the Malay Muslims and indigenous peoples who make up half of the population. The Bumiputera, notes *The Economist*, trust UMNO "to defend racial laws that give them a leg up over their ethnic Chinese and ethnic Indian compatriots," with access to higher education, government jobs and social and economic benefits. Through "gerrymandered electoral districts, compliant courts and the use of colonial-era sedition laws," UMNO has managed to divide the opposition, muzzle the press and survive a series of corruption scandals and internal fissures to retain its grip on power.[24]

Malaysia's borders are not only geographical and physical, but ethnic, social and political. Ethnic groups—not only the Chinese and Indians but indigenous groups in East Malaysia—feel marginalized.

Everything Works Here

In January 1997, Stephanie and I flew to Kuala Lumpur (usually known as KL) from Tashkent in Uzbekistan. At that time, we were

---

24. "Politics in Malaysia: No more Mr. Nice Guy," *The Economist*, August 29, 2015.

living in Bishkek, the capital of Kyrgyzstan, where I was teaching on a Fulbright faculty fellowship. It was the middle of winter—a cold one, even by Central Asian standards—so we decided to head south for the semester break. At that time, there were only two possible destinations, both from Tashkent—Bangkok or KL. A university colleague and his wife were working in KL and offered to show us the city. We boarded the bus from Bishkek for the overnight journey on snow-covered roads to Tashkent. The next day, we were relaxing by a hotel pool, drinking fresh squeezed lime juice.

The first thing that struck us about Malaysia—and it said as much about where we'd come from as where we'd come to—was that everything seemed to work. We had spent the last six months in a country that, less than five years after the collapse of the Soviet Union, was going through profound economic, social and political changes. We were used to things *not* working—no stock on the shop shelves, no money in the banks, no heating in the apartment or classroom, buses that ran out of petrol, trash piled up in the streets, government offices with no one on duty. In Malaysia, the phones worked. There were no power outages. The streets and sidewalks were clean, the buildings well maintained. Everything was available in the stores. We spent much of our second day walking around a small mall, ogling consumer goods we hadn't seen for months, something we would never do in the US. We had become so used to the maxim "If you see it, buy it, because you may not see it again," that we quickly filled our shopping bags. We had come with a long list of stuff we could not get in Kyrgyzstan.

We stayed the first three days in Shah Alam, a sprawling suburban area west of KL in the Klang Valley. Take away the tropical vegetation, the mosques and the signs in Bahasa Malay, and we could have been in any US metropolitan area with freeways, office blocks and malls. In downtown KL, we visited museums, the impressive Victorian railway station, and the Petronas Twin Towers which, at 1,483 feet high, was at that time the tallest building in the world. The towers were not yet open to the public, so we just had to imagine the view.

Chinatown sprawls across a dozen blocks with temples and fine

British colonial-era buildings. Its heart is Jalan Petaling, decorated with Chinese lanterns and lined with street stalls, selling everything you can imagine and probably a few things you can't. More upscale is the Central Market, the former food market on the bank of the Klang River, which was saved from demolition and converted into a market for traditional arts and crafts, a category which apparently includes cameras and mobile phones.

On our last day in the city, we joined thousands of pilgrims and onlookers for the Hindu Thaipusam festival, held in the Tamil month of Thai which falls in late January or early February. It is dedicated to the deity Lord Murugan, who embodies valor, youth, beauty, power, and perhaps a few other virtues I've neglected to mention. It culminates at the massive limestone Batu Caves, one of the most popular Hindu shrines outside India.

The festival began in 1892, two years after an Indian trader, inspired by the scepter-shaped entrance to the main cave, built a temple and statue of Lord Murugan. It begins with a procession from a temple in KL with a silver chariot bearing a statue of Lord Murugan pulled by two bulls. Devotees accompany the chariot along the eight-mile route. On their shoulders, some carry offerings of milk in brass or clay pots on huge decorated carriers called *kavadi*. The heaviest *kavadi*, six feet tall and weighing up to 150 pounds, are built of bowed metal frames which hold long skewers, the sharpened ends of which pierce the skin of the bearers' torsos. We were told they go on a strict vegetarian diet for a month or so before they attempt this mind-over-body feat. After bathing in the nearby Sungai Batu (Rocky River), the devotees climb the flight of 227 stairs to the shrine where priests sprinkle consecrated ash over the hooks and skewers before they are removed. There's no blood shed.

Other pilgrims, while not emulating the *kavadi* bearers, display their pain management by piercing their bodies with dozens of hooks; some had limes or little silver jugs attached to them. Others had skewers running through their cheeks and tongues. Small children, some with their heads shaven, struggled up the steps clutching simple clay pots with milk. All were fulfilling, in their own way, vows of thanks and penance to Lord Murugan.

A Beach Town without the Beach

After five days, Stephanie and I escaped the noise and traffic of KL for the mountains. The country's highest peaks, including Mount Kinabalu, at 13,435 feet half the height of Mount Everest, are in East Malaysia. In peninsular Malaysia, a spine of uplands, with some mountains more than 6,000 feet high, runs down from the border with Thailand until it peters out south of KL. Except where they've been cleared for agriculture, they're covered with jungle.

We took the bus northeast for 120 miles, the last 60 on twisting mountain roads, to the Cameron Highlands. The region is named for William Gordon Cameron, an explorer and geologist who in 1885 was commissioned to map the border area between the States of Pahang and Perak. Lying between 2,500 and 5,000 feet above sea level and with gentle forested slopes, the highlands were suitable for the cultivation of tea, coffee, fruits and vegetables. The British decided it was a good place to establish hill stations where the crowd at the Coliseum Café could escape from the sweltering summer heat of the lowlands. By the 1930s, a road had been built from the main north-south coastal route, and the Cameron Highlands boasted three hotels, two boarding schools, a military camp and a golf course, surrounded by nurseries, orchards, vegetable farms and tea plantations. Development was halted during World War II and the Emergency, but today the Cameron Highlands is one of the most popular resort areas in the country.

We stayed in the small town of Tanah Rata. In Malay, the name means flat ground—just enough level land for one main drag, called Jalan Besar (Big Road) with stores and an array of restaurants, but not much else. Stephanie likened it to "a beach town without the beach." We stayed at a small guesthouse run by an amiable Malay guy who inexplicably shortened his real name, Kalamedin, to Bob. There was not much to do except take walks, read, and play cards. We attempted one jungle walk, which ended in a scramble up a slope where the monsoon rains had partly washed away the path. And we toured one of the lush green tea plantations that cover the slopes around the town. The tea tree is Tanah Rata's cash crop, with black, oolong, white, and green tea all coming from the same leaves but processed differently to create the tea varieties. Most of the workers are Tamils, originally from South India and Sri Lanka. Their settlement reminded me of an Appalachian coal camp—a single row of company houses, a store, and a school, surrounded by the plantation with the tea processing factory up the hill. And a Hindu temple instead of a Baptist church.

In the Name of the King

European explorers and military commanders did not show much imagination in naming the places where they built forts and trading posts. After they pulled up their boats on the shore under the gaze of perplexed native inhabitants, the commander would plant the flag in the sand, say a prayer and claim the territory for the monarch. "By the grace of God, this land shall forever be in the realm of His Imperial Majesty ..." At this point, the speaker might pause and turn to a subordinate. "We've been at sea for two years. No news from home. Is George still on the throne?" The muddled conversation among the crew that followed might be worthy of a *Monty Python* skit. "It's what's-his-name, I think he was the Prince of Wales." "Charles?" "No, it's William or James." "You're sure it's not the Duke of Norfolk?" "Nah, he's a Catholic." Finally, the commander would reassert his authority, and make an educated guess: "In honor of the king, we will call the fort George Town." If there was a new monarch on the throne by the time his dispatch reached London, someone could discreetly change the name.

It's understandable why explorers, merchants and military commanders would name places after royalty. Whether or not they were loyal subjects, it did their military or business careers no harm to be able to report that the monarch's name now graced some far-flung colonial trading post. In place-naming, the French had it easiest because all their kings from 1610 until the 1789 revolution were called Louis. Most of the Dutch kings in the same period were called Willem. It was more challenging for the British who had James, Charles, William, Mary, Anne and George.

Royal Navy captain Francis Light got it right on July 17, 1786, when his small force landed in a swampy patch of jungle on Penang Island, off the northwest coast of the Malay Peninsula. George III had been on the throne since 1760 and, despite the loss of his American colonies three years earlier, was still reportedly in good health. For Captain Light, it was a safe bet to name the fort George Town. Over his 60-year reign, George III lent his name to many other places around the world. Three more Georges who succeeded him added to the tally. Today, in addition to the settlement on Penang Island, there are four Georgetowns in Australia, four in Canada, four in the Caribbean, three in Africa, two in India and, amazingly for the nation that rebelled against the monarchy, almost 50 in the US.

Captain Light was not confronted by native inhabitants, perplexed or otherwise, because he had done a deal with the Sultan of Kedah, the northernmost kingdom in the Malay peninsula. The Sultan, facing a threat from the kingdom of Siam to the north, agreed to cede Penang Island to the British East India Company in return for military protection. The island, about one third the size of Singapore, was strategically situated at the northern end of the Strait of Malacca between the peninsula and the island of Sumatra, on the main route for commerce with China and the Spice Islands. Captain Light developed George Town as a free port, allowing merchants to trade without having to pay tax or duties. The goal was to draw traders from Dutch-controlled ports in the region, principally Malacca to the south. Sea traffic grew rapidly, and by 1792 George Town had a population of 10,000. It would become the base from which the British began colonial expansion in the peninsula.

By the early nineteenth century, farms on Penang Island were producing nutmeg, cloves and pepper, making George Town a center in the spice trade. In 1826, the island became part of the Straits Settlements, a loose grouping of British colonies that included Malacca and Singapore. After the opening of the Suez Canal in 1869, with steam ships taking over international commerce, George Town became the major export point for the peninsula's tin mines. Its growing wealth attracted trading firms and banks, making it a financial center. Population growth strained public services such as water, sanitation and health care and the crime rate increased, culminating in riots in 1867, when rival Chinese triads clashed in the streets. Britain took over direct control of the Straits Settlements from the East India Company. Public health care and transportation improved, and the police cracked down on the secret societies.

In World War II, Japanese forces carried out a systematic purge of what they believed to be hostile elements among the local Chinese population. George Town became a base for the Japanese Imperial Navy and German U-boats operating in the Indian Ocean shipping lanes. Allied planes from India bombed the port and warehouses, while ships laid mines to impede shipping. The island was liberated in August 1945.

After Malaya gained independence in 1957, the Malay-dominated government decided to invest in developing KL and the nearby cargo facilities at Port Klang. George Town lost its status as a free port and went into an economic decline that lasted almost half a century. Colonial-era buildings fell into disrepair. In response, NGOs and the private sector launched a campaign to revitalize the center, and in 2008 it was named a UNESCO World Heritage Site.

The city and island still have a rich ethnic mix, with Malays, indigenous tribes, Chinese, Tamils from southern India, and Europeans. The Chinese population includes an ethnic sub-group, the Peranakans, descendants of immigrants from southern China who arrived in the Malay Peninsula between the 15th and 17th centuries. They have left their mark in distinctive architecture and the hybrid Nyonya cuisine that uses typical Malay spices. The intermingling of ethnicities and religions has given George Town an eclectic assortment of colonial and Asian architectural styles. Walking around the historic district, we found Confucian and Hindu temples on almost every street, and the occasional church. Although all the streets now have official Malay names, many residents still use the shorter, more familiar English names. Penang Island is one of the most popular tourist destinations in the country, with beaches and shopping malls. Now that most commercial cargo traffic is handled through the port of Butterworth on the mainland, George Town's Swettenham Pier has become the busiest port-of-call in Malaysia for cruise ships.

The city is famous for its banana leaf restaurants, where your place setting is simply that—a large banana leaf. You order your main dish—chicken, beef or fish—and the waiter serves you rice, vegetable dishes and meat on the leaf. You eat everything with your fingers. It's an acquired skill, and Stephanie and I did our best to imitate the dexterity of the locals. We failed miserably.

On Island Time

From George Town, we crossed back to the mainland and headed east by bus on a mountain road with breathtaking views of the highlands and jungle. Our destination was Kota Bharu on the east coast, near the border with Thailand. In Malay, the name means "new city" or "new fort." During the nineteenth century, the city became the capital and commercial center of the Sultanate of Kelantan, which grew prosperous from its tin and gold mines and agricultural economy. The sultans built impressive palaces, royal buildings, and mosques.

We had arrived during Ramadan when Muslims fast during the day. More than 90 percent of the local population are Muslim, so for breakfast and lunch we had to rely on Chinese and Indian restaurants. At night we joined the Malays who broke their fast about 7:30 p.m. to eat at the night market. We dined on chicken and beef satay, *murtabaks*, the savory or sweet stuffed pan-fried bread, coconut milkshakes with scoops of ice cream, and fresh-pressed cane sugar juice. After dinner, we retired to the roof garden of our guesthouse to play cards.

From Kota Bharu, we boarded a ferry for the two-hour trip to Perhentian Kecil, one of two small islands in the South China Sea. In Malay, "Perhentian" means "stopping point," a reference to the islands' traditional role as a waypoint for traders between Bangkok and the Malay Peninsula. For centuries, the islands had a sparse population of fishermen, but today there are more tourists than locals.

There are no jetties on Perhentian Kecil. Our ferry pulled into a bay, and a small motorboat came out to pick up the passengers. We waded through the warm water to the beach. There are no cars or roads on the island. Just one fishing village and palm-fringed coral sand beaches with backpacker hotels and small restaurants. We stayed in a hut with a straw roof a few feet from the beach. There were outside showers and no electricity; at night, your light comes from a Coleman lantern.

The water was warm and clear, wonderful for swimming. One day we rented masks and snorkels and swam out to the reef at the edge of the bay. The turquoise-blue waters were teeming with tropical fish—cuttlefish, parrotfish, clownfish and rays—dodging in and out of the coral. Later in the day, as we played cards at the bar, one of the hotel staff emerged from the water with a huge tuna he had speared. "Your dinner!" he shouted. On another day we took the short jungle path to the other side of the island to go swimming. The Perhentian Islands are home to numerous species of monitor lizards, venomous spiders, and geckos. Later, as we were having a drink at the Iguana Bistro, one of its regular customers showed up—a seven-foot iguana. Perhentian Kecil—it was about as close to a tropical paradise as any I've seen.

The Jungle Railway

Our final destination was Malacca (today called Melaka), the colonial port city on the west coast, south of KL. To reach it, we had to travel diagonally southwest through the mountain region in the middle of the peninsula. We decided to take the train, romantically described in the *Lonely Planet Guide to Southeast Asia* as the "jungle railway." All the southbound express trains ran at night, so we opted for the day train to see the countryside. We should have asked about arrival times because it turned into an 18-hour marathon (the bus from Kota Bharu to Malacca does the trip in about half the time). The problem is that it's a single track almost all the way. Because we were on the local train, we had to give way to all the northbound expresses. We would stop at a station, pull out to the points, back up onto the second track, and wait—sometimes for 60 to 90 minutes—until the northbound train sped past. At one point, a fellow traveler made the unhelpful calculation that we were doing an average of nine miles an hour. We were treated to fine views of the jungle and remote villages, but we seemed to stop everywhere. We reached the end of the line, a town called Gemas, at about one o'clock in the morning. We took the bus into Malacca the next day.

Controlling the Sea Lanes

"Whoever is Lord of Malacca has his hand on the throat of Venice." Tomé Pires, the Portuguese envoy, writing soon after the capture of the city in 1511, was thinking about what today we would call the supply chain. Malacca is strategically situated midway along the narrow, 550-mile strait between the Malay Peninsula and the island of Sumatra, connecting the Indian Ocean with the South China Sea and the Pacific Ocean. For centuries, it has been a major shipping lane, linking China, Japan and Southeast Asia with India, the Arabian peninsula, East Africa and the ports of Europe. By capturing the city, Portugal was able to grab a share of the lucrative spice trade with the Moluccas (Spice Islands), as well as the commerce in glassware, camphor, textiles, perfume and precious stones.

From the seventh century, the maritime empire of Srivijaya, based in Sumatra, had controlled two maritime choke points— the Strait of Malacca and the Sunda Strait between Sumatra and Java. By the mid-fifteenth century, the rising power in the region was the Malacca Sultanate, founded by the Malay ruler of Singapore, Iskandar Shah. Malacca's trade expanded and the city became a cultural and educational center for Islam and Malay language, literature and the arts.

On August 24, 1511, the Portuguese general Alfonso de Albuquerque and a force of 1,200 captured the city. They spared the Chinese and Burmese population but had the Muslims massacred or sold into slavery. The Dutch, who were building an empire in the East Indies, captured Malacca in 1641 with the help of the Sultan of Johor, whose ancestors had been booted out by the Portuguese. In an 1824 treaty, the Dutch traded Malacca to the British East India Company for part of the island of Sumatra, and it later became one of the three colonies in the Straits Settlements.

Today, the city retains many vestiges of its colonial past. Near the harbor are the ruins of the original fort, *A Famosa* («The

Famous» in Portuguese), and a small gatehouse, the *Porta de Santiago*, among the oldest surviving European architectural remains in Southeast Asia. In the eighteenth century, the Dutch used existing Portuguese fortifications to build a larger fort with cannons facing east to guard against landward attacks. Nearby, the well preserved *Stadthuys* (city hall), with its distinctive red exterior and clocktower, was built in 1650 as the office of the Dutch Governor.

We climbed the hill to Saint Paul's Church, originally built in 1521, the oldest church building in Malaysia. The eighteenth century Christ Church, built in Dutch colonial style, began its spiritual life as a Dutch Reformed Church before switching to Anglicanism after the British arrived; its graveyard indicates the diversity of the population with tombstones in Portuguese, Dutch, Armenian and English.

Malacca boasts more than 30 museums, dedicated to the usual topics—history and ethnography, maritime trade, Islam—and to a few unusual ones such as stamps, toys and kites; one is housed in a submarine. With a lively Chinatown on Jonker Street, it's a favorite weekend getaway for people in KL and Singapore and attracts many foreign visitors, especially from China, Taiwan and Indonesia.

Lost in the Mallosphere

Since that first visit in 1997, I've returned to KL four times to teach workshops. My hosts usually book me into the Federal Hotel, a high-rise on Bukit Bintang (Star Hill) in the heart of the city's premier shopping district. I don't mind shopping, but I've never thought of it as a recreational or cathartic experience; it's something I have to do, and if it doesn't take too much of my time, then all the better. The idea of taking a one or two-week vacation to go shopping and flying thousands of miles and spending money on hotels and meals to do so, strikes me as strange, but I've seen enough people doing it to realize that I may be in the minority. Certainly, as a business traveler at the Federal Hotel, I was a misfit among all the other guests on their shop-till-you-drop orgies. Tour buses disgorged their human cargo, many sporting color-coded group stickers, into the lobby. They wandered around the sprawling hotel, taking videos of each other. The Federal has high-priced souvenir and jewelry shops, an upscale Chinese restaurant, an Irish pub, a Japanese bar, a night club and a revolving restaurant on the roof. Breakfast is in the faux-Hawaiian Kontiki restaurant, with bamboo-roofed love seats, a Hawaiian/oldies muzak mix and absolutely no place to plug in a laptop.

The real shopping experience is in the numerous multi-level malls on Bukit Bintang and the side streets. The behemoth is the 48-story, twin-towered Berjaya Times Square, with its Big Apple-themed sections. In square footage, it claims to be the 13th largest shopping mall in the world; it boasts more than 1,000 retail stores, 65 food outlets, a hotel, and an indoor theme and amusement park with a roller coaster and archery range where you can work off any excess energy you have left after hours of retail therapy. There are the high-end malls such as Pavilion and Starhill Gallery with their luxury brands; the formerly high-end Lot 10 has sunk into the mid-range to join Fahrenheit 88, the former KL Plaza, renovated and rebranded to reflect the average temperature in the country; the more down-market Sungei Wang Plaza is patronized by teens and less affluent shoppers. The 12-story Plaza Low Yat ("Malaysia's largest IT lifestyle mall," whatever that means), which used to be a rather seedy place where you could pick up pirated software and movies, has reinvented itself as a respectable retail mall. There are at least seven large malls, and several smaller ones, within a three-block radius of KL's so-called Golden Triangle. The main point of discussion on the travel websites is whether you need two or three days to cover them all.

For me, a couple of hours was enough. In the vast mallo-sphere, my usually reliable sense of direction deserted me. It's a rabbit warren of entrances, exits, levels and connecting tunnels and walkways with thousands of small stores. Malls over, under and beside other malls. Squeezed between them at street level are cheap luggage stores, money changers and massage parlors. The narrow passages are crowded, and signs everywhere warn of pickpockets.

Most evenings I walked the short block from Bukit Bintang to

Jalan Alor ("Alor" means city, so this is simply City Street). It is lined with low-priced restaurants—most of them Chinese, with some Thai, Vietnamese and Indian—that fill the sidewalk and half of the street itself. The décor is basic—wooden tables and plastic lawn chairs—but there's no need for ambience or table cloths when you have a front-row seat to an Asian street scene. People of all ethnicities are out walking. Porters with hand carts deliver fruits and vegetables. Vendors wander among the tables hawking lottery tickets, glow-in-the-dark toys, watches, sunglasses, and selfie sticks. I strolled by the restaurants advertising their signature dishes—clay pot vinegar pig trotter, frog porridge and special fish head—and check out a Vietnamese. There's braised snail with salt, grilled blood cockles, steamed pork womb with onions, and that truly indigenous Vietnamese specialty, bread with baloney. I sat down among the tanks of live fish, and unadventurously ordered grilled beef, vegetables and steamed rice.

My favorite place is Wong Ah Wah (WAW), a Chinese restaurant at the southern end of the street, recognizable by the incongruous Mickey Mouse logo on its sign. It occupies a full three storefronts, with one more housing a large kitchen, full of smoke and interesting smells. Unlike other restaurants, where hawkers tempt customers by waving menus in front of them, WAW does not need the promotion, because it's almost always full. It has a thick menu of reasonably priced dishes—fish of all types, cooked many ways, barbecue chicken wings (and many other chicken and pork dishes), two pages of frog dishes and creative vegetable dishes such as grilled potato leaves with garlic.

Urban Hijau

In the middle of KL, surrounded by high-rises and mega-malls and under the haze that daily shrouds this city of eight million, lies a green oasis. On a sloping half-acre plot, a small group of volunteers raises a wide variety of vegetables, fruits and herbs. This is Urban Hijau (Green), a pioneering project that encourages urban farming through permaculture methods. "Traditionally, Malays were farmers," my guide Saqib Sheikh told me, "but in large cities, people often don't know where their food comes from, and gardening is no longer part of the culture."

One of the reasons is KL's urban crowding and high proper-ty prices. The Urban Hijau group is fortunate. The landowner, herself an urban farming enthusiast, rents the group the plot for a nominal 1 *ringgit* (25 cents) a month. The concrete foundation and pillars of the house she once planned to build are now the location for workshops and produce markets. Outside the gate, there's a drop-off point for plastic bottles that are filled with sand to form the walls of mandala gardens, designed so that volunteers can work without stretching. Clay tiles purchased to build the house roof line other mandalas. Wood chips and not-so-fresh mushrooms make for good compost. Most beds are nourished with goat manure. "We can use almost anything," said Saqib.

Because of Malaysia's hot, humid climate, volunteers harvest almost every week, year-round. There's spinach, eggplant, beans, bananas, papayas, sugar cane, rice, medicinal plants such as roselle, a type of hibiscus, and a fish pond. The group has built a drip irrigation system to conserve water. On the edges of the terraces, one volunteer was planting vetiver, a rooted grass that strengthens the soil to prevent erosion.

"I'm not a farmer," said Saqib, "but each of us contributes our skills. I do the marketing, the events, social media, fundraising." Urban Hijau was formed by graduates of a permaculture class who firmly believe in participatory decision-making. "We all have day jobs," said Saqib, "so sometimes it's difficult to meet. We make a lot of decisions on WhatsApp."

The Super Nice Express to Alor Setar

"I need to take a bus to Alor Setar," I told Neelem, my workshop driver, when he picked me up at the Federal. "Why would you want to go there?" he asked. "There's nothing but rice paddy fields."

I said I planned to visit my friend Adrian Budiman, who was teaching at the Universiti Utara Malaysia (University of Northern Malaysia). Could Neelem recommend a bus company? I'd checked on the web, and there were several that took the highway 280 miles up the west coast to Alor Setar, capital of the State of Kedah and the major city north of George Town, less than 40 miles from the border with Thailand. On the return trip that evening, he reported back. "Super Nice Express. Very fast, efficient and comfortable." I bought the ticket at Puduraya, the central bus station, the next day and e-mailed Adrian to tell him I'd be in Alor Setar by mid-afternoon at the latest. "Super Nice Express?" he wrote back. "That's probably one level down from the Super Duper Nice Express."

At Puduraya, it seemed that every bus company had a gimmick or slogan, apart from the usual Express (Ekspres) or Executive or Luxury in its name. If you want to go to Singapore, take the "Smiling Bus." For mystery and suspense, travel on the Matahari Ekspres. Or the Backpacker Ekspres to the Cameron Highlands, which Stephanie and I had visited in 1997. In the dark, humid underground bus parking area, thick with diesel fumes, I wandered up and down, trying to match the number scrawled on the back of my ticket with the bus license plate. The bus arrived half an hour late, and it wasn't the Super Nice Express but the Jasmine Express. Half an hour out of the city, we stopped at another bus station and were told to change buses. Evidently, the Jasmine was supposed to shuttle us here and then go on to another destination. We waited in the hot sun for 30 minutes until we boarded the Shamisha Holiday Express and, at last, got on the highway north.

Our next unexplained stop was on the other side of the highway toll booth. Ten minutes later, the Jasmine Express rolled up and let off one passenger who hadn't made the change. I hoped that we were now finally on our way to Alor Setar and would probably arrive about 90 minutes later than scheduled. I settled down to look at urban and rural Malaysia flashing by. Suburban KL, which seemed to grow by leaps and bounds every time I visited, sprawls over the low hills, with new residential and commercial developments. North of the city, most of the hill country has been taken over by palm oil plantations, one of Malaysia's main agricultural exports. Then the highway climbs through a range of jungle-covered limestone mountains, the stone exposed in sheer cliffs. Every couple of miles, there was a concrete and cement factory with a limestone quarry. We stopped for lunch at the Agro Mall, a sprawling development with a WalMart-size hypermarket, a food court, children's playground, and a mosque. At 1:00 p.m. on Saturday, it was packed. Someone told me that local families often take a short trip to the service area on weekends to shop and have lunch.

As we headed north, passing the suburbs and industrial areas east of Penang Island, we entered the coastal plain, and the palm plantations gave way to rice paddies. The State of Kedah is Malaysia's rice bowl, accounting for half of national production. Many paddies were still festooned with the debris of the recent national election—the flags of the ruling (and victorious) UMNO, white scales of justice on a blue background. Adrian later told me that all flags—the Malaysian equivalent of yard signs—were supposed to have been removed after the election, but the rice farmers hadn't bothered; perhaps the flags provided them with useful markers for planting and harvest.

About 3:30 p.m., we exited the highway again and pulled alongside an SUV with its trunk open. The bus driver loaded boxes stored in the luggage compartment into the car, then smoked a cigarette while talking to the driver. Twenty miles south of Alor Setar, we pulled over again to allow a group of passengers from another bus to board. At about 6:15 p.m., we reached Alor Setar. A journey advertised as a 5 ½ hour trip had taken almost eight hours. "Are you sure you took the Ekspres?" Adrian joked when I joined his family for dinner at a fish restaurant on the beach.

Across the Border for Lunch

In an Islamic nation, Kedah is one of the most conservative states. Almost all women wear the headscarf and Adrian's university is in session Sunday through Thursday, leaving Friday (the prayer day) and Saturday as the weekend. By contrast, in KL, Friday is a working day with a two-hour (or longer) lunchtime break for prayers. Alcohol is readily available (if pricey) in KL, but you won't find any in Kedah. Yet a few miles north on the highway is the border with Thailand where temptation beckons for not-so-strict Muslims. This is a major commercial truck route (keep driving north and you'll reach Bangkok) and a busy border crossing, with many Thais commuting to Malaysia for work. For those on the

Malaysia side, it's a quick trip for lunch or shopping at the large duty-free store in the no-man's-land between the border posts.

Adrian and I parked at the duty-free and walked over the border to the town of Dannok. The Malaysian passport officials were all business; the Thai officer hit Adrian up for a 1 *ringgit* (25 cent) "service charge" but didn't charge me. Dannok is a scruffy border town, with small hotels, restaurants, fruit and vegetable markets and street hawkers. After the almost sterile cleanliness of some Malaysian cities, it was somewhat reassuring to see litter on the streets. And Dannok is a lot livelier than the Malaysian towns on the other side of the border, especially at night when the bars and clubs open. I wandered down a side street and came upon the red-light district—skimpily-clad girls hanging out in open air restaurants and darkened storefront signs advertising the "Sexy Karaoke Club" and "Girls, Girls, Girls." Just a few hundred yards away was conservative Islamic Kedah. Only in a border zone can two contrasting worlds come so close together.

Chapter 11

The Highlands of Thailand

★ ★ ★

No Pain, No Gain

"Maybe you should try a massage at Wat Pho?" my colleague Greg Emery suggested to Stephanie over dinner in Bangkok. "I had an old knee injury from football and they really helped me."

Stephanie did not have a sports injury, but four months earlier she had suffered a nasty fall. Late at night, she had got up to answer the phone and, in the dark living room, tripped over a large lump in the middle of the floor. It was our dog, Tyke, a black Labrador. Tyke wasn't hurt. Stephanie sustained a spiral fracture of the right humerus, the long bone in the arm that runs from the shoulder to the elbow.

"I don't need to operate—it will heal itself," the orthopedic surgeon told her after looking at the X-rays. It didn't. The right arm was numb, and Stephanie had difficulty driving and lifting objects. A neurologist concluded that some nerve endings had been damaged but assured her they would heal in time. For two months, she went to physical therapy but felt no improvement. She decided that the therapy was not helping and quit.

I was scheduled to travel to Thailand at the end of November, as a member of an Ohio University faculty team accompanying about 40 students who would work with students from Bangkok University on projects for businesses and non-government organizations. Stephanie said she would join me for a vacation after the projects were completed; her mother, Marge, heard about it and decided she wanted to come too. They flew to Bangkok at the end of my second week and joined Greg for dinner on the second night.

The temple complex of Wat Pho, some of whose buildings date from the late seventeenth century, is in the center of Bangkok, just south of the Grand Palace, the residence of kings since 1782. Wat Pho houses the largest collection of Buddha images in Thailand, including a 46 meter long reclining Buddha. The temple is considered to be the first public university in Thailand, and taught its students religion, science, and literature through murals and sculptures. A school for traditional medicine and massage was established in 1955, and now offers courses in Thai medical practice, pharmacy, midwifery, and, luckily for Stephanie, Thai massage.

Stephanie and Marge took an autorickshaw—in Thailand, it's called a *tuk-tuk*—from the hotel the next morning. At Wat Pho's medical pavilion, they decided to go for "the whole shebang," the one-hour hot herb treatment, a bargain at about US $6. The language barrier proved no problem for Stephanie, who has a background in improvisational comedy. She pointed to her upper arm, then used her hands and a snapping sound to indicate that it had been broken and wiggled her hand to show it was numb. The therapist, a squat, muscular woman in her 30s, nodded and motioned to her to lie on the massage table. She started working the muscles and bones, pushing, pulling and prodding at precise pressure points. Stephanie gritted her teeth and tried to smile, but at one point yelled out in pain.

Her tormentor smiled. "No pain, no gain," she replied. Apparently, these were the only English words she knew.

At the end of the session, Stephanie's arm felt sore, but the numbness had disappeared. The traditional Thai massage had worked its magic. She has never felt the numbness again.

Three weeks later, back in the US, she called our medical insurance company to relate the story. "How much did you and I spend on physical therapy?" she asked, almost rhetorically. "It was useless. For much less, I could have flown to Bangkok, gone to Wat Pho for the massage, had a nice meal and flown home."

The customer service representative said she would note the comment. As far as Stephanie knows, Bangkok flights and Thai massages are still not listed as approved medical procedures.

Leaving Bangkok

I was more than ready to leave Bangkok. I'd had a jam-packed two weeks in the city. Days full of meetings. Hours stuck in the city's notorious traffic jams, trying to figure out whether I would be one or two hours late for the next appointment. The city's *wats*, canals and other sights were mostly blurs, glimpsed from taxis and *tuk-tuks*. I was working as teacher, counselor, planner and all-around problem solver. I didn't get much sleep.

One night, a student knocked on my door at 2:00 a.m. "Left my billfold in a cab on the way back to the hotel from a club. We need to report it." The student and I took a *tuk-tuk* downtown to the tourist police. Although I knew the chances of recovering the billfold were remote, especially because the student didn't have a clear recollection of where he had been that evening, we went through the routine of reporting the loss. The officer looked across at the table. "Your son?" he asked. I smiled. The student was a light-skinned African-American. Just as some Americans think Thais, Malays, Vietnamese and Indonesians all look the same, so the officer could not distinguish between us. "My student," I answered. I got back to the hotel at 5:00 a.m. and was up two hours later to help teams prepare for their final presentations.

After their successful trip to Wat Pho, Stephanie and Marge joined me to see some of the sights I had missed. We joined the students for a Saturday tour of Ayutthaya, the ancient Thai capital north of Bangkok which for almost 400 years was a major trading, cultural and religious center, with links to China, trading states in Southeast Asia, France, Spain and Holland. We visited the wonderful teak house built by Jim Thompson, a World War II US intelligence officer who became a silk trader and disappeared mysteriously in the jungle in the 1960s. We took a waterbus along a canal, ending up in Chinatown where the streets were closed for parades in honor of the king's 76th birthday.

Chilling in Chiang Mai

The next morning, we took the 90-minute flight to Chiang Mai, 450 miles northwest of Bangkok. Thai colleagues told me that the 11-hour daytime train trip was the more interesting way to travel, offering an ever-changing panorama of rural Thailand, of rice paddies and jungles, villages and temples. It was a good way to decompress after the hustle, bustle, noise, pollution and rip-offs of Bangkok. But not everyone likes to travel the way I do, and I had to go with the group decision.

Although Chiang Mai is the second largest city in the country and the provincial capital, its population in 2001 was less than 200,000 (compared to an estimated 10 million living in the Bangkok area). There were none of the snarling jams that turned the three-mile taxi trip from Bangkok University to the hotel into a 90-minute ordeal. In Chiang Mai, you could hop on a *tuk-tuk* or *songthaew* (literally "two rows), a converted pickup with bench seats in the back and a cap, for about 25 cents and be almost anywhere in the city in 10 minutes; we also heard the *songthaew* called a monkey taxi, probably because you feel like you're swinging in the trees as you hold on.

Chiang Mai, founded in the late thirteenth century, was the political, religious, economic and cultural center of a series of regional kingdoms. As a prosperous trading center, it was also on the itinerary for invading armies. The Burmese took the city twice and ruled it for more than 200 years from the mid-sixteenth century. A moat was built to help repel invaders, and in 1800 the Thai king, who recaptured the city from the Burmese in 1775, had his viceroy, Chao Kavila, build monumental brick walls around the inner city. Under Kavila, who also built a river port, Chiang Mai became an important regional trade center. Teak merchants from Burma moved there, building mansions and *wats* to show that their wealth came with divine blessing. The railroad arrived in 1921, finally linking northern and central Thailand. Word soon spread that the northern capital, surrounded by misty mountains, was a great place to unwind and go shopping for arts and crafts. The tourists have been coming ever since.

Wated-Out

Chiang Mai has a long list of must-see historical sites, including a dizzying number of *wats* (at least 300). We joined the students for a visit to Wat Phra That Doi Suthep, about 10 miles northwest of the city, in a spectacular location on the slope of the 5,000-foot Doi Suthep peak, with sweeping views of the city. The *wat*, established in 1383, is one of the north's most sacred temples; you approach it by climbing the 300 steps of a staircase built in the form of a giant serpent. In the city, we visited several *wats*. It's easy to get "*wated*-out," just as tourists in France, Germany and Italy feel weary and confused after visiting a dozen cathedrals and churches in a single day. Too many arches, columns, statues, tombs and relics. Too many towers, *stupas* and Buddhas.

For most of the students, the highlight of the Chiang Mai trip was a two-hour elephant ride. Each elephant had a *mahout*, who had worked with his elephant for its whole life. Our caravan of elephants crossed a small river and wound up through jungle paths. Halfway along the trail, Stephanie and I stopped to buy a bunch of bananas for our elephant, but that didn't hold him for long; with an average consumption of 25 kilos of vegetable matter a day, elephants are constantly eating leaves and vegetation, breaking off whole branches with their trunks.

The next day, a group of about 20, led by an American who's worked in Thailand for 30 years, traveled to a Hmong village. The Hmong hill tribes in Vietnam and Laos sided with the US in the Vietnam War and many had to flee, some to the US. In northern Thailand, the government encouraged them to settle in villages and stop growing opium, their major cash crop. Now they grow vegetables and flowers and make distinctive handicrafts. This was a remote village, inaccessible to the tour buses, and we had a fascinating visit, seeing homes and learning about Hmong history and customs. Unlike other hill tribes that have adopted Western ways, the Hmong have worked hard to maintain their traditions.

On the way back to Chiang Mai, we stopped in a Karen village. With its modern houses, cars and satellite dishes, the contrast with the Hmong village was palpable. This region of northern Thailand remains an unstable area. The hill tribes have traditionally moved freely across the borders of Thailand, Myanmar, Laos and China's Yunnan province, and have resisted government attempts to settle them. In Myanmar, the opium trade has financed armed conflicts, with the Karen, Shan and other tribes fighting for autonomy or independent homelands.

Shopped-Out

The high-rise hotel where we were staying with the students was modestly priced but was crowded with tourists on cheap package tours. The companies running the tours had names such as Overseas Adventure Travel and Jungle Tours but as far as we could tell most of the touring took place in shops, and the major adventure was trying to figure out if someone was selling you real silk or a real sapphire. The Chiang Mai area is Thailand's major handicrafts center, and we were advised to buy here rather than in Bangkok because the prices were lower and selection better. The industry is highly organized, with buses pulling up to huge stores selling jewelry, silk, lacquerware and handicrafts, disgorging their passengers to spend their dollars, pounds, euros, yen and yuan.

Most tour companies get kickbacks (sorry, I meant to say "commissions") for taking their customers to specific stores. If you understand that's how the system works, that's fine. Just don't believe your friendly tour guide when he says he'll get you that "special discount" because the store manager is his cousin.

The students experienced this form of free enterprise after the elephant ride. The buffet lunch was at an orchid farm where, of course, you could buy jewelry and knick-knacks made from orchids. Then it was on to a handicrafts "village" where we saw people making umbrellas and fans and were encouraged to visit the showroom. After that, a huge jewelry emporium, where we were treated to a promotional video before being ushered into the store. By that time, about half the students had had enough, and wanted to go back to the hotel, so we hustled up a couple of vans and divided the faculty team. I stayed with the group as they went on the lacquerware and silk factories, and the silver emporium. After being *wated*-out I felt shopped-out.

My Heart's in the Highlands

After the students left (some heading home, some for the beaches of the south), Stephanie, Marge and I moved to a small guesthouse in the inner city. It was nice to unwind, hang out in cafes and pubs, and shop on the markets. Chiang Mai has a large expatriate community (mostly Americans, British, Australians, French and Germans). For them, the city has all the cultural advantages of Bangkok, but fewer of the disadvantages. They run trekking companies, restaurants, guesthouses, pubs and other small businesses.

Stephanie and I lingered in a second-hand bookstore owned by an American. "Highlands," a track from the 1997 Bob Dylan album, *Time Out of Mind,* was playing. The song's title is thought to be borrowed from the poem "My Heart's in the Highlands" by Scottish poet Robert Burns, whom Dylan later cited as his greatest influence. We pored over the large selection of English language books while Dylan wandered from a conversation with a waitress in a Boston restaurant to the Scottish hills, horses and hounds. And so on, *non sequitur.* But not *ad nauseam.* At that time, "Highlands" was Dylan's longest known studio recording at 16½ minutes ("Murder Most Foul," released in 2020, is 23 seconds longer), but it fit my post-Bangkok decompression mood perfectly. I imagined that many people had come to Chiang Mai in the Thai highlands in the 1970s and 1980s to smoke opium and bond with nature, and just stayed. Their hearts were in the highlands. Somehow, it did not seem like such a crazy idea.

ata

Chapter 12

The Maldives:
Island and Nation Building

★ ★ ★

You're a small island nation in the Indian Ocean and you're running out of land. What do you do? Simple. You build another
island. Just find a large enough area of coral reef on an atoll that's
a few feet below sea level, dump concrete blocks on top of it, add
fill dirt and sand, plant a few coconut palms and you have a new
island. Then add a harbor and start building apartment blocks.

It's called Hulhumalé (New Malé in the native language of
the Maldives, Dhivehi). Malé atoll, the capital, is one of the most
densely populated urban areas in the world, with about 145,000
people living in an area of just 3.6 square miles. Walk around the
island (even at a leisurely pace, it takes less than an hour and a
half). It's completely built up. To make space for a new building,
an existing one has to be demolished.

With congestion and a severe housing shortage, the only option
is to expand to nearby islands or build new ones such as Hulhumalé, a five-mile, 20-minute commute by ferry from Malé. Despite
projections that rising sea levels may submerge the Maldives
within the next 75 years, Maldivians believe they're here to stay
and are building for the future. Existing islands are being extended
and their sea defenses strengthened, and new islands are planned.

The reclamation of Hulhumalé began in 1997; seven years
later, when it was officially inaugurated by President Maumoon
Abdul Gayoom, it had apartment blocks, a school, a mosque, a

hospital, government offices and commercial buildings. It is, so to speak, built up, in that it is several feet higher above sea level than other islands. Construction has continued in phases, with roads, apartment blocks, houses and commercial and industrial plots added. A causeway links Hulhumalé to the next atoll to the south, Hulhulé, the site of the international airport.

The Housing Development Corporation (HDC), the government agency developing the island, displays a timeline of satellite imagery from 2007 to 2018, as construction progressed. While the engineers were dumping sand and gravel, the marketing team was dredging up large deposits of lavish prose to describe the project: "Emerging from beneath the waves, the city of Hulhumalé remains a beacon of development for the Maldives."

Hulhumalé is branded as a "youth city" and a "smart city" with fiber optic networks and unspecified "green" architecture and energy sources. Maldivians and expatriates are being enticed to buy beachfront condos. HDC lists "the top 25 reasons" for companies to invest in Hulhumalé, at least half of which involve tax breaks or the ability to protect investments. By 2016, the population had risen to 40,000, with an eventual target of 240,000. If Hulhumalé ends up with that many people, it may start feeling as crowded as the capital, because it has a land area of only 1.5 square miles. Of course, the government can just keep on reclaiming more coral reef to expand the island. Its policy is to encourage people to move from distant islands to Hulhumalé and other islands in the center of the archipelago where there are better job prospects and access to public services. In total, about two thirds of the total population of Maldives could eventually be concentrated into six islands.

Hulhumalé, now the Maldives' fourth-largest island, is its most ambitious and expensive island reclamation project, but not the only one. Some islands are designated for specific purposes. There are fishing islands and picnic islands and resort islands. And an island for dumping trash.

Landing in Malé

Most foreigners in the Maldives are there for a vacation. From the airport, they are whisked away by seaplanes or fast launches to luxury private island resorts, where they go snorkeling in the tropical waters, relax on the beach and enjoy fine dining. My Maldives adventure was more prosaic—one week in Malé in 2012 to lead a workshop on legal issues in media, sponsored by the Asia-Pacific Institute for Broadcasting Development and the Maldives Broadcasting Commission.

I was told that when you fly into Malé, all you see on either side of the plane is water and you mentally brace yourself for what US airline stewards call "the unlikely event of a water landing." And then, suddenly, you're on the ground. I didn't have that experience because my flight from Colombo, Sri Lanka, arrived in the dark at 2:00 a.m. at Velana International Airport on the "airport island" of Hulhulé. I boarded the ferry for the choppy 10-minute crossing to Malé. The previous year, the government had announced plans to build a 1.3 mile bridge from Hulhulé to the capital, but the plans stalled, and funding dried up when the charismatic but controversial president, Mohamed Nasheed, was forced to resign. Eventually, the Chinese stepped in with US $200 million in funding and the 1.3 mile Sinamalé bridge (also known as the China-Maldives Friendship Bridge), the first inter-island bridge in the country, was opened in 2018.

Lots of Islands, Not Enough Land

The Maldives lie just north of the equator, 300 miles southwest of the southern tip of India and 450 miles southwest of Sri Lanka. At last count, the archipelago consisted of 1,192 islands, most of them too tiny to appear on any but the largest-scale maps. They are grouped in a double chain of 26 atolls, composed of live coral reefs and sand bars, situated on top of a 600-mile long submarine ridge that rises abruptly from the Indian Ocean and runs north to south. About 200 islands are inhabited, with fishing villages strung around the edges of the atolls; another 90 are private resort islands, with more being developed.

The archipelago is spread across about 35,000 square miles of the Indian Ocean, an area as large as Portugal or Hungary or the US State of Indiana, making the Maldives one of the world's most dispersed countries. Paradoxically, it is also one of the most

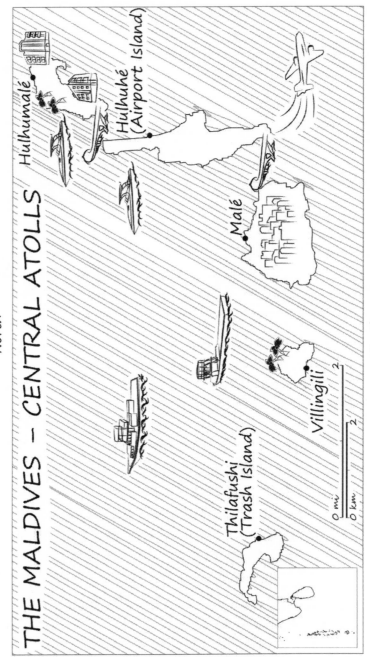

THE MALDIVES – CENTRAL ATOLLS

North

South

Hulhumalé

Hulhulé
(Airport Island)

Malé

Thilafushi
(Trash Island)

Villingili

0 mi   2
0 km   2

densely populated because there's a lot of sea and not much land. The population of more than half a million is squeezed into less than 120 square miles of land. If you gathered all those small islands together, you would have an area a little smaller than the city of Detroit or Philadelphia, albeit with much nicer weather. In any case, the 1,192 islands and 120 square miles of land are dodgy statistics, because more than 80 percent of the land is less than one meter above sea level. The UN's Intergovernmental Panel on Climate Change has warned that, at current rates, the rise in sea level will make most islands uninhabitable by 2100.

The government wants to keep as many islands as it can above water for as long as possible, not only to protect inhabitants but because the islands define the Maldives' 200-nautical mile Exclusive Economic Zone (EEZ). Under the United Nations Convention on the Law of the Sea, the surface of the ocean is open to all shipping, but what lies beneath is national property. Historically, the convention has been used mostly to protect domestic fishing industries. That's important for the Maldivian economy in which fishing provides employment for about 25 percent of the population. Because the archipelago stretches across such a wide area, its EEZ totals about 331,000 square miles—twice the size of California. If oil or other mineral resources are discovered on the ocean bed, as they have been in other areas of the Indian Ocean, the Maldives could strike it rich by licensing drilling rights. In some island nations, the real estate that lies under the sea is more valuable than the land above it. However, the land must be above water to claim the sea around it. If the predictions of rising sea levels hold, the Maldives stands to lose both.

Trading Buddhism for Islam

There's no consensus about the origin of the name "Maldives," although the most commonly accepted version is that it derives from the Sanskrit *mālā* (garland) and *dvīpa* (island), which would make it the "garland of islands," the kind of slogan tourist promoters would invent, even if it did not have a historical basis.

According to legends from the southern atolls, the Maldivian kingdom has existed for 2,500 years. The early settlers probably came from what today is south India. Buddhism arrived during the third century BC when the Emperor Ashoka expanded his dominion across most of the Indian subcontinent. The Maldivian kings promoted the religion, and most archaeological remains are from Buddhist stupas and monasteries.

The Maldives are strategically located on shipping lanes across the Indian Ocean. From the tenth century, Arab ships, trading between the Middle East and the Malay Archipelago, stopped off to take on provisions and trade with the locals. The most commonly traded items were cowrie (sea snail) shells, which were widely used as currency in Asia and the East African coast, and coir, the saltwater-resistant fiber of the dried coconut husk, which was stitched together and used for rigging on trading *dhows*. Religion followed trade and after more than a thousand years of Buddhism, Maldivians converted to Islam by the mid-twelfth century. The last Buddhist king took the title of Sultan and founded the first of a series of six Islamic dynasties.

From the sixteenth century, European colonial powers vied for trading rights. The Portuguese, sailing from their colony in Goa, were the first to arrive in 1558, but were booted out 15 years later after an ill-advised attempt to impose Christianity on the population. From the mid-seventeenth century, the Dutch, who had replaced the Portuguese as the dominant power in Ceylon (Sri Lanka), established trading posts, but wisely left the sultans in charge of local politics and religion. After the British expelled the Dutch from Ceylon in 1796, the Maldives became a British protectorate. It remained an Islamic state with the sultan as ruler. Its defense and foreign relations were controlled by Britain which later established a Royal Air Force base on a southern atoll.

The Sea is Rising

Independence came in 1965. Three years later, the monarchy was abolished, and a presidential republic established. The next decade was marked by factional infighting, but in 1978 Maumoon Abdul Gayoom began the first of six terms as president, ushering in an era of political stability and economic progress, with tourism and foreign investment growing.

In April 1987, a tidal surge caused severe flooding in Malé, damaging breakwaters, retaining walls, the harbor, jetties, and apartment blocks. With aid from Japan, Gayoom had a massive concrete seawall built around the city. He was the first president to warn about the danger of rising sea levels, telling the 1992 United Nations Earth Summit: "I stand before you as a representative of an endangered people. We are told that as a result of global warming and sea-level rise, my country, the Maldives, may sometime during the next century disappear from the face of the Earth." The Maldives was the first country to sign the Kyoto Protocol in 1997.[25] In December 2004, the Indian Ocean tsunami swept across the island chain. Six islands were totally destroyed, 14 had to be evacuated and 57 others were flooded, causing major damage to property and infrastructure. More than 100 people lost their lives and total damage was estimated at more than US $400 million.

In 2008, a reform candidate, Mohamed Nasheed, was elected president, promising to end corruption and restore political and civil liberties. His administration inherited a huge debt, and an economic downturn following the 2004 tsunami and the 2008 financial crisis. Nasheed did not endear himself to the conservative political and religious establishment by imposing taxes on goods and services and introducing social welfare benefits, but his warnings about climate change were probably his political undoing. In November 2008, concerned by forecasts of rising sea levels, he announced plans to use tourism taxes to purchase new land in India, Sri Lanka, and Australia. "We do not want to leave the Maldives," he said, "but we also do not want to be climate refugees living in tents for decades."

Already under fire for his secular policies and economic and social reforms, the president's comments on climate change got him into hotter-than-tropical water with the tourism industry. His climate change campaign, which featured TV appearances in the US, including *The Daily Show with Jon Stewart* and *The Late Show with David Letterman*, and the world's first underwater

---

25. Jon Hamilton, "Maldives builds barriers to global warming," *NPR Morning Edition*, January 28, 2008.

cabinet meeting, with ministers in scuba diving gear, attracted global attention, but did not go down well at home. In late 2011, political unrest grew, with opposition groups claiming Nasheed's policies were undermining Islamic practices and traditions. Nasheed resigned in February 2012 after a police and army mutiny. Although he won most votes in the first round of new presidential elections in late 2013, the result was annulled by the Supreme Court and Nasheed was arrested and imprisoned.[26] Maldivians told me that his gloom-and-doom messages had a serious impact on the tourist trade.

In the period immediately after Nasheed's resignation, when rival groups vied for influence, street protests in Malé were a weekly event. On a Friday night in September 2012, I watched from the balcony of a restaurant as a noisy opposition march made its way along the main east-west drag to the national stadium. The march was also playing live on the big-screen TV a few feet from my table. Friday is the prime day for public protests in Islamic countries because most people have the day off and protests usually start after Friday prayers. This one was a peaceful affair, with lots of speeches, flag-waving and marching. It also had a sound track, with a truck with large speakers pumping out what sounded like Maldivian reggae and the demonstrators gently rocking to the beat. At least the government allowed the march to be held, and the police did not intervene, stationing themselves on the side streets.

At times, the TV coverage looked like amateur video as the camera jerked suddenly in one direction or another. I figured out that the videographer did not have a vantage point but was pushing through the crowd to reach the spot where the party leaders were speaking. When the camera eventually reached the main speaker, a supporter nudged her, and she turned around

26. Nasheed reentered politics in September 2018 when the party of President Abdullah Yameen, which borrowed millions of dollars from China for the bridge and other infrastructure projects, suffered a surprise election defeat. Nasheed, now Speaker of the parliament, has claimed that the loans have created a "debt trap" that will allow China to dominate the Maldivian economy and influence its politics. Anbarasan Ethirajan, "China debt dogs Maldives' 'bridge to prosperity'," BBC News, September 17, 2020.

to face the camera. In every country, politicians know there's a larger audience on TV than on the street.

"Sun-Kissed Beaches and Tranquil Lagoons"

There are three Maldives. The best known is the Maldives of the tourist brochures—pristine sandy beaches, waving palm trees, and upscale resorts where the alcohol flows freely (if expensively) and the service staff (mostly migrants from Sri Lanka) open doors, place imported flowers in your air-conditioned room, crew the yachts, take out the trash and serve you cocktails on the beach. It's the tropical idyll. There are 90 so-called resort islands (that means the island is owned by a private company or individual). They are described in the *Hello Maldives* brochure as "enticing tourists with their sun-kissed beaches and tranquil lagoons, the turquoise-blue waters studded with pristine corals and the swaying coconut palms, splashing rich hues of jade, azure, turquoise and sapphire shades so quintessentially tropical." Whoever wrote this gushing copy could benefit from a strong dose of adjectival antidote.

The growth of the tourism industry in the last half century has been remarkable. In the early 1970s, the Maldives, with a population of 100,000, was one of the world's 20 poorest countries, its economy largely dependent on fisheries and trading local goods. It was a series of small, undistinguished blobs on the map of the Indian Ocean, and on no one's list of tropical destinations. The first two tourist resorts were opened in 1972. Since then, tourism has transformed the economy. In 2019 more than 1.7 million visitors came to the islands. Tourism is the single largest contributor to GDP, accounting for two thirds of foreign exchange earnings. More than 90 percent of government tax revenue comes from import duties and tourism-related taxes. The development of tourism has created jobs in other sectors, particularly in fishing, retail, and construction.

I did not visit any resort islands and was not particularly interested in doing so. I spent my time in the second Maldives—the city of Malé, home to one quarter of the country's population of more than 500,000, with a visit to Villingili, an island west of Malé with a population of a couple of thousand (and reportedly only five cars).

The Capital, Malé

Malé has a limited number of tourist sites. There's the Mulee'aage, the official residence of the president, built in the British colonial bungalow style and completed in 1919. Close by is the Medhu Ziyaaraiy, the tomb of Abdul Barakat Yoosuf Al Barbary, a religious scholar from Morocco who is credited with bringing Islam to the Maldives in 1153. Across the road, the Old Friday Mosque (Hukuru Miskiy) was built in 1658 in the reign of Sultan Ibrahim Iskandar I. Like other mosques in the Maldives, it's constructed of coral boulders; although the coral is soft and easily cut to size when wet, it makes sturdy building blocks when dry. Its original thatched roof was later replaced by wood joists and a metal roof. It's surrounded by a seventeenth-century cemetery with intricately-carved tombstones.

Malé is the commercial and transportation hub of the country with the largest seaport, businesses, banks and media. It's a crowded, lively place, with many small shops and cheap restaurants. Why pay resort prices when you can have fresh tuna kebab with fried rice and a soda for US $6? The main drag is lined with shops selling clothes, shoes and children's toys and crowded with pedestrians and motorbikes. Almost everything—construction materials, petrol, clothes, meat, fruit and vegetables—has to be imported (mostly from India, Sri Lanka and Malaysia) so prices are high.

About one in five people in the Maldives works in the fishing industry, the second-largest foreign exchange earner after tourism. Indeed, that's what most people did until the tropical paradise was discovered by the wealthy sun-seekers and people got TVs, Nikes and mobile phones. At one time, the stocks of tuna, blue fin, yellow fin, mullet and other species were plentiful, but over-fishing has led to a decline and the imposition of strict limits on catches by commercial boats. Although nets are used to catch small fish such as sardines for bait, only line fishing is allowed for larger fish which is why fishing boats need large crews. Jadullah Saeed, one of my workshop participants, told me that fishermen use a hook that pops out of the mouth of the fish as he swings it onto the boat. When you're catching fish one by one, that's the most efficient way to do it.

At the Malé fish market, shoppers and restaurant owners bid on the catch, then take the fish to a counter where a line of men expertly and speedily gut and fillet them. Maldivians have many recipes for fish. They can be grilled with spices and served with a vegetable fried rice, cooked into a curry or barbecued—as a whole fish or as kebabs. The most common item in the hole-in-the-wall restaurants in Malé is a deep fried whole fish, seasoned with curry. Cheap and delicious, you eat it cold with your fingers. Of course, you can buy Western food but why would you want to? All the meat is imported from Sri Lanka and India. The chicken on the lunchtime buffet at my hotel was edible but the "beef" was tough. Beef? I doubt it. As in Nepal, most "beef" is actually "buff" (water buffalo).

There's no pork, of course, because the Maldives is an Islamic country. And while the resort tourists enjoy their beach parties with US $50 bottles of Cabernet, the rest of the country is entirely dry. It's difficult to figure out the strength of religious feeling, because every Islamic country adopts a different posture depending on who it's talking to and what's on offer in foreign aid. When you ask Saudi Arabia to build infrastructure, you emphasize the deep, conservative faith of the population. "Thanks, we'll take the hospitals, schools and roads. If you also want to build a mosque, that's OK—we'll give you the land." When you're talking to Western countries and asking for money, you're a moderate, secular Islamic nation that respects human rights and allows girls to go to school. Although you see fully veiled women on the street in the Maldives, most wear the *hijab* (headscarf) or do not cover their heads at all. However, dress is modest with little bare skin showing. Males are required to wear shirts when swimming at public beaches. At my first (and regrettably last) dip in the ocean at Villingili island, middle-aged women dressed in black robes and with their heads covered were paddling around. A perfectly normal sight in the Maldives.

Taking Out the Trash

After my circuit of Malé island, I stopped for lunch at a small restaurant near the fishing harbor. Tuna steak, rice, salad and, to my disappointment, a plastic bottle of water. It seemed to symbolize another challenge for an island nation with a growing population and economy but so little land: where does the trash go?

Only in the Maldives could the answer be—there's an island for that. It's called Thilafushi. Like Hulhumalé, it's an artificial island but with a much less desirable environment.

By the early 1990s, with the capital facing a major garbage disposal problem, the government decided to create a landfill in a five-mile long lagoon to the west. It was formally inaugurated—if that's what you do with an island landfill—when the first load of trash arrived by landing craft on January 7, 1992. In the early years of operations, deep pits were excavated, and the sand extracted used to build concrete walls around them. When the pit was filled with waste, a layer of construction debris was dumped on top and the surface levelled out with sand. As the pits filled and were topped off, the government decided to lease the new land to companies for industrial purposes. Today, Thilafushi is Malé's industrial district with factories for building and repairing boats, cement packing and methane gas bottling, and warehouses.

It's estimated that an average of 300-400 tons of trash is dumped each day, with an increasing amount coming from the tourist resorts (all those empty Cabernet bottles). Bluepeace, the main ecological movement in the Maldives, has described the island as a "toxic bomb." It claims that batteries, asbestos, lead and other potentially hazardous waste is mixed with the municipal solid waste, and that dangerous chemicals leak into the ocean. With increasing trash traffic, boat crews sometimes had to wait hours for trucks to arrive to pick up the trash. In frustration, some started dumping it straight into the lagoon. In December 2011, a surge of waste floating in the lagoon drifted out to sea, forcing Malé City Council to temporarily stop shipments and launch a clean-up operation. A BBC reporter who visited the island the next year described it as "apocalyptic."[27] But there's no good alternative in a nation whose economy is so heavily dependent on tourism. The trash keeps coming and Thilafushi will keep growing.

---

27. Charles Haviland, "Maldives 'Rubbish Island' is 'overwhelmed' by garbage," BBC News Asia, December 8, 2011; "'Apocalyptic' floating island of waste in the Maldives," BBC News Asia, May 20, 2012.

The Other Maldives

I did not see the third Maldives, but I would love to before it disappears forever. It was described to me by Jadullah, the oldest (he was in his late 40s) of my workshop participants.

Because the islands lay on the sea routes to the Malay Archipelago and China, Arab, African, Indian and Malay ships and traders left their mark, making the islands racially and culturally diverse. Jadullah grew up on an island that was a transit point between the north and south Maldives. Sometimes, he told me, he skipped school and went down to the harbor to talk with fishermen and traders from other islands; occasionally, he sneaked on board one of the ferries or trading ships as it sailed out and stayed up all night under the starlit sky listening to stories about the other islands. Each group of islands around an atoll, he said, has its own culture, traditions, dishes and may have had little contact with other islands.

Those cultural differences are disappearing. The trading schooners have given way to diesel-powered boats. Small aircraft reach the main regional centers and seaplanes the remote islands. Maldivians are travelling for work and education, mostly to Sri Lanka, India and Malaysia. There are daily international flights to Abu Dhabi, Doha, Kuala Lumpur, Beijing, Moscow, London and other European cities. And the population is more mixed. Most of the staff working in the resorts and the hotels and restaurants of Malé are Sri Lankan. With the government encouraging people to move from remote islands to Hulhumalé and the other central atolls for jobs and better public services, the Maldives of Jadullah's childhood may soon be just a memory.

_♣_

Chapter 13

Pakistan: On High
Alert in Karachi

★ ★ ★

"You're going to Pakistan?" friends and colleagues ask. "Don't
you know it's dangerous? There's a US State Department
travel advisory."

The comment, sincerely offered out of concern for my safety,
nevertheless shows how we tend to categorize countries along a
continuum from "really safe" to "dangerous" to "you-must-be-
out-of-your-mind-to-go-there." Our assessment is usually based
on a mental image formed over the years from media reports
and other sources, such as travel advisories. Pakistan is usually
stuck in the "dangerous" category, along with Iraq, Afghanistan,
Syria, Somalia, Yemen, the Democratic Republic of Congo and
whatever other countries are currently experiencing terrorist
attacks or civil conflict. By the same token, the United Kingdom,
France, Germany, and other Western nations are considered "safe,"
even though all have experienced terrorist attacks.

Pakistan, with a population of about 220 million, is the fifth
most populous country in the world and has the second largest
Muslim population (after Indonesia). From the coastal plains of
Sindh to the Northwest Territories bordering Afghanistan to
the Punjab, which was divided between India and Pakistan at
partition, it is a remarkably diverse country with many ethnic
groups, regions, landscapes, and cultures. For two centuries, the

port city of Karachi—my destination for a two-week workshop—has attracted migrants from all over South Asia; it has small but influential Hindu and Christian populations and an educated middle class, many of whom have studied overseas.

Is Pakistan really a more dangerous country than Mexico? Is Karachi a more dangerous city than Tijuana or Juàrez? Honestly, I can't say because I've never been to Mexico or its border cities, and, even if I had, I might be forming an opinion based on personal experience—how uncomfortable I feel in a place—rather than on data. What I can say is that most media reports and travel advisories are based primarily on recent incidents that occur in one city or area of the country and may not reflect the overall security situation. In other words, it's dangerous to travel in one area, but the rest of the country is pretty safe. On the Semester at Sea round-the-world voyage, Kenya was not the only country dropped from the itinerary because the program managers, no doubt consulting with their lawyers and risk managers, considered it too dangerous. There was civil unrest in Hugo Chavez's Venezuela, so we did not dock at Maracaibo. Instead, we went ashore in the safer communist haven of Cuba and heard Fidel Castro praise his understudy Chavez in a three-hour speech.

I've been to Pakistan three times and, based primarily on conversations with Pakistani colleagues, have constructed my own mental map of where I'm willing to travel. I feel pretty safe in the political capital, Islamabad, where I've conducted two workshops. I would not venture into the tribal areas of the North-West Frontier Province that border Afghanistan without a really good reason, and only then with Pakistani colleagues. In 2010, I felt uncertain about the commercial capital of Karachi, which had a reputation for violence, including some high-profile assassinations. In 2002, the South Asia bureau chief for the *Wall Street Journal*, Daniel Pearl, who was investigating alleged links between Richard Reed, the so-called "shoe bomber," and Al-Qaeda was kidnapped in Karachi and killed by his captors. On the positive side, my workshop invitation had come from GEO TV, the country's largest commercial network. I figured they would make sure nothing bad happened to me on their watch. As it turned out, they went to every length to protect me.

I am not trying to make a case against travel advisories, but I wish they were more location-specific, rather than designating a whole country or region as dangerous. Over the years, I've come up with a smartass reply to the question, "Do I read the travel advisories?" "Of course I do," I reply. "Usually on the plane when I'm leaving."

A City of Migrants

The East India Company captured Karachi in 1839. A decade later, Sir Henry Bartle Edward Frere arrived to serve as commissioner for the province of Sindh and set about transforming the city and province. As colonial administrators go, Frere stands out as one of the more enlightened and progressive. In 1851, he issued a decree making it compulsory for administrative officers to use the local Sindhi language instead of Persian. A committee he appointed settled on a standard Sindhi language script, and Frere promoted the publication of Sindhi-language books. He used the model of the British Penny Post system, with its low and uniform rate for sending mail, to reform the provincial postal system. His administration promoted economic development in Sindh and built roads, railroads, and cargo facilities to transform Karachi into a major seaport. When the American Civil War halted the transatlantic cotton trade with the Confederate states, Sindh offered a new supply chain. Steamers on the Indus River transported raw cotton from the interior to Karachi where it was shipped to British textile mills. The port also handled grain exports from British India's breadbasket, the wheat belt of Punjab. In 1863, a year after Frere left to take up his new appointment as Governor of Bombay, construction began on Karachi's Venetian-Gothic style town hall, to be named for the administrator. After independence in 1947, Frere Hall became the national library and houses a collection of more than 70,000 books, including rare and hand-written manuscripts.

Throughout its history, Karachi has been a magnet for migrants escaping conflict or religious persecution or seeking better economic opportunities. During the colonial era, it attracted traders and laborers from all over British India. The father of Pakistan's future leader, Muhammad Ali Jinnah, a textile merchant from Gujarat, moved his family to the booming port city in 1875; Jinnah was born the next year in the family's upscale rented apartment in the Wazir Mansion. At that time, Sindhis and Balochis (from the neighboring province of Baluchistan) made up the majority of the population, but as the city grew its demographics changed. More than half a million Muslims, the *Muhajirs* (the Arabic term for migrants), mostly Urdu-speaking middle-class refugees from North India, fled to Karachi soon after partition in 1947; at the same time, most of the city's Sindhi-speaking Hindus left for India.

By the mid-1960s, Karachi had begun to attract Pashtun and Punjabi migrants from northern Pakistan; by some estimates, Karachi is home to the world's largest urban Pashtun population, most of whom work as laborers and transport drivers. When Bangladesh gained independence in December 1971 after a nine-month liberation war, Urdu-speaking Biharis who wanted to remain Pakistani citizens moved to Karachi. Over the next 20 years, as Bangladesh emerged from the economic devastation of the conflict, almost three million ethnic Bengalis emigrated to Karachi. This period also saw an influx of almost one million Afghan refugees fleeing the Soviet–Afghan War, and smaller numbers escaping from post-revolution Iran. The 2010s saw another influx of Pashtun refugees fleeing conflict in North-West Pakistan and widespread flooding. By this time, Karachi had become known not only for its ethnic diversity but for its high rates of violent crime, gang warfare, sectarian violence, and extra-judicial killings.

How Dangerous Is the City?

Karachi has an unenviable, and today statistically undeserved, reputation as a dangerous city, ruled by gangs and terrorists, rife with corruption and street crime. In 2010, the year I visited, more than 300 people, including several high-profile political leaders, were assassinated in the city. In August, the assassinations sparked riots in which 35 were killed and 80 wounded.

Crime rates had been rising since the late 1980s, when Pashtuns fleeing the Soviet invasion of Afghanistan had arrived, opening up channels for smuggling arms and drugs. In the 1990s, criminal mafias with political connections became powerful, controlling much of the commercial transport system, water tankers and the sand and gravel industries. Since the early 1980s, the city has been controlled by the Muttahida Qaumi Mahaz (MQM) party, which represents the majority Urdu-speaking population, descendants of the *Muhajirs*. The MQM holds most parliamentary seats in Karachi but its dominance is challenged by the Pakistan People's Party (PPP), which finds support mostly among the Sindhis, and the Awami National Party (ANP) which represents the fast-growing Pashtun population. The MQM and the PPP have ties to Karachi's underworld, with the MQM running a large and violent criminal racket, extorting protection payments from businesses. PPP leaders are accused of using their control of the Sindh provincial assembly to enrich themselves. Each party blames the others for the assassinations and violence. The national government points the finger at banned sectarian groups and the Pakistan Taliban, which raises funds in Karachi. The role of the military and secret service was as it always is in Pakistan. Murky.

In 2013, security forces, led by the paramilitary Pakistan Rangers, moved in to crack down on criminal gangs, the MQM, and Islamist militants. That year marked the highest ever recorded number of homicides in Karachi's history, with more than 3,200 people dying from acts of terror or crime. By 2015, when 650 homicides were recorded, the rate had dropped by 75 percent, and by 2017 the number was down to 381. The number of kidnapping and extortion crimes also dropped dramatically, although street crime levels remained high. As a result of the operation, Karachi went from being ranked the world's sixth most dangerous city for crime in 2014 to 93rd by early 2020. With the drop in crime rates, real estate prices have increased sharply, and more upmarket restaurants and cafés have opened.

Smart TV

GEO (the word in Urdu means "live") was launched as a news channel in 2002 with a skeleton staff and almost no advertising. It grew rapidly, and by the time of my visit had a staff of 2,500, three domestic networks (news, entertainment and sports), and studios in other cities in Pakistan and Dubai in the United Arab Emirates (UAE). Since then it has added a headline news channel and a second entertainment channel. Its international channels are aired in the UK and on some satellite systems in the US. Fast growth created challenges, particularly in human resources, so GEO invested heavily in training. My job was to help the managers, who came from departments including news, documentary, sales, IT, engineering, and programming, to develop more systematic and creative training programs. There was a sense of energy and risk-taking in the organization that you sometimes do not find in more established media companies.

GEO's edgy and sometimes controversial news and talk programs often anger the political and religious establishments but attempts to censor content or take GEO off the air have always failed. Advertising on the entertainment and sports channels supports news coverage. The smartest decision by GEO's founders was to locate its satellite uplink facility not in Pakistan, where it could be subject to surprise government technical inspections or mysterious power cuts, but in Dubai Media City. The government may harass or threaten GEO managers and journalists at home, but it's not going to risk jeopardizing relations with the UAE which provides aid and has come to Pakistan's assistance after natural disasters such as earthquakes and floods.

The Metal Detector and Me

The workshop was held at the Carlton Hotel, a few miles out of the city, in a large flat, sandy area reclaimed from the Arabian Sea. GEO chose the Carlton because of its security precautions. At one time the hotel had four entrances; three had been closed and the remaining entrance had a guard post and barrier. Even after you entered, you could not drive all the way to the main entrance but had to park behind concrete barriers about 100 yards away. The entrance was manned by a uniformed security guard and a hotel staff member who, with his white tunic, maroon waistcoat and plumed hat, looked as if he'd stepped out of the palace guard for an eighteenth century Maharajah or off the set of a TV period drama.

I always approach metal detectors and scanners with trepidation.

Surely, there's something in my backpack or briefcase that will trigger an alarm or look suspicious. I am always ready to spread out the contents, turn on my laptop and audio recorder, and explain why I'm carrying power adaptors and other accessories. I dutifully empty my pockets of coins and pens. After the first few here's-what-I-have-that-you-may-want-to-check performances at the Carlton, I realized that the guards were simply not interested in what I was carrying, even if it triggered the alarm on the metal detector. All they did was smile and say, "Good evening, sir. I hope you are enjoying your stay at the Carlton." My backpack was never opened and inspected for concealed weapons. It all seemed to me to be a problematic case of reverse ethnic profiling. Surely, white Western males in their 60s should be subject to the same scrutiny as everyone else.

I explored the area around the hotel the day I arrived. There wasn't much to see. Much of the area looked like a construction site with large patches of flat land between expensive houses—the Pakistan versions of McMansions—and apartment blocks, and newly paved roads without sidewalks. There was a small commercial district a couple of miles away with banks and shops, but overall it was a drab, uninteresting landscape. The area is known by the name of the agency that administers it, the Defence Housing Authority (DHA). It was established in 1980 to provide affordable housing for the families of retired officers and later handed over—no doubt at a knockdown price—to a company established by former military officers. Since then, the DHA has become a major commercial developer, selling building plots to wealthy civilians, and building clubs, marinas, and golf courses. Today the DHA is one of the city's most affluent suburbs, with its own local government and police force, separate from the city of Karachi. Its growth is one indicator of the continuing power of the military in Pakistani society and politics. The military has stakes in many areas of the economy and former military officers can amass fortunes in the private sector.

Escape from the DHA

The road from the DHA to central Karachi runs along the Arabian Sea coast. This is Clifton Beach where middle-class Karachi goes to play. The road signs say, "Keep Clifton Green," although there's not a blade of grass or a tree in sight. The water is probably too polluted for swimming (the west end of the beach ends at the container port) but it's a pleasant walk or—for the more adventurous—a camel ride on the sand.

Returning from the city one night, my hosts from GEO's Human Resources department, Shehla and Ishfan, asked if I wanted "barbecue tonight" and then started laughing. The hottest (or rather coolest) restaurant on Clifton Beach is called Barbecue Tonight. We ate dinner on the rooftop—barbecued spicy chicken *botti* with *nan* bread and salad and fresh lime juice—enjoyed the cool breeze and looked out over the lights of the city. At 11:00 p.m., the restaurant (on three floors with hundreds of tables) was just starting to fill up as families and groups of young people arrived.

Downtown Karachi was as I had expected—bustling and polluted. For 20 years after independence, the city served as Pakistan's political capital. In the late 1950s, in an attempt to build national unity, Pakistan's leaders decided to shift the seat of government away from the southern port and began construction of a new capital near the city of Rawalpindi in the northeast. Islamabad (City of Islam), a planned city, became the capital in 1967. Karachi remains the country's leading industrial and financial center, with the port handling more than 90 percent of foreign trade. Industries include textiles, cement, steel, heavy machinery, chemicals, and food products. The Pakistan Stock Exchange and the headquarters of most public and private banks are on I. I. Chundrigar Road, known as "Pakistan's Wall Street." Most multinational corporations are headquartered in Karachi. And this is only the formal part of the city's economy. In a city of more than 15 million, it's estimated that the informal sector employs more than two thirds of the workforce.

Karachi's streets are filled with buses, cars, trucks and autorickshaws. Traffic patterns were, well, unpredictable, and if there were any center lines on the roads, no one paid attention to them. Some intersections were staffed by policemen who whistled and waved their arms around enthusiastically, but the theatrics appeared to have no effect on how or where people drove. On the buses, the cheap seats were on the roof; pickup trucks loaded with goods weaved in and out, with young men perched on the rear fenders. Many vehicles had dents and scratches, victims of much-too-close-encounters. There are some positives. Because Pakistan has to import most of its oil but has abundant supplies of natural gas, most vehicles have been converted to run on Compressed Natural Gas (CNG). And, especially in the DHA, vehicles have to negotiate speed bumps; many are at traffic lights, preventing vehicles from making quick starts and no doubt reducing accidents.

The Great Leader

There's no Old Karachi, as such, but rather small pockets of colonial-era architecture scattered throughout the city. On a Sunday afternoon, my GEO hosts and I visited Quaid-i-Azam (Great Leader) House, also known as Flagstaff House. From 1944, it served as the residence of the father of the nation, Muhammad Ali Jinnah, the British-trained lawyer and politician who led the All-India Muslim League from 1913 to August 1947 when Pakistan achieved its independence. Jinnah became Pakistan's first Governor-General but died just over one year later.

The house, designed by the British architect Moses Somake, was built in the British Raj style, which combined traditional Indian architectural forms with Western styles, including Victorian Gothic and Neoclassical. The interior rooms have been well preserved with the original 1940s furniture. It is not difficult to imagine Jinnah sitting at his desk, composing letters to Mahatma Gandhi, Jawaharlal Nehru, the British Viceroy, Lord Mountbatten, and the other political movers and shakers of the day, and taking telephone calls late at night.

The Quaid-i-Azam had had a long, distinguished, and tempestuous political career. After returning from legal training in London in 1897, the 20-year-old Jinnah set up practice as the only Muslim barrister in Bombay. He soon became involved in politics and quickly rose to prominence in the Indian National Congress. In his early career, he favored Hindu-Muslim unity, but broke with Congress and Gandhi over its policy of *satyagraha* or non-violent resistance. By 1940, he had become convinced that

Muslims should have their own state and in that year, the Muslim League passed the Lahore Resolution, demanding a separate nation. During World War II, while leaders of the Congress were imprisoned, the League gained strength, and in elections held shortly after the war, won most of the seats reserved for Muslims. Ultimately, the Congress and the Muslim League could not reach a power-sharing formula for a single state, leading all parties to agree to the independence of a predominantly Hindu India, and a Muslim-majority State of Pakistan.

For a few months after independence, while communal violence wracked other provinces and cities in Pakistan, Karachi and Sindh remained relatively peaceful. Riots broke out in January 1948, after which most of the province's Hindu population left for India. Karachi, designated as the first capital of Pakistan, became the main destination for the *Muhajirs*. Almost half a million had arrived by May 1948, and at least 100,000 each year until 1952. The influx dramatically changed the city's demographics. In 1941, Muslims made up 42 percent of Karachi's population; a decade later, the city's population had tripled, and Muslims made up 96 percent of the total. Urdu replaced Sindhi as Karachi›s most widely spoken language.

As Pakistan's first Governor-General, Jinnah worked to establish the new nation's government and policies, and to aid the *Muhajir* refugees, supervising the establishment of refugee camps. But the strain of years of hard work was taking its toll. Since the 1930s, Jinnah had suffered from tuberculosis, a condition made worse by his relentless working routine and smoking habit. Besides the papers on his desk sat his tin of Craven A cigarettes—he had smoked more than 50 a day for the previous 30 years—and a box of Cuban cigars. Many years later, Mountbatten stated that if he had known Jinnah was so ill, he would have stalled, hoping his death would avert partition.[28] Jinnah died of pneumonia at age 71 in September 1948, just over a year after Pakistan gained independence. His sister, Fatima, lived at Quaid-i-Azam House until 1964. In 1985, the building was acquired by the Pakistan

---

28. Akbar S. Ahmed, *Jinnah, Pakistan, and Islamic Identity: The Search for Saladin* (London: Routledge, 2005), p. 10.

government and conserved as a museum.

Jinnah is widely revered as the father of the country, and every year thousands come to pay their respects at his mausoleum, the Mazar-e-Quaid, a gleaming white-arched structure, designed in a 1960s modernist style, and inaugurated in 1971. We arrived as the honor guard was changing, with the officer barking out orders and a bugler playing Taps. It was formal, but also rather moving. There's a small museum (admission seven cents, even for foreigners) where many of Jinnah's personal possessions have been assembled—from his barrister's robes and suits to a dinner service, his golf clubs and two cars from his private collection, including an immaculate 1938 Packard.

As-Salamu Alaykum, Pardner!

My GEO liaisons were, if anything, over-solicitous. Any time I wanted to go anywhere, Shehla and Ishfan showed up with a car and driver. They were good companions and reduced my shopping expenses by at least one third with their aggressive bargaining.

They also liked to spring surprises on me. One night, after I shopped for *pashminas* for Stephanie on the sprawling Denna market, they suggested we go to Zamzana, a street in an upscale district known for its wide range of restaurants. We turned down a side street to be welcomed by a young man sporting Levis, a denim shirt, scarf, and cowboy hat. Welcome to Gun Smoke, where the old West comes alive in modern Karachi. The interior of the restaurant is lined with cowboy kitsch, including a few cattle skulls, and there's country music on the sound system. The menu offers buffalo wings, steaks, and burgers. I went for the Whiskey River BBQ Burger with fries and coleslaw, and it was quite good. Wild West popular culture travels well.

Let It Snow ...

For a surreal experience, the Gun Smoke was matched only by the Carlton Hotel muzak mix that included "Let It Snow, Let It Snow, Let it Snow" and "Santa Claus Is Coming To Town" as the temperature rose into the mid-90s outside. The muzak was briefly interrupted by power cuts, which occurred seven or eight times a day. Usually, the power was off for only a couple of minutes while the system switched from the grid to the hotel's back-up generator, but it knocked out the Wi-Fi, which was flakey at the best of times. Pakistan has major electricity supply problems, with rolling power cuts in almost every city. This has a major effect on industrial production because factories never know when they will have power. One day, the power in many areas of Karachi was out for 6-8 hours.

If power is in short supply, human labor is abundant. Everywhere I went, there was always someone to open the door, carry a bag or run an errand. At the small grocery stores, "self-service shopping" meant having an employee follow you around, carrying the basket, as you shopped. At the Carlton Hotel, one staff member had the uncanny knack of knowing exactly when I'd be in the bathroom during workshop breaks. He would run over to turn on the faucet, hand me a towel, then grin and say, "money, money, money." There were always three or four staff at reception and more in the lobby, and a dozen waiters standing around in the restaurant. The hotel's main business is meetings and wedding receptions, so it needs a large labor pool. As the welcome letter from the management stated, "The requirement and tastes of our guests vary from individual to individual. However, we are here to cater to your needs and mood swings." Mood swings? Do they have a shrink on the staff?

I Hate that I Love America

Most of my lunch and tea break conversations with the GEO TV managers focused on their opinions and perceptions of the US, and how Americans viewed their country. They were all interested in US politics, media, and culture. A few had visited, but since 9/11 it had become difficult to obtain a visa. At the same time, they were concerned about US interference in Pakistan, particularly drone attacks and covert operations, and about how the country was stereotyped in US media.

"Please tell your friends Pakistan is not all tribesmen with AK-47s and women in *burkas*," said Shams Kamzi, who headed

GEO's documentary unit. Shams told me he was editing a new documentary that examined the ambivalent feelings of Pakistanis who had studied and worked in the US. It was entitled "I hate that I love America."

Chapter 14

Mongolia: Borders on the Steppe

* * *

Counting Sheep

If you're looking for an outdoor job with lots of travel, some on horseback, and camping out under the stars, I have the career for you: become a data collector in rural Mongolia.

In land area, Mongolia is the eighteenth largest country in the world. At 604,000 square miles, it's about the size of Iran, three times the size of Spain, or more than twice the size of Texas. Yet its population of about 3.25 million puts it in the demographic minor league with countries such as Bosnia, Armenia, and Jamaica. Compared with US states, it has as many people as Utah or Iowa. Almost half of them live in the capital, Ulaanbaatar, commonly abbreviated as UB. Another half million live in smaller urban centers. That leaves almost one million who are technically classified as rural. Most of the time, they're on the move with their herds of sheep, goats, horses, yaks, cattle and camels.

According to the World Bank, Mongolia has the lowest population density of any country in the world—an average of two people per square kilometer. For what it's worth, that's a 100 percent increase on the previous World Bank benchmark year of 1961 when the country had an average of one person per square kilometer. Such averages do not mean much. At any time, but especially in winter, there are many square kilometers with no people at all, or just a herder family passing through. That's because Mongolia has little land that can be cultivated. Three quarters of the land area is grassland steppe, suitable only for grazing. There are mountains to the north and west and, in the south, the vast Gobi Desert, searing hot in summer, bitterly cold in winter. The Gobi offers jaw-dropping, photogenic landscapes for travel documentaries, but it's not a place where you'd actually want to live, which is why its population density is close to one person per square kilometer.

Those jokes about "more sheep than people" play well in rural Mongolia because livestock numbers have been steadily increasing. According to the national statistics office, which has been conducting livestock censuses since 1918, the country had a record high of 66.46 million animals in 2018. That's about 20 animals for every person. Sheep (46 percent) and goats (40.8 percent), whose cashmere wool is the main source of income for herders, accounted for most of the total. There are smaller numbers of cattle, yaks, horses and camels.[29] The increase sounds like good news for all concerned—herders, consumers and government tax collectors—but it comes with a long-term environmental cost as pasturelands in some regions are overgrazed.

In any case, you have to wonder about the accuracy of the census, conducted in a 10-day period in December when most of the country was covered in deep snow and travel was hazardous. Did the data collectors survey the herds and hope they didn't count the same sheep twice? Did they show up at the family *ger*—the traditional felt tent—and ask the patriarch about the size and composition of his herd? Or did they stay at their computers in their offices in UB and wait for herders to self-report using the app on their mobile phones?

It's a little like asking people how much property they own or how much they earned without requiring titles or pay slips; when tax time rolls around, it's a natural human tendency to under-report. Around the campfire, drinking *airag* (fermented mare's milk) or vodka, herders like to boast about their livestock; in rural Mongolia, social status is measured by the size of the herd. But when census time comes around, the herder knows the information will

---

29. "Number of livestock animals in Mongolia rises to over 66 mln," *Xinhua*, December 27, 2018.

be shared with the tax authorities. He's more likely to be modest about what he owns, or claim he lost livestock in the latest winter storm. What's a data collector to do? Ride out and look for dead sheep? Bottom line: in 2018, there may have been more than 66.46 million livestock, and the animals-to-people ratio even greater.

Keep counting those yaks.

My colleague Chuck Ganzert contemplates a camel ride at Gorkhi-Terelj National Park, then decides against it.

A Dedication

I made my first trip to Mongolia in October 2004, when I conducted an analysis of the staffing, resources and programming of Mongolian National Radio and Television (MNRTV) for UNESCO and led a management workshop. In April 2005, I worked with my colleague Chuck Ganzert from Northern Michigan University to install computers at MNRTV, teach staff digital audio editing, and hold a workshop on training techniques.

I returned in October 2005 as a member of a team from the Open Society Institute that was advising MNRTV on how to transition from being a government agency into a public service broadcasting organization. This chapter is dedicated to the memory of Chuck who died unexpectedly from a stroke in 2016 at the age of 63. He was a wonderful colleague and his technical skills, patience and rapport with the MNRTV staff helped make the project a success.

Tent City

In the communist era, Mongolians needed permission from the authorities if they wanted to move from one place to another, or from the countryside to a town. Those controls ended when the country became independent in 1990, and since then rural depopulation has accelerated. UB, which had about half a million residents before 1990, has seen its population triple. Although part of the increase is due to natural demographic growth, most people left rural areas to seek better economic opportunities or were forced to leave because they could no longer survive as herders.

UB lies in a shallow depression between four hills. Outside the downtown area, with its high rises and public buildings, are districts of Soviet-era apartment blocks, the prefabricated concrete *khrushchevkas,* built to meet the post-World War II housing shortage, and the more shoddily-built *brezhnevkas,* built from the mid-1960s. Beyond the apartment districts, the city is ringed by a tent city of *gers* that are home to an estimated 800,000 people, about half the city's population.

On my daily commute from the downtown Bayangol Hotel

North

South

RUSSIAN FEDERATION

CHINA

Suhbaatar

Khentii Mountains

Gorkhi-Terelj National Park

Gobi Desert

Erenhot

Ovu Tolgoi

ULAANBAATAR

Tavan Tolgoi

OMNOGOVI

Khangai Mountains

Altai Mountains

400

400

0 mi

0 km

to MNRTV, I passed clusters of *gers* in small family encampments called *hastas*—half a dozen *gers* and perhaps a metal-roofed brick house, surrounded by a fence with cars parked on the rough driveway. Some *gers* have been upgraded for urban living, with the wooden frame covered with canvas or synthetic materials instead of felt and animal hides, a diesel generator to supply electricity and a satellite dish; some have small gardens. However, as in other informal settlements, most lack access to electricity, running water and sewage systems. The *ger* districts are not connected to UB's piped central heating system that, as in other Soviet-era cities, supplies apartment blocks, schools and public buildings. It's needed, because UB has the unenviable distinction of being the coldest capital city in the world, with nighttime temperatures of − 40 Celsius common from November to March. In the tent city, *ger* dwellers use stoves, burning coal, animal dung and other materials. Toxic winter emissions make UB one of the most polluted cities in the world.

The city is constructing schools and paved roads in the *ger* districts and has invited private developers to build high-rise apartments to rehouse rural families. Yet unemployment levels are high, and families cannot afford to pay for rent and utilities. Many who were born and grew up in a *ger* prefer the traditional dwelling. "Public officials," *The Guardian* noted, "may struggle to coax the *ger* dwellers to swap their felt and canvas for bricks and mortar. Mongolians' attachment to their *gers* is both practical— they are warm in winter and cool in summer—and emotional."[30]

Other Mongolians have fled to warmer climes for employment. There are large migrant worker populations in South Korea, Japan, and Western Europe. There are more Mongolians—four million of them—in China's Inner Mongolia region than in Mongolia itself, although they are vastly outnumbered by Han Chinese who have been encouraged to migrate to the region to work in factories and on farms.

Mongolia's size, its severe climate and its poor transportation

---

30. "Nomads no more: Why Mongolian herders are moving to the city," *The Guardian*, January 5, 2017; Peter Geoghegan, "Life in Ulaanbaatar's tent city is hard—but Mongolians won't give up their gers," *The Guardian*, September 3, 2014.

infrastructure present major challenges to economic development and communication. How, for example, is the mail delivered?

Neither Snow nor Rain nor Heat nor Gloom of Night ...

The short answer is: with difficulty, and certainly not the next day. Even in UB, many streets outside the center do not have names, and houses and apartments do not have numbers. Navigating the informal *ger* settlements is even more challenging.

Administrative divisions do not mean much to herding families, even if they have abandoned their nomadic lifestyle. On the maps in city hall, UB is neatly divided into numbered residential neighborhoods called *khoroolol*, the equivalent of the *mikrorayon* (micro-region) in Soviet cities. Mongolian colleagues told me that most people do not know in which *khoroolol* they live. Instead of street addresses, people use landmarks—large buildings, retail stores, parks, Buddhist temples, public monuments. "My apartment? Next to the Italian restaurant behind the hospital. Fourth floor, green door." When a retail business advertises in a newspaper or on a billboard, it includes a map with landmarks. It can be difficult for non-residents to figure out where they are going, but this form of navigation comes naturally to Mongolians. Out on the steppe, they used natural landmarks such as mountains, rocks, and streams, and gave them names. Finding your way in the city is not much different. Berlin Fast Food is across the street from the taxi stand on Liberty Square, the Los Bandidos Mexican restaurant a couple of doors down on the street opposite the Peace and Friendship Building.

Official addresses, even when they exist, mean even less outside UB. Yet the mail does arrive, thanks to the fearless couriers of Mongol Post, who seem to literally embody the unofficial motto of the United States Postal Service: "Neither snow nor rain nor heat nor gloom of night stays these couriers from the swift completion of their appointed rounds." Well, all except for the swift part.

Mongol Post has been delivering mail since 1924, and in rural areas has learned to rely on unofficial networks, especially for the last leg of the journey. Let's say you go down to UB's Central

Post Office on Peace Avenue, the main east-west drag, to mail a package to your relatives in western Mongolia. Perhaps it's a birthday present, or a box of AA batteries for the transistor radio, so the family can listen in the evening and receive weather reports. Although the family is on the move and has no address, you know that their pastures are in a certain *bag,* a sub-district. Your package will first be delivered to the *aimag* (provincial) center. From there, it will go to the *sum* (district) center, probably by bus or van, and then to the *bag* where the general store doubles as a government center and post office. It can take up to two weeks for a package or letter to reach the *bag.* The postmaster knows the names of each herder family in the *bag* and where they have pitched their *ger.* If your relatives don't stop by in a few days to pick up supplies, he'll entrust the mail to someone who is riding out that way or a child going home from school.

Or maybe the postmaster will call your relatives to tell them he has a package. In most areas of Mongolia, the mobile phone network works pretty well.

Mongolia's Family and Friends Plan

It's a busy Saturday afternoon in UB, with the stores and restaurants crowded. Yet the long-distance telephone counter at the central post office is deserted, with a bored clerk surveying rows of empty phone booths.

At one time, there would have been lines to make calls. Now the action is out on the street, with roaming mobile phone vendors doing brisk business. They will sell you a phone or top up your time. If you don't have a phone, they'll charge you 600 *tugriks* (that's about 25 cents at the arithmetically head-spinning rate of more than 2,600 to the dollar) to make a short call on one of their phones.

The nationwide landline network was built by Soviet engineers, with the telephone usually arriving before the road. A Polish journalist told me that when he first visited UB in 1975 there were no paved roads leading out of the city, and only one railroad line. To reach an *aimag* center, you drove—probably in a GAZ-69, the rugged, bone-shaking Soviet military-style jeep—along the rutted tracks that followed the telephone poles.

It was always expensive to build and maintain the network in a country with long distances and scattered communities. With a harsh winter climate and thousands of roaming animals with sharp horns, phone lines could be down for weeks, leaving some communities almost isolated. Making a long-distance call on clunky Soviet-era telephone technology was also an act of faith. You called the operator to book the call. If you were lucky, the operator would call back in an hour or so and connect you. If you were very lucky, you would actually be able to have a conversation above the static.

Most Mongolians, who did not have phones at home, made the trip—on foot or horseback—to the post office and waited in line. People developed resourceful ways to keep in touch. To reach a family member who was out with the herd, you called the *bag* post office and left a message with the day and time you planned to call. Someone would get a message to the relative to come to town.

In the late 1990s, Mongolia, like other developing countries, decided it wasn't worth making further investments in its patchy and difficult-to-maintain landline network. It made the technological leap, building mobile phone towers that now reach most rural areas. The development was spurred by foreign investors, particularly mining companies that needed an efficient network to serve their remote locations. Mobile phones have transformed not only how Mongolians stay in contact but how they do business. Herders can check livestock prices, order feed and supplies and even file a report for the annual livestock census. Leather and cashmere dealers can negotiate directly with suppliers without heading into town with a load of carcasses and bags of wool and waiting for them to arrive.

What about the social consequences? Will mobile phones have an effect on Mongolian family relations, especially among the younger generation? Some argue that the mobile phone may strengthen family ties by making it easier to stay in touch with relatives. That's important in a country where, largely for economic reasons, families have become more dispersed, with members living in UB or overseas. The mobile phone offers families a relatively cheap way to stay in contact. And without having to wait in line at the post office.

From Khans to Commissars

For centuries, the land that today is Mongolia was loosely ruled by a motley collection of nomadic tribes, whose territorial control ebbed and flowed across the steppe. In 1206, Genghis Khan founded the Mongol Empire, which eventually became the largest contiguous land empire in history, stretching from Beijing to the Balkans. His grandson Kublai Khan conquered China, establishing the Yuan dynasty that lasted almost a century until 1368 when the Ming dynasty from the south forced the Mongols to retreat north to their traditional homelands. Except for a couple of periods of relative unity, they went back to business as usual as warring nomads. The Manchu rulers of the Qing dynasty absorbed Mongolia in the seventeenth century and encouraged the spread of Tibetan Buddhism across the steppe. After the collapse of the Qing dynasty in 1911, the northern region, called Outer Mongolia, with aid from the Soviet Union, declared independence; Inner Mongolia remained part of China. For the next 70 years Mongolia was a Soviet satellite state, essentially a buffer zone between the USSR and China. Soviet troops were stationed there, and Moscow subsidized the country's education, health care and social services. Mongolia's leaders were Russian-educated, and Russian was widely spoken. Eighty percent of Mongolia's trade was with the USSR, and 15 percent with other socialist countries.

On a clear day, I climbed the steps to the Zaisan Memorial at the southern edge of UB. It offers a panoramic view of the city and a powerful reminder of how closely Mongolia was in the Soviet orbit for most of the twentieth century. The memorial honors Soviet and Mongolian soldiers killed in World War II. The circular murals are Soviet public art at its most realistic and evocative, depicting scenes of friendship between the people of the USSR and Mongolia. The scenes include Soviet support for Mongolia's independence declaration in 1921, the defeat of the Japanese Kwantung Army by the Soviets on the Mongolian border in 1939, victory over Nazi Germany, and peacetime achievements such as Soviet space flights, including Soyuz 39 which carried Jugderdemidiin Gurragchaa, the first Mongolian to go into space.

Soviet-era mural featuring cosmonaut Jugderdemidiin Gurragchaa, the first Mongolian to go into space.

Mongolia had its own peaceful democratic revolution in early 1990. This led to a multi-party system, a new constitution, and a painful transition to a market economy. When the socialist trading bloc collapsed, Mongolia lost its guaranteed markets. The economy, based largely on livestock raising and mineral extraction, went into freefall. The loss of social subsidies plunged the country into a budget crisis and resulted in cuts in government services, including education and health. By 1998, one third of Mongolians were living below the poverty line and the country was heavily dependent on foreign aid.

Borders on the Steppe

Just like the cowboy of the American West, the life and independence of the Mongolian herdsman has been overly romanticized. He sits high and proud in the saddle, watching over his herd, armed and ready to defend it from wolves or rustlers. At night, he gathers with his family in the *ger*, and, like the cowboy by the campfire with his guitar, plays the *morin khuur*, the traditional bowed stringed instrument, and tells tall stories of brave ancestors who defied the elements and invaders to defend their lands and their herds. He knows his winter and summer pastures, and can name each low hill, each rock outcrop, each stream. He teaches his children how to ride and care for the livestock. He is a master eagle hunter. Out on the steppe, there are no fences, no pesky settlers trying to break the sod and raise crops. The herdsman is at one with the earth and the endless sky, free to drive his livestock wherever he wishes.

Except that he is not, and probably never was. The term "nomad" is misleading because it implies absolute freedom to roam. Yet in every pastoral society there has always been at least a loose system—administered by a local ruler, a government agency or by mutual agreement among herders—to regulate access to pastures. Under the Manchus, Mongolia was divided into districts called *hoshuu*, within which each herding family was assigned to a smaller unit, a *sum*, and a sub-unit, a *bag* (the administrative system that still exists today). In a landmark study, *The Headless State,* social anthropologist David Sneath challenges the traditional image of the steppe as a region dominated by fierce nomads organized into clans and tribes and shows that local rulers established administrative systems. In terms of pasture, this meant that "each family owned no land as such but had a recognised area of pasture that it used in the different seasons, and of these the rights to the exclusive use of winter pasture (*ovoljoo*) tended to be the most strictly enforced."[31]

In practical terms, there wasn't much difference between the Manchu system and the twentieth century communist collectives called *negdels.* The *negdel* system regulated access to pastures, limited the size of herds (and thus the amount of gazing land needed), maintained water wells and kept a central supply of fodder to distribute in winter. The shift to a market economy disrupted a system that, despite inefficiency and corruption, at least guaranteed herders a basic living. When the herds were privatized, each herder became responsible not only for raising livestock, but for selling the meat, carcasses, and wool. With long distances and a poor road

31. *The Headless State, Aristocratic Orders, Kinship Society & Misrepresentations of Nomadic Inner Asia* (New York: Columbia University Press, 2009).

network, some moved closer to towns and increased the size of their herds without regard to quality. Most pasture land near towns now suffers from over-grazing while remote areas are under-grazed.[32]

The main culprits are the cashmere goats, whose highly-prized hair is the most important source of income for herders. Cashmere is Mongolia's third largest export (after copper and gold), making it the world's second-largest producer of raw cashmere after China. The goat population has increased almost fourfold from seven million in 1999 to 27 million today.[33] Unlike sheep, which literally graze on the grass, goats dig out and eat the roots, making regrowth harder; their sharp hooves also damage the upper layer of the pasture, which is then swept away by the wind. Some areas, such as those on the northern fringe of the Gobi Desert, are becoming desert-like.

And then There's the Weather

They have a name for it in Mongolia—the *dzud*. It is a periodic weather phenomenon when an unusually hot, dry summer is followed by an unusually cold winter. Summers have been getting hotter; since the 1950s, the average temperature in Mongolia has risen by 2.07 degrees Celsius, more than double the average global increase of 0.85 degrees over the past century. A dry summer reduces the growth of grass, while the harsh winter means that more fodder is needed.

Without the safety net of the *negdel* fodder distribution system, herders are left to literally forage for their animals, drying and storing cut grass during the summer months. In some regions, the grass that once grew tall and thick can no longer supply enough winter fodder. On the northern edge of the Gobi Desert, a 68-year-old herder told a reporter that the autumn rains no longer come, the grass is shorter and thinner, the river beds dry. "When I was 17 or 18," he said, "we had a lot of rain, a lot of grass, and we could harvest the grass in the autumn. ... Now

---

32. "The last best place," *The Economist*, December 21, 2002.

33. Beth Timmins, "Cashmere and climate change threaten nomadic life," BBC News, March 5, 2020.

the climate has changed so much—you can say we only have two seasons now."[34]

In a harsh winter, herders will try to save their prized cashmere goats, keeping them close to the *ger* or even inside with the family, but may find it impossible to feed the whole herd. When the snows melt in April, the steppe is littered with livestock carcasses. From 1999 to 2002, Mongolia was hit with three consecutive *dzuds*, resulting in a combined loss of 11 million animals. These disasters were eclipsed by the *dzud* of 2010-2011 when eight million livestock—about 17 percent of the total population—were killed. About 9,000 families lost their entire herds while a further 33,000 suffered a 50 percent loss. Some families were forced to move to the *ger* settlements of UB.

Safety in Radio

"Livestock losses in the eastern *aimags* were much lower than in the west last winter. We really believe our radio weather forecasts made a difference."

I met with Purevdash Baaran, Director General of Mongolian National Radio (MNR), in April 2005. Mongolia had not had a *dzhud* the previous winter, but herders had still suffered livestock losses. Why were they worst in the west?

Although Mongolia has a relatively high literacy level, distribution of newspapers and magazines is costly and difficult because of poor roads and transportation. Electrical service is not generally available outside *aimag* centers, except in mining camps, and power cuts are common. Through its network of transmitters, broadcasting on AM long wave and short wave in rural areas and FM in urban areas, MNR is the only medium of mass communication that reaches the whole country.

Purevdash told me that for several months in late 2004, power cuts in western *aimags* took MNR transmitters off the air. Herders wrote to MNR, complaining they were receiving no information about current events, and, more importantly, no weather forecasts.

---

34. "Nomads no more: Why Mongolian herders are moving to the city," *The Guardian*, January 5, 2017.

In a country with extremes in climate, Purevdash said, frequently updated weather information is essential. An unexpected snowfall can leave a herd scattered across the steppe; livestock are lost, and sometimes herders lose their lives trying to reach stranded animals. "But if you know the snowstorm is coming the day before, you can gather your herd around the *ger* and provide them with feed," he said. "In the eastern *aimags*, we were able to warn herders in advance, but that wasn't the case in the west, and that's why the losses were higher." Even though many herding families now have mobile phones, radio remains an important medium for news, business, health information and education. In rural areas, it can save livelihoods—and sometimes lives as well.

I asked Purevdash what kinds of radios herders used. He smiled. "Some of them still have the old metal Latvian-manufactured transistor radios manufactured in the 1950s. They were standard issue in communist times, but they're no longer made and can't be repaired." Cheap, plastic Chinese transistors were available but were not rugged enough. Purevdash said that some families could not afford batteries, and even if they could, might have to ride many miles to buy them. After the disastrous *dzud* of 2000-2001, the Mongolian Red Cross issued an international appeal to supply radios to herders and distributed about 16,000 (mostly Russian battery models) to needy families. Red Cross officials with whom I met told me that the program had reached only a small percentage of the rural population and they were searching for donors to fund new distribution rounds. I asked about the battery issue. "We'd like to distribute radios that can be powered in different ways," said Red Cross Secretary General Rabdan Samdandobji. "By battery, by hand-crank and by solar power. We have plenty of that—an average of 270 sunny days a year."

Where Dinosaurs Roam

On a cool, crisp, sunny day in early October, my MNRTV hosts invited me to join them for a picnic in the Gorkhi-Terelj National Park, about 50 miles northeast of UB. "You've been stuck in the city all week," my interpreter Batzorig said. "We need to show you the real Mongolia."

A few miles out of the suburbs, we entered a landscape of rolling pasture lands and low hills. The sky was blue, the land various shades of brown; with the summer over, there was little grass left for grazing. We passed herds of sheep, cattle, and yaks. As the road wound up into the Khentii Mountains, the vegetation became sparser and the settlements fewer. At one overlook, we stopped at a stone cairn decorated with Buddhist prayer flags.

As we descended into the next valley, Batzorig pointed to a group of *gers* nestled below the cliffs. "That's our lunch place," he said. "You'll also see some animals you haven't seen before." He said it with a sly grin. The national park has several tourist *ger* camps, where you can rent a tent for a picnic or an overnight stay and have a romantic out-on-the-steppe experience with none of its hazards or inconveniences of actually having to live and work out of a *ger*. But it was not the clean and well-appointed *gers* that I noticed as we pulled into the camp.

"You didn't tell me we were having lunch at a theme park!" I protested mildly. The area was dotted with life-size (well, I assume their makers had done their scientific homework) models of dinosaurs, who looked ready to devour our picnic lunch and then us too. "Guess they wandered up from the Gobi looking for new pastures," said Batzorig.

Dinosaurs roam ger camp.

Batzorig's explanation was geographically accurate, although about 80 million years off. In the Cretaceous Period, the Gobi was not the rugged, barren, searing hot desert it is today. Instead, it was "a dinosaur's paradise of vast valleys, freshwater lakes and a humid climate." These conditions, according to paleontologists, "make the Gobi Desert the largest dinosaur fossil reservoir in the world." On expeditions to Mongolia in the 1920s, the American explorer and naturalist Roy Chapman Andrews—the inspiration for the Indiana Jones character—excavated numerous fossils and found the world's first dinosaur egg nests, a crucial discovery that was to change the way in which paleontologists interpreted their discoveries. In two years in the Gobi, Andrews's team unearthed more than 100 dinosaurs, and took them back to the American Museum of Natural History in New York City, where many stand today.[35]

The Gobi is still rich with fossils. Under Mongolian law, any that are found are state property and their export is forbidden, but in this vast, sparsely populated region it's impossible to enforce the regulations and smuggling continues, with high prices paid at auctions.

There's Gold (and Copper) in them thar Hills

Most of the digging in the Gobi today is not for fossils but for minerals. Mongolia's mineral wealth is immense, valued at between US $1 and $3 trillion, the vast range indicating that no one knows what is still to be discovered. Minerals account for 90 percent of the country's exports, making the economy susceptible to swings in world markets and prices. Three minerals—coal, copper and gold—dominate the market, although the country also exports iron, tin, tungsten and molybdenum, used in high-strength steel alloys. Since the late 1990s, the expansion of the mining sector has been fueled by China's industrial and residential construction boom. Most mining companies are based in Canada, Australia, the UK, US, and Russia (with the Mongolian government owning minority stakes), but their largest customers are in China.

---

35. Beth Timmins, "Dinosaurs: Restoring Mongolia's fossil heritage," BBC News, November 23, 2019.

Mining has created an economic boom in some areas. Two decades ago, Ömnögovi in the South Gobi was the least populated province in Mongolia. Today, it has the country's two largest mining operations and a fast-growing population. Tavan Tolgoi (Five Hills) has the world's largest reserves of coking coal, estimated at 7.4 billion tons. Every day, trucks depart the massive mine for the 150-mile trip south to the Chinese border. It's a rough, unregulated two-lane highway and accidents are common; when trucks reach the border, drivers often have to wait two or three days to clear customs. The government is raising funds to build a railroad to carry coal more cheaply and efficiently. South of Tavan Tolgoi, just 60 miles from the Chinese border, is the Oyu Tolgoi (Turquoise Hill) copper and gold mine which some analysts predict may eventually account for 30 percent of Mongolia's GDP. The deposit was discovered in 2001 by the Canadian company, Ivanhoe Mines, and is now a joint venture between Ivanhoe, the UK-Australian multinational Rio Tinto and the Mongolian government. The mine has 2,500 employees on site and has built a paved road to the Chinese border.

These two mining operations have led to an economic boom in a once remote province, with business people arriving to open truck stops, auto repair shops, hotels, stores, restaurants, and bars. The environmental costs have yet to be measured. In a region already experiencing drought and desertification, mining companies draw water from rivers and lakes for their operations. In 2011, contractors for the Oyu Tolgoi diverted a river, drying up local water wells and threatening herders' livelihoods. The parties came to an agreement on environmental management and compensation, but tensions persist.

The business end of mining is concentrated in UB, where mining companies have their offices, banks and contracts with PR and lobbying firms. Billboards around the city feature smiling Mongolians in hard hats against a background of heavy equipment gouging into the landscape with slogans such as "Mera— meeting your everyday blasting needs." The streets are clogged with imported cars and SUVs. At the Hotel Bayangol, where I stayed on my three visits, my not-so-scientific survey of the breakfast crowd suggested that at least half were in the mining business—geologists, engineers, equipment suppliers. The discovery of a mineral deposit, even a high-value one, does not mean that it is commercially viable to exploit it. A mine needs a skilled workforce, infrastructure, a supply chain for materials and a market for its products. In Mongolia, if you need a road or railroad, you'll likely have to build it yourself. A Canadian mining executive summed up the calculation: "There are a lot of costs here. A mineral deposit needs to be at least three times the size of one in Alberta to make it worth exploiting."

The growing number of expatriates working in UB has been good for the restaurant and bar business. After long stints at remote mining camps, in baking hot or sub-zero temperatures, they want more than the typical Mongolian greasy spoon restaurant can offer. Ethnic restaurants—French, German, Italian, Mexican, Turkish, Korean—have popped up all over the city along with the usual collection of Irish pubs.

Mongolia's politics and economy continue to be shaped by its two larger and more powerful neighbors. As *Washington Post* correspondent Edward Cody put it: "When Mongolians look north, they see the Russian colossus that controlled them for most of the twentieth century. When they look south, they see 1.3 billion Chinese, hereditary adversaries whose booming growth and insatiable appetite for raw materials touch almost everything that happens in the Mongolian economy."[36] When China is buying copper and cashmere, Mongolia's economy flourishes; when China reduces demand for natural resources, and commodity prices fall, Mongolia suffers.

UB-2

Soviet planners had the annoying bureaucratic habit of numbering everything—from factories to shops to restaurants. Even memorable places ended up with prosaic names. UB-2 sounds like the name of a Siberian rap group. In fact, it's a resort hotel on the edge of Gorkhi-Terelj National Park, the gateway to

---

36. Edward Cody, "Feeling the squeeze of China and Russia, Mongolia courts U.S.," *The Washington Post*, February 12, 2006.

some of the most spectacular scenery and varied wildlife in the country. When I was there, it was still stuck in an engaging time and price warp, one of the best deals around for budget travelers.

Chuck and I had decided to hold the workshop for MNRTV department heads out of the capital, so that the participants would not be distracted by daily work demands. In contrast to my trip to Gorkhi-Terelj on a crisp, sunny day the previous October, we did this one in a howling snowstorm—a 21-seater bus with 26 passengers, luggage and four cases of Korean beer. In good weather, the 50-mile trip usually takes about two hours. On the snow-covered roads, it took more than three hours. We arrived as it was getting dark. As far as I could tell, UB-2 was where the road ended.

Opened in 1964, UB-2 was one of hundreds of seaside, lakeside and mountain resorts all over the Soviet Union and its satellite states where workers and their families escaped factories and cramped apartments for a two-week summer vacation. In its heyday, it was probably one of the best, offering breathtaking views of the Khentii mountain range, hiking, horseback riding, rafting, rock climbing and (for the hardy) dips in the icy-cold water of the Tuul River. In the evenings, there were family activities and games.

UB-2, a rundown Soviet-era resort with breathtaking views of the Khentii Mountains.

The scenery hasn't changed. The park is part of a 1.2 million hectare (almost three million acre) wilderness area stretching north to the Russian border. Horses, sheep, goats, camels and yaks graze on Alpine meadows dotted with wildflowers below snow-capped 10,000-foot peaks. The cool, silent woods along the banks of the Tuul River offer short, easy walks among the northern birch, larch and fir. The park is home to wolves, bears, deer, marmots, lemmings, moose and more than 250 species of birds.

Unfortunately, UB-2 was not as well preserved as the nature surrounding it. Guest rooms featured peeling wallpaper, rickety furniture and windows sealed with caulking to keep out the draught. There were power outages, and the water supply was erratic. The portraits of Stalin had been replaced with watercolors by local artists but, in most respects, not much had changed since the 1960s.

Furnishings and facilities aside, you could not beat the price. The single rooms cost less than US $7 a night. Chuck and I were rewarded with US $10-a-night three-room suites, which had the same décor, furniture and leaky windows as the standard rooms, but with more square footage of threadbare carpet. There was no water supply to the shower. I wished they had given us the option of staying in the UB-2 camp, where you could rent a *ger* with thick carpets and a wood burner and accommodate six people for under US $30 a night.

The restaurant served hearty, inexpensive meals of *buuz* (steamed dumplings filled with mutton or beef), stews, mountain trout, and perch from Khövsgöl, Mongolia's second-largest freshwater lake. There were pool and ping-pong tables, and one TV in the lobby that seemed to be permanently tuned to a station featuring white-suited, lip-syncing Mongolian boy bands, and female vocalists in elaborate evening gowns.

Chuck and I had been warned that if the participants did not have an activity in the evening, they would likely spend it with a bottle of vodka, and snooze until the midmorning coffee break the next day. After pool, ping-pong and group TV viewing, what was there left to do? We decided against an evening lecture on US politics and history. Instead, we would teach them to do American traditional dance. After scouring the stores in UB, we found a

CD of Celtic music. It was by bands neither of us had heard of but that didn't matter. All we needed was two 16-beat A parts and two 16-beat B parts. I called simple dances, and everyone had a great (and relatively sober) time. An American couple on vacation—the only other guests at UB-2—joined us. It must have seemed slightly surreal to them to be dancing the Virginia Reel at a rundown resort in a Mongolian national park, but it gave them a good story to tell back home. After dancing, the group gathered in Chuck's suite and sang traditional Mongolian songs. It was a beautiful, moving end to the day.

ↄ▓ↄ

Chapter 15

Central Asia's Fergana Valley: Border Wars

★ ★ ★

As the crow flies, Kyrgyzstan's second and third largest cities—Osh and Jalalabad—are just 30 miles apart, on the south and north sides of the Fergana Valley. The highway from Osh runs north 15 miles to a bustling border town, its bazaar a major distribution point for imported Chinese consumer goods. On the Kyrgyz side, it's called Kara-Soo; on the Uzbek side Qorasuy (both mean Black Water). Cross the bridge and it's a straight shot north past the industrial town of Khanabad before crossing back into Kyrgyzstan for the final few miles to Jalalabad.

It would be a simple trip if not for regional politics. For three quarters of a century, the internal boundaries of the Soviet Socialist Republics (SSRs) were marked on administrative maps but made little difference in the daily lives of people who crossed them freely—often daily—for work, school, shopping or to visit relatives. The only sign that you were crossing from one SSR to another might be a small commemorative welcome plaque or a police post. It was only after the collapse of the Soviet Union in December 1991, when each SSR became an independent country, that the notional boundaries became national borders.

I made my first trip to Kyrgyzstan four years later to establish a training and resource center for journalists in Osh. Nine months later, Stephanie and I moved into an apartment in Bishkek, Kyrgyzstan's capital, where I was starting a one-year (later extended

215

to 16 months) stint as a Fulbright Senior Scholar in Journalism and Mass Communication. From 1998 to 2012, I made six more visits to Kyrgyzstan for media consulting, workshops and conferences, lived in Kazakhstan for six months on a second Fulbright Fellowship, and made trips to Tajikistan and Uzbekistan.[37] Over the course of 15 years, I crossed Central Asian borders many times—on flights and in cars, buses and *marshrutkas* (the shared minibuses). Sometimes, I had a visa; sometimes, I had to use charm, bad Russian and an occasional bribe to get through.

Messy Borders

Border spats in the Fergana Valley have simmered and boiled since 1991. At Qorasuy, the Uzbek authorities destroyed the bridge, stifling the local economy. Local people, used to bureaucratic paranoia, improvised, using rope walkways to cross the stream. The bridge has since been rebuilt but the border is still tightly policed by Uzbek border guards, who claim they are trying to keep out arms, drugs, and Islamic terrorists. Even if you make it across, you may not reach Jalalabad because the border crossing back into Kyrgyzstan is periodically closed. Most drivers from Osh take a circuitous 65-mile, two-hour route via the Kyrgyz town of Uzgen. Osh and Jalalabad are separated by only a slim wedge of eastern Uzbekistan, but it's faster to drive around it than face delays and fines at the border posts.

It wasn't always that way. In October 1996, Stephanie and I made the 550-mile overland trip from Bishkek to Osh. We paid US $75 to a driver, Jorobev, a burly Kyrgyz in his mid-40s, who looked as if he could handle himself if we ran into bandits in the mountains. We set off at 6:00 a.m. in his battered but mechanically well maintained Soviet-made Lada 300, the trunk stacked with our luggage and his commercial cargo—two cases of vodka he was planning to sell in Osh.

Fourteen hours and two mountain ranges later, we were weaving our way in the darkness down a twisting mountain road, with

---

37. Read more in my first book, *Postcards from Stanland: Journeys in Central Asia* (Ohio University Press, 2016).

North

South

UZBEKISTAN

KYRGYZSTAN

TAJIKISTAN

Fergana Mountain

To Bishkek

Uzgen

Kara-Soo

Osh

Jalalabad

Khanabad

Andijan

Fergana Valley

Naryn River

Kokand

SHAKHIMARDAN (UZ)

SOKH (UZ)

VORUKH (TJ)

Pamir Alay Mountain

Syr Darya River

0 mi   50
0 km   50

steep cliffs to the left and a dizzying drop (with no guard rail) on the right to the gorge of the Naryn River. We slowed down at the border crossing near Jalalabad, but the barrier was open, and no guards in sight. As we crossed back into Kyrgyzstan at Qorasuy, the Uzbek guards pulled us over. They were looking for drugs, and two Westerners traveling in a small car late at night aroused suspicion. One guard spoke English. He seemed less interested in Jorobev's vodka cache than in promoting tourism. "Why are you passing through and not visiting Uzbekistan?" he asked good-naturedly. "It is a wonderful country, and the people are so friendly." We said we'd heard that too and would love to see Samarkand and Bukhara on a future trip.

Six months later, I did the return trip north, more comfortably, in a Toyota Land Cruiser with a staff member from the US embassy. The driver opted to take the longer route via Uzgen to avoid crossing into Uzbekistan. We had heard that Uzbek and Kyrgyz border guards sometimes shifted their posts short distances to block roads. It was not a matter of sovereignty, of claiming a few feet of an apricot orchard or cotton field as national territory. It was simply what poorly-paid government employees had to do to survive. If you move your barrier to the roadside, you can hit up drivers for fines or invented transit fees. At one village on the north side of the Fergana Valley, two Uzbek border posts stood literally 50 yards apart, on either side of a stream. The driver knew exactly what to do. Just ahead of the first border post, he cut off on a dirt road up the valley for half a mile, crossed the stream and headed back down on the other side, rejoining the main road a short distance from the second post. Like the townspeople of Qorasuy, the locals had figured out how to get around an artificial border.

Mountain Borders

More than 90 percent of Kyrgyzstan's land area—the size of Austria and Hungary combined, or the US State of Montana—consists of mountains, with 40 percent over 3,000 feet high. To the east, the Central Tian Shan range forms a natural border with China's Xinjiang Province, rising to Pik Pobedy (Victory), at 24,111 feet the second-highest point in the former Soviet Union. North of Bishkek, the Kungey Ala Too range forms the border with Kazakhstan; to its south the Kyrgyz Ala Too range runs east-west to the deep mountain lake of Issyk-Kul. The Fergana range straddles the middle of the country, with Jalalabad in its southern foothills. South of Osh, the Pamir Alay range, stretching west from the Tian Shan with peaks rising to more than 16,000 feet, forms the southern border with Tajikistan. For most of human history, the mountains have provided summer pastures for herds of sheep, goats, and horses. Except in the valleys, the soil is too thin and rocky to be cultivated. This was a land without borders, where identity was defined by religion, family, clan and place.

The major concentrations of Kyrgyzstan's population are in two large valleys—the Chuy in the north, with the capital Bishkek, and the Fergana in the south, with Osh and Jalalabad. About half the country's population of 6.5 million live in the south. The north is more industrialized and secular, oriented to Kyrgyzstan's larger and more prosperous Central Asian neighbor, Kazakhstan, and to Russia and the West. The south is more agricultural, conservative, and Islamic, looking to Uzbekistan and further west to Iran. Some northerners fear separatism, Islamic fundamentalism, and the influence of Uzbekistan in the south; some southerners believe the government in Bishkek exploits their region, while short-changing it on tax revenue and social services. Polls show that most people in Kyrgyzstan consider the differences between the north and south to be the major challenge to national unity.

Soviet Gerrymandering

The borders of Central Asia began to be defined in the late nineteenth century when the armies of Tsarist Russia conquered the khanates of the region and subdued the tribes of the mountains and steppe. Sporadic revolts broke out against Tsarist rule. The *basmachi* (derived from the Turkic word *baskinji*, meaning "attacker") movement began in 1916 when the Russian army began drafting Muslims for service in World War I, and local officials imposed taxes and confiscated livestock. In the turmoil that followed the 1917 Bolshevik Revolution, with civil war raging between the White and Red Armies from the Urals to the Far East, political leaders took advantage of the power vacuum and declared independent republics in Central Asia. Most revolts were short-lived and brutally suppressed, their leaders murdered or sent to Siberian prisons. Although sporadic resistance continued, by the mid-1920s the Soviets had regained control over the region.

For the socialist state, religious, ethnic and clan loyalties represented a threat to stability. The Soviets feared that traditional ties could foster support for Islamic, social or political movements. Intellectual and religious leaders still talked privately of a Greater Turkestan or a Central Asian caliphate. The Soviets attempted to counter pan-Islamic and pan-Turkic tendencies by constructing nationalities, giving each a defined territory with national borders, along with a ready-made history, language, culture, and ethnic profile. Your loyalty was no longer to your tribe, village, or faith, but to your nationality as a Kazakh, Kyrgyz, Tajik, Turkmen or Uzbek and to its Soviet Socialist Republic (SSR). The Uzbek and Turkmen SSRs were created in 1924, the Tajik SSR in 1929. In 1926, most of present-day Kyrgyzstan became the Kara-Kyrgyz Autonomous Soviet Socialist Republic (ASSR) and a full Kyrgyz SSR in 1936. In the same year, the Kazakh SSR was formed.

While promoting new national loyalties, the Soviets realized that too much nationalism could be dangerous. In a parallel effort to solidify control, they shifted around ethnic groups to ensure that none was dominant in a specific area. The policy of divide and rule created artificial borders between ethnically-mixed SSRs. The medieval cities of Samarkand and Bukhara, historically major centers of Tajik culture and with large ethnic Tajik populations, ended up in the Uzbek SSR. Osh, with its predominantly Uzbek population of traders and arable farmers, was a classic case of ethnic gerrymandering. As Central Asia scholar Madeleine Reeves points out, if the Soviets had drawn boundaries exclusively along ethnic lines, the nomadic Kyrgyz would "end up with a Kyrgyz republic that had no cities of its own: a worrying prospect for a state preoccupied with thrusting 'backward' populations into Soviet modernity."[38] Their solution was to make Osh, with its Uzbek majority population, the Kyrgyz SSR's southern capital.

Independence came suddenly to all Soviet republics. In December 1991, Soviet citizens in each SSR suddenly found themselves citizens of an independent country with the artificial borders drawn in the 1920s. In border regions, nomadic families were no longer free to move their herds between winter and summer pastures; some arable farmers could not reach their wells or found their irrigation ditches cut. Buses stopped at the border and people could no longer travel easily to visit relatives or trade or shop on the market. In the Fergana Valley, the borders cut through the middle of towns such as Qorasuy and villages, sometimes through the middle of houses. Although most of the valley is in Uzbekistan, the northern panhandle of Tajikistan (Sughd *oblast*, with a population of more than two million) juts into the valley, physically, economically, and culturally separated from the rest of the country by the Pamir Alay. Uzbekistan literally bisects southern Kyrgyzstan, the border zigzagging in and out of the foothills of the Fergana and the Pamir Alay.

A Divided City

At least from the fifth century BC, Osh has been a crossroads city, a trading center attracting people of many races, religions, and cultures. It lies in the east of the Fergana Valley, where the Ak Burra River, flowing out of the Pamir Alay, emerges from its gorge and flows into the once-mighty Syr Darya, on its way to the Aral Sea. Osh was on a branch of the Silk Road that ran east along the Fergana Valley, crossing the Pamir Alay to Kashgar in China. By the sixteenth century, it was a religious and trading center with mosques and madrassas, busy markets, and wealthy merchant homes.

In the Soviet era, Osh was the administrative center of an *oblast* (province) in the Kyrgyz SSR, and its demographics began to change. Like other trading cities in the Fergana Valley, most

---

38. Madeleine Reeves, "A Weekend in Osh," *London Review of Books,* July 8, 2010, 17.

of its population was ethnically Uzbek. From the 1960s, as the Soviet Union began building textile and other industrial plants in the south, ethnic Kyrgyz were encouraged to move from the countryside to take factory jobs. The growth in the Kyrgyz population led to conflicts with the Uzbeks. Most were arable farmers and traders who feared they might lose their land and businesses in an independent Kyrgyzstan where ethnic Kyrgyz dominated politics. They wanted to protect their culture and traditions, including the use of the Uzbek language, particularly in schools and media. As long the authorities maintained tight control, the tensions remained largely dormant. When the empire began falling apart, they exploded.

Inter-ethnic violence broke out before independence. Clashes between gangs of Kyrgyz and Uzbeks began in Uzgen in June 1990 and spread to Osh. The police stepped in, sometimes using excessive force; some policemen supported their own ethnic group by taking part in the riots. In the countryside, Kyrgyz herders on horseback terrorized Uzbek farmers and attacked *chaikhanas,* the traditional Uzbek teahouses. Army units moved in and closed the border with the Uzbek SSR to stop Uzbeks from joining the conflict. Official estimates from the three days of fighting put the death toll at more than 300, although unofficial estimates claim it was closer to 1,000. After independence, ethnic Kyrgyz came to dominate both the national government in Bishkek and the regional and local administrations in the south, including the police and the tax authorities.

The most serious inter-ethnic violence in the region occurred in 2010, in the midst of a severe economic depression. The resignation of Kyrgyzstan's president, Kurmanbek Bakiyev, whose power base was in the south, triggered anti-government demonstrations which spiraled into clashes between Kyrgyz and Uzbeks in Osh. The violence spread to Jalalabad and other towns as groups looted and set fire to homes and businesses. Uzbeks became the scapegoats for the country's economic woes. Rather than blame a corrupt president for the mess, it was easier to target Uzbek shopkeepers and traders.

The interim government granted shoot-to-kill powers to its security forces, most of whom were ethnic Kyrgyz. Witnesses reported that security forces handed out weapons, uniforms, and vehicles to Kyrgyz mobs. Armored personnel carriers moved into the Uzbek *mahallas* (neighborhoods) to remove makeshift barricades, clearing the way for attacks by armed men and looters. Uzbekistan moved troops to the border to stop the clashes spilling over. Official figures put the death toll at more than 470, but the figure included only those whose deaths were recorded. Uzbek sources claim that more than 2,500 Uzbeks were killed. According to international organizations, more than 400,000 people were displaced, with 110,000 fleeing across the border to Uzbekistan, causing a major humanitarian crisis.

Tensions in the south remain high. Uzbek schools have been pressured to switch to Kyrgyz-language instruction. Uzbek-language signs have been removed from public places; Uzbek media have been closed or forced to sell out to Kyrgyz interests. Many Uzbeks feel unwelcome in a country where they have lived for generations.

Low Gas Pressure in Osh

For natural resources, Kyrgyzstan and Uzbekistan are mutually dependent. Uzbekistan needs to keep the water from mountain rivers flowing for irrigation. Southern Kyrgyzstan needs Uzbekistan's natural gas and electricity for its factories and homes.

In the Soviet era, central planners made sure that the water, gas and electricity flowed both ways. Uzbekistan depends on the water from two great rivers, the Syr Darya, flowing out of the Fergana, and the Amu Darya, flowing out of the Pamir Alay, to irrigate the cotton and rice crop and fruit orchards of the Fergana Valley. Moscow told officials in the Kyrgyz SSR when to release water from their reservoirs into the Syr-Darya, and how much to release. In return, the Uzbek SSR sent its natural gas and electricity from its coal-fired power plants to the factories and central thermal heating plants of Osh, Jalalabad, and other towns.

After independence, the countries struck a barter deal—summer water from Kyrgyzstan in exchange for winter gas and electricity from Uzbekistan. Kyrgyzstan wanted to increase domestic energy production by boosting hydroelectric capacity but had to wait until the dams filled up after summer to start producing power. Both countries started selling their resources on a cash-only basis, and both complained that the other was not paying its bills on time. The victims in the energy wars were the people of southern Kyrgyzstan who endured frequent, unscheduled power outages and (even when the supply was on) low gas pressure.

I made half a dozen trips to Osh during my Fulbright Fellowship and several more on later trips to the region. Rather than stay at the cavernous, over-priced Hotel Intourist with its surly reception staff and dodgy plumbing, I usually rented an apartment in a suburb and took a cab or *marshrutka* to the university or media resource center. That's what Stephanie and I did on our visit in 1996. By mid-October, it was already chilly, and the bazaar vendors were doing a brisk business in small, electrically hazardous Chinese space heaters. Uzbekistan had reduced the gas supply several months earlier, so it was available only for cooking, and the pressure was low. The local government said it could not pay Uzbekistan until more people paid their utility bills, but to unemployed industrial workers, teachers who had not been paid for months, and retirees who had seen the value of their pensions plummet, food came before utility payments.

In such circumstances, you learn to adapt; when the gas flame on the stove is low, you switch your pan to the hot plate, another fast-selling bazaar item. Bathing required careful planning. In the morning, we put two large pans of water on the stove or hot plate, went back to bed for half an hour, and then took a standing bath.

The Rocky Road to Sokh

If you really want to experience extreme border tensions in southern Kyrgyzstan, try traveling to Sokh.

It's an agricultural area in Kyrgyzstan's Bakten *oblast*, south of Osh, with a population of about 60,000. In the 1920s, it was a center of a *basmachi* uprising against the Red Army. Most of its residents are rice and potato farmers. There's nothing to distinguish it from other agricultural areas in Bakten. But it is part of Uzbekistan.

Sokh is one of Uzbekistan's five enclaves within Kyrgyzstan. Tajikistan has one enclave, Vorukh, in Kyrgyzstan, and one in Uzbekistan.

Until recently, Kyrgyzstan had one, Barak, in Uzbekistan.[39]

How did they come into being? One story is reminiscent of the legend of the enclaves on the India-Bangladesh border—that the rulers of two princely States, the Maharaja of Cooch Behar and the Faujdar of Rangpur, put up small chunks of land or villages as wagers in chess games. As this story goes, Sokh and the other four enclaves were lost by a Kyrgyz SSR communist official in a card game with his Uzbek counterpart. In another version, topography was the deciding factor; because the main road along the Sokh River runs north to the Uzbek SSR, it was given the territory, leaving the more mountainous terrain to the east and west for the Kyrgyz SSR. In another version, the enclaves were allocated based on the language and ethnicity of their inhabitants. This is plausible for the smaller Uzbek enclave of Shakhimardan, the native home of the Uzbek poet Hamza, where nine out of ten inhabitants are ethnic Uzbeks. And for the village of Barak, the former Kyrgyz enclave in Uzbekistan near Qorasuy. But not for Sokh, where almost all inhabitants are ethnic Tajik. Education at its 28 schools and three professional colleges is in Tajik. The local newspaper, *Sadoi Sokh* (the Voice of Sokh) is printed in the Tajik language.

Sokh has been a border sore spot since 1991. Kyrgyzstan has consistently rebuffed the demand for a 10-mile corridor along the river valley to connect Sokh with mainland Uzbekistan. This is a mountainous country, and a corridor would effectively cut Bakten *oblast* into two parts, making it difficult for Kyrgyz citizens to travel. Currently, Sokh residents need to travel almost 100 miles through several border and customs posts to reach Uzbekistan. Kyrgyz citizens travelling between the eastern and western parts of the *oblast* also face checkpoints. Not to mention land mines.

In 1999, Uzbekistan's capital, Tashkent, was rocked by a series of car bombs. The president, Islam Karimov, produced intelligence

---

39. Rashid Gabdulhakov, "Geographical Enclaves of the Fergana Valley: Do Good Fences Make Good Neighbors?" Central Asia Security Policy Briefs #14 (OSCE Academy, Bishkek); "Sokh Enclave: Two Decades of Simmering Tension," Radio Free Europe/Radio Liberty, January 7, 2013; "Convoluted borders are hampering Central Asian Integration," *The Economist,* October 31, 2019.

reports that claimed terrorists from the Islamic Movement of Uzbekistan (UMI) were using Sokh as a base for operations. Uzbekistan sent troops to the enclave and laid land mines along the border. Kyrgyzstan claims that mines were laid on its territory and that several of its citizens were killed by mines or gunfire while trying to cross the border. Uzbekistan says the borders hamper economic development in the enclave where unemployment is high, and many young people have left to seek work in Russia. For Kyrgyzstan, it's a matter of national pride and sovereignty. Uzbekistan has long been regarded by its neighbors as the regional bully. Surrendering land, even in a territory swap, would make the government look weak.

To the west, the situation in Tajikistan's enclave, Vorukh, is even more dangerous. Like Sokh, it's a sizeable area—about 50 square miles—with a population of about 30,000. In April 2013, Kyrgyzstan began constructing a road to bypass the enclave; Tajik officials said the road was on disputed territory and would allow the Kyrgyz to blockade the enclave. Local residents attacked the construction crew. Several months later, eight border guards, Kyrgyz and Tajiks, were injured in an hour-long shootout. Kyrgyzstan responded by closing its border with Tajikistan for the next three months, but tensions remain high. A shootout at another border post in the Fergana Valley in 2019 left four guards dead.

The border between Kyrgyzstan and Tajikistan runs for more than 600 miles, but only half of it has been delineated. In this case, the Soviet cartographers of the 1920s may be partly to blame for sloppy work because both sides rely on conflicting historical maps.[40] Despite many meetings, the two governments have not agreed on a single mile since 2006. No one really cares about who owns some rocky outcrop in the Pamir Alay, but when the border descends to mountain pastures and river valleys where people live and farm, it's a contentious issue.

Regional tensions have eased since 2016 when the authoritarian Karimov, Uzbekistan's president since independence, died. His successor, Shavkat Mirizyoyev, ordered the opening of more border posts and signed border agreements with Kyrgyzstan

---

40. "The post-imperial chessboard," *The Economist*, April 2, 2014.

and Tajikistan. A land swap was agreed to eliminate Kyrgyzstan's Barak enclave in Uzbekistan. But Sokh is still stuck. One resident boarding a bus from Uzbekistan for the long journey home summed up the historical irony well: "We haven't been able to travel freely since Soviet times."

Chapter 16

Tbilisi: Crossroads of Eurasia

★ ★ ★

An Unassuming Academic Façade ...

On my first visit to the Georgian Institute of Public Affairs (GIPA) in 2011, I was glad my driver knew where he was going. We turned off Rustaveli Avenue, the main drag in downtown Tbilisi, and wound through a maze of side streets towards the Mtkvari River. After parking on the street, the driver pointed me towards an alley. I cut down between a construction site and an apartment building that looked as if it was about to collapse; later, I learned that it used to house the GIPA Faculty of Law. Outside the entrance to GIPA sat an abandoned car; across the courtyard was a single-story house, with laundry hanging on the line.

It was an unassuming academic façade; a couple of the letters on the GIPA sign had sagged, and someone had scrawled over the logo. I passed the café and radio studio (tucked into a closet under the stairs) and climbed three flights of uneven stone stairs to the Caucasus School of Journalism and Media Management (CSJMM). Two medium-sized classrooms with rickety chairs—test it before you sit on it, warned Ana, one of the faculty members—and computers pushed back to the wall to make space for the desks. The dean's office, barely larger than a closet. The faculty office, crammed with papers and books, a few framed newspaper front pages and a poster for the 1974 Jack Lemmon/Walter Matthau movie *The Front Page*. That was it. And my job was to help the school become the leader in journalism and media education in Georgia? What on earth had I gotten myself into?

My first trip to Tbilisi, the capital of the former Soviet Republic of Georgia, had been 18 months earlier as an invited speaker at a media conference sponsored by the Organization for Security and Cooperation in Europe. Now I was launching what was supposed to be a four-year USAID-funded project to build staffing, curriculum, and facilities at CSJMM, which for years had been struggling from grant to grant, yet still turning out excellent graduates. The project was part of a larger (US $14 million) program to develop journalism in Georgia, run by a USAID contractor, the International Research and Exchanges Board (IREX). The program had one of those acronyms that can only be dreamed up by Beltway bandits competing for US government contracts—G-MEDIA. It stood for an awkward-sounding medley of aspirational words: Georgian Media Enhance Democracy, Informed Citizenry and Accountability.

As with most USAID-funded projects, this one had taken several months to get going. I was given an impressive title, Senior Journalism Education Advisor, and a contract full of jargon on "capacity building," "measurable indicators," "enhancing free media" and "results-oriented strategies." I boned up on the lengthy G-MEDIA work plan, and thought about how CSJMM could fit into it, only to be told that the plan was still being negotiated with USAID and that I should not be in a rush to do anything except attend meetings and write concept papers. As time went by, I developed a better understanding of GIPA's potential and needs but seemed to understand less and less about what IREX wanted me to do.

On that first visit to CSJMM, I soon forgot about the cramped conditions, broken furniture, and grungy décor. You can fix buildings and buy equipment. People are more difficult to fix. Fortunately the school had very good people—dedicated faculty with strong professional backgrounds who loved to teach, a roster of industry professionals for part-time teaching, and top-notch graduate students from Georgia, Armenia and Azerbaijan. Although there was a Georgian-language program, the flagship journalism program was taught in English. I sat in on the orientation for the Azerbaijani and Armenian students who had arrived for spring semester. The students asked a lot of questions and were not afraid to offer their opinions.

Coffee with Giorgi

The GIPA café would make a good set for a movie scene—dark and dingy, with paint peeling from the walls, beat-up tables and benches with chipped surfaces and uneven legs. The air was thick with cigarette smoke and the smell of fried onions. Students in coats and scarves drank strong Turkish coffee and engaged in earnest debate. I wanted to believe they were discussing post-Soviet politics, human rights, philosophy, or underground art movements, but more likely they were griping about their research paper assignments and comparing their smart phone features. But it was an engrossing scene—think Paris Rive Gauche, Greenwich Village in the 1930s, Prague 1968. Art, politics, literature, revolution. Hollywood would spend thousands to re-create the scene. At GIPA, it was for real.

The café is where I met GIPA's rector, Giorgi Margvelashvili. Giorgi had an office somewhere in the old four-story building, but he seemed to do most of his business in the café. After working at universities in Central Asia, I was accustomed to meeting a university rector (roughly equivalent to a provost or vice chancellor) in a large, lavishly furnished office, with a picture of the country's president hanging on the wall behind an enormous desk and a table (symbolically several inches lower than the desk) with chairs for visitors. I tend to dress up because I know the rector will be well-dressed, ready to meet visiting politicians and foreign dignitaries. At the GIPA café, I felt conspicuously overdressed in my sports jacket and dark pants. Giorgi was in jeans, boots, and a dark shirt, with a scarf wrapped around his neck. A stocky man in his mid-40s, with close-cropped hair, he looked like the sort of character you would try to avoid on a street corner at night.

This was Giorgi's second spell as rector. He had served from 2000 to 2006, helping to build the quality and reputation of

GIPA, one of the country's first private, post-graduate institutions. From 2006 to 2010, he headed GIPA's research department and became a frequent commentator on politics and society in Georgia. By 2012, two years into his new term as rector, he had become a vocal critic of the pro-Western government of the reformist Mikheil Saakashvili, who had come to power in the Rose Revolution of 2003 and served two consecutive terms as Georgia's president. Saakashvili cultivated close alliances with the US and NATO. In 2005 President George W. Bush paid a high-profile visit to Georgia. After he left, the main airport highway was renamed (to the astonishment of most US visitors) George Bush Street. There's a billboard of George, smiling and waving, at the underpass where the road begins.

Although Georgia experienced economic growth under Saakashvili, the president came under criticism for human rights violations in his crackdown on corruption. Police used strongarm tactics in interrogations and raided opposition media. Judges imposed harsh prison sentences, sending Georgia's prison population soaring. Business leaders were pressured to make contributions to Saakashvili's political party. Street protests became more frequent and violent.

When the Georgian Dream coalition, bankrolled by tycoon Bidzina Ivanishvili, defeated Saakashvili's party in the October 2012 elections, Giorgi swopped his jeans and boots for business suits to become Minister of Education and Science. In 2013, he comfortably won election to the presidency with almost two thirds of the vote, but during his four-year term he fell out with Georgian Dream over constitutional reforms that weakened the power of the presidency. He did not seek re-election when his term ended in December 2018.

In 2011, the future President of Georgia impressed me as smart and pragmatic, with a clear grasp of what was possible, given the State of the Georgian economy and politics. GIPA had done well under his leadership, and he wasn't sure he needed aid or advice from anyone, certainly not a US government agency. When I briefed him on what IREX expected from GIPA in return for investments in facilities, equipment, and training for CSJMM, he was skeptical. "You really think the student radio station can turn a profit at the end of two years?" he asked as I shared a spreadsheet showing revenue projections. "Does IREX know anything about the state of the economy? No radio station in Georgia makes money—most are supported by businesses or politicians." Giorgi's meeting with the IREX Chief of Party ended with sharp words on both sides.

IREX assigned me other credulity-straining tasks such as a four-year projection of CSJMM's revenue-earning training courses: which courses would be taught, who would teach them, how they would be marketed, how many people would enroll and the likely net profits. Everyone agreed that GIPA needed to plan, but it was unrealistic to provide that level of detail at the beginning of the project. I sensed that USAID was getting cold feet about IREX's grand plan and had moved to add a new set of unrealistic targets and benchmarks to the work plan. Then, if these were not met, the Washington bureaucrats could claim it was someone else's fault.

I had several tense discussions with the IREX Chief of Party. A few weeks later, after returning to Kazakhstan's capital, Astana, where I was on a Fulbright Fellowship, IREX shut down communication with me. The IREX media chief in Washington then called to tell me there had been a change in strategy and my services were no longer needed. I had already booked an April flight to Tbilisi and arranged to take a vacation with Stephanie and her mother, Marge, after my work was done. I decided not to change my plans. I contacted CSJMM and volunteered to teach classes for a week. Although IREX was waffling about its media development strategy, and whether CSJMM would be part of it, I had made a personal commitment to the staff and students. I no longer had an official position, but I wanted to offer what I could.

The Crossroads of Europe and Asia

It's a cliché, but tourism campaigns and business boosters keep using it: their city is at "the crossroads of Europe and Asia." Some of the claims are pretty iffy, resting on carefully selected historical data and ignoring anything that does not fit the narrative. The strongest "crossroads" contender is, of course, Istanbul, which straddles the Bosphorus Strait between European and Asiatic Turkey. However, Georgia's capital is a worthy rival.

Tbilisi is situated in the narrow winding valley of the Mtkvari River, which rises in northeastern Turkey (where it is called the Kura) and flows east through Georgia, its tributaries carrying snowmelt from the southern Caucasus, and entering the Caspian Sea in Azerbaijan. For centuries, Tbilisi was the head of navigation on the Mtkvari and an important river port. During the twentieth century, extensive irrigation for agriculture and the building of reservoirs and hydroelectric plants substantially reduced water flow, halting commercial traffic. Today, the only boats on the Mtkvari in Tbilisi are those offering tourist excursions.

Georgia's capital, Tbilisi, in the valley of the Mtkvari River.

With the medieval fortress of Narikala on a hill overlooking the old town, and its narrow, twisting cobbled streets and stone churches, Tbilisi recalls Eastern European cities such as Prague or Budapest. Yet the Asian influence is evident in the architecture, with brightly-painted decorative wooden balconies on older houses, some of which were once *caravanserais* (inns).

233

Traditional architecture in Tbilisi's old town.

Tbilisi was once a major trading center, where routes from Istanbul, Tehran, Baghdad, Damascus and other cities converged. It was a place to rest and stock up on supplies before the hazardous journey through the passes of the Caucasus or across the Caspian Sea to the cities of Southern Russia, or to the Silk Road routes through Central Asia.

The city was founded, probably in the fourth century, on the site of hot sulfur springs. According to legend, a local king was out hunting when a pheasant fell into the spring and was conveniently cooked up for dinner. Tbilisi takes its name from the Georgian word *tbili* (warm). Over the centuries, the crossroads city has been conquered and liberated many times—by the Persians (three times), the Mongols, the Turks, and the Russians. In the last Persian invasion in 1795, thousands were killed and much of the city burned to the ground. The Russians rebuilt it in imperial style in the nineteenth century. In between invasions, the Georgians made it their capital.

Georgia has always been at the mercy of its larger and more powerful neighbors. The most recent conflict came in August 2008 when Russia invaded on the pretext of defending the rights of citizens in the breakaway regions of South Ossetia and Abkhazia. Thousands of ethnic Georgians were forced to flee their homes, although many returned later. Russia promptly declared the two regions independent republics; Georgia and most of the international community consider them to be Russian-occupied. With Vladimir Putin continuing to flex his military muscle with the annexation of Crimea and the conflict in eastern Ukraine, no one is placing bets on Georgia regaining its lost territory anytime soon.

Big, Bad Mama Russia

It's one of history's ironies that the man whose iron rule transformed the Soviet Union into an industrial and military power was born into a poor family in Gori in eastern Georgia in 1878. In his early life, the shoemaker's son, Joseph Vissarionovich Dzhugashvili Stalin, studied at a seminary in Tbilisi and wrote passable Georgian poetry before being radicalized by Marxist-Leninist doctrine. After the 1917 Bolshevik Revolution he rose quickly in the communist party ranks, and effectively ruled the Soviet Union from the mid-1920s until his death in 1953.

Despite his ruthless, bloodthirsty record, despite forced collectivization, mass starvation and political purges that claimed millions of citizens' lives, Stalin remains a popular figure in Russia today. In a 2017 poll, the largest number of respondents (38 percent) named him as "the most outstanding person in world history," citing his leadership in the Soviet victory in World War II. Putin, a self-confessed admirer of Stalin, came in second, four points behind, in a tie with the beloved nineteenth century poet, Alexander Pushkin.

Stalin is still revered by some Georgians who are nostalgic for the certainties of the old Soviet-era order, but many more revile the republic's most famous son, almost as much as they dislike his understudy, Putin. Over the years, Stalin memorials have been

North
RUSSIAN FEDERATION
Caucasus Mountains
ABKHAZIA
Black Sea
SOUTH OSSETIA
Mtkvari River
Gori
TBILISI
Batumi
TURKEY
ARMENIA
AZERBAIJAN
0 mi 50
0 km 50
South

dismantled, most recently in 2010 when authorities removed a statue from Gori's central square. Under a 2011 law, dozens of Soviet-era monuments and symbols were demolished and street names which evoked Georgia's communist past were changed.

Although governments can pass laws to try to erase historical memory, culture changes more slowly. Many former Soviet republics are still closely bound to Russia by trade and transportation links, with the poorest partly dependent on remittances from the migrant workers who clean the streets and work on construction sites in Russian cities. For better or worse, Russian is still used as a language of convenience and commerce. On my first visit to Tbilisi in 2009 for the media conference, Russian was the only shared language for the participants from Georgia, Armenia and Azerbaijan. For the younger generation in Georgia, learning English is the key to advancement in education or professional life. Those who grew up in the Soviet era had to learn and use Russian, so it's still widely known, if less often spoken. My taxi driver from the airport spoke no English, but he understood my Russian.

In November 2009, just over one year after the invasion, relations between Russia and Georgia remained tense. The war halted direct flights between Moscow and Tbilisi, so my colleague Andrey Richter from Moscow State University had to travel via Istanbul, more than doubling his flying time. At the airport, his passport was closely inspected. If he had had stamps for South Ossetia or Abkhazia, he would likely have been denied entry. Antipathy between the two countries continues. Sometimes it's subtle. Many Russians love Georgian cuisine, but they don't like to call it Georgian; Russian restaurants advertise their fare as generically *Kavkaz* (Caucasian).

Power Cuts

In 2011 Tbilisi was still off the map for most Western tourists, although foreign investment was increasing, and business visitors pushed up hotel and restaurant prices. It was difficult to find a decent hotel room in the city for less than US $100 a night. Stephanie arranged an apartment rental for almost three weeks for just under US $700. It was in the Saburtalo district, just outside the downtown area but easily reached by subway (65 cents) or cab (US $2-$3). The apartment block was rather rundown, and had a funky, noisy elevator that cost the equivalent of a nickel for each ride. Our apartment was on the seventh floor, so it was worth the nickel. It had two bedrooms, a kitchen, large living area with satellite TV and Internet, and a balcony with a view of the city and hills. The electrical system was, well, not exactly up to code but the place was comfortable.

We experienced one or two power cuts a day but none of the neighbors seemed to be concerned. A decade earlier, power cuts had been frequent, and some parts of the city had only 2-3 hours of power per day. Like other former Soviet republics, Georgia experienced an economic collapse after independence, and recovery was slow. Through the 1990s, unemployment was high and corruption rife. Until 2003, power blackouts in Tbilisi were frequent because a group of what a GIPA colleague called "energy bandits" was selling power from Georgia's hydroelectric plants in the South Caucasus to other countries and pocketing the revenues. The really dark days—when there was electricity for only a couple of hours a day or none at all—are in the past, although many stores had diesel generators that are used when the power was out to preserve refrigerated goods.

Gimme that old Time Orthodox Religion

Tbilisi is stunningly beautiful, with its ancient churches, winding cobbled streets, and small squares. Some of the nineteenth century apartment buildings are dilapidated and need more than stucco patch and new paint, but I've always felt that a little genteel, post-Soviet decay makes a city more interesting. I never tired of wandering the narrow streets, with hole-in-the-wall shops selling *khachapoury* (the Georgian cheese bread) and other baked goods, small basement restaurants and *babushkas* selling fruit and vegetables out of apartment doorways. Several streets near the river have been given a facelift, and have trendy restaurants, bars, boutiques, and shops selling pottery, carpets, and religious icons.

The Georgian Orthodox Church, which was quietly tolerated in Soviet times, is a major force in society and politics.

Independence brought a religious revival, with more than 90 percent of Georgia's citizens claiming in public opinion surveys that they were believers. Tbilisi is dotted with churches, most with elaborate interiors and icons; the oldest have frescoes from the ninth century. Neglected by the Soviets, many churches have been cleaned and restored, and hold masses three or four times a day.

Georgian Orthodox Church. More than 90 percent of Georgia's citizens claim to be believers.

One rainy day, I stopped in at the Anchiskhati Basilica of St. Mary, the oldest surviving church in the city, built in the sixth century. It's a small church (I have no idea why it qualifies to be a basilica) with a stunning interior of high arches and frescoes. A mass was in progress, and the singing from the choir of half a dozen women, resonating through the church, was almost hypnotic.

It's difficult to gauge the depth of devotion, but the signs are everywhere. People walking on the street pause in front of churches to cross themselves, and often give money to *babushkas* begging at the church gates. Taxi drivers speeding to the airport on George Bush Street slow down and cross themselves when passing a church (I did not observe similar reverence for the George Bush billboard). Religion is apparently a better enforcer of speed limits than the city police.

Stephanie, Marge and I had arrived a few days before Easter. The churches were packed every day. On Easter Sunday, all the TV channels ran non-stop live coverage of services at the cathedrals, full of worshippers holding candles and mobile phones to take pictures. There are no seats or pews in Georgian Orthodox churches, so congregational crowd control is an issue. For major religious events, the police were on hand to maintain order, as people pushed towards the priests as they performed rituals. There is also a strict dress decorum, with women fully dressed and covering their heads with scarves. Marge was criticized by one churchgoer for wearing sandals (even though she was also wearing socks).

Giorgi, who drove us to the cathedral at Mtskheta, the ancient capital outside Tbilisi, said that the church was a major property owner, and had amassed considerable wealth since the country became independent. This gave it political and economic power. Because it is conservative, it is generally viewed as a force for social stability, as is the Roman Catholic Church in other countries. Politicians are careful to declare their support for the church, attend major religious events, and consult with church leaders, especially on social issues.

How Do You Say, "Black Pepper?"

Almost everyone Stephanie and I met—in shops, restaurants or on the street—was friendly and hospitable. Stephanie charmed them by speaking a few words of Georgian, and on rainy days she worked hard to master the alphabet. It's like no other alphabet I've ever seen, but Stephanie declared that it was both logical and phonetic. Soon she was sounding out signs and simple words. Of course, her vocabulary was limited, but ranged from the familiar ("Hello," "Goodbye" and "Thank you") to the more technical.

240

How many foreigners know the Georgian for black pepper? I stuck to my Russian, which seemed to be understood by most people and served us well in traveling, shopping, and eating out.

We spent one morning ambling around the *Dezerter* bazaar near the main railroad station. The market earned its name during the 1921 Red Army invasion which toppled the country's Social-Democratic government, installed a Bolshevik regime and incorporated Georgia into the Soviet Union. Soldiers fleeing the fighting would drop off their weapons and uniforms at the market, so the name "deserter" stuck. Renovated in the early 2000s, it's a maze of stalls selling fruits, vegetables, second-hand clothes and household goods. Stephanie bought spices, bean seeds, persimmons and pomegranates, and interesting greens that she added to salads and soups.

We visited the outdoor Ethnographic Museum on the hill above Vake Park, where traditional houses and farm buildings, most of them built from logs, have been reassembled. Sadly, it was rather rundown, with some buildings closed and others in need of repair. Our guide told us that in Soviet times, many groups came to visit, but since independence government funding had been cut and the number of visitors had declined sharply. Most foreign visitors head for the ski slopes of the Caucasus, the Black Sea resorts or wine country. It's part of the Georgian National Museum, so perhaps they can fix it up (and pay the guides more than US $200 a month) when the economy and tourist revenues improve.

Even if Russians prefer to call it *Kavkaz* (Caucasus), Georgian cuisine is well renowned throughout the former Soviet Union and is gaining attention in the West. Hearty soups, stews of pork, lamb and veal with onions, freshwater fish, potatoes, peppers and spices, chicken and pork *shashlik* (kebab), *khinkali* (dumplings filled with meat or vegetables), goat's cheese, the famous *khachapouri* (cheese bread) which comes in many forms from pizza-like slices to pies, and the unleavened flat bread, baked fresh in little shops all over the city. The dry red and white wines, which come mostly from the Khakheti region east of Tbilisi, are excellent and reasonably priced and wine production will likely increase if Georgia joins the European Union.

After our visit with Giorgi to the ancient capital of Mtskheta, we stopped at a roadside restaurant for a late lunch. "You should try the *lobio*," Giorgi advised. It's a tasty dish made from red kidney beans and served with *mchadi* (corn bread) and marinated vegetables.

It was, indeed, tasty and filling. "You're eating Georgian cowboy food," Giorgi teased. I think he'd told that joke before.

ato

Chapter 17

On the Continental Divide
in Russia's Southern Urals

★ ★ ★

Stuck in the Mud

After a week in March in Yekaterinburg, I was tempted to sum
up the city in a few words. Mud, mobile phones, beer, religion,
history. And more mud.

In 2007, I spent a month in Russia's Southern Urals region
on a fellowship program from the International Research and
Exchanges Board (IREX). I was attached to the US consulate
in Yekaterinburg with the grandiose title of "US Embassy Policy
Specialist." No one explained to me what a "policy specialist" was
supposed to do and, as far as I could tell, my teaching and research
on local media had absolutely no effect on US policy towards
Russia. Nevertheless, it was a good experience, mud and all.

The mud was everywhere. On the roads, the sidewalks, in the
courtyard of my apartment complex, and all over the cars. I've
never seen anything like it, and now I know why some Russians
hate this season with its long, slow thaw. There's no snow on the
buildings, but it's still in the parks and piled up on the sidewalks.
"If there is one Russian word a springtime visitor to the country
should know," writes Miriam Elder in *The Guardian*, "it is *slyakot*,
a wonderfully onomatopoeic term that translates, simultaneously,

as 'slush' and 'mud'."[41]

Elder was battling the mud in Moscow. The city, she wrote, "has almost no drains on its roads, leaving melting snow and mud puddles to stagnate with nowhere to go. The roads, battered yearly by winter, look more like concrete Swiss cheese slices, riddled with holes and uneven paving." I'm sure Yekaterinburg's roads and sidewalks were in no better shape than those of the capital city.

The role of mud in Russian history should not be underestimated. It's difficult enough to move food and supplies through winter snows, but the mud that clogs rural roads in spring can delay or halt commerce, causing urban food shortages. In wartime, Russia's greatest natural allies have always been its large landmass and climate: the Russian winter and lack of supplies halted Napoleon's advance in 1812 and the Nazis in 1941. You have to wonder: if the French or German armies had not retreated and dug in for the winter, would they have been able to advance in the spring? Or would they have been, like everyone else, stuck in the mud?

In Yekaterinburg, the locals were used to the mud and walked briskly, sometimes with a mobile phone in one hand and a bottle of beer in the other. It was a surprise to see so many young people—not just men, but women—walking around with open bottles and guzzling at bus stops and street corners. I did not see any public drunkenness, and the drinking seemed to be a social thing, but it's easy to understand why the country has such a problem with alcoholism. About one quarter of the aisles of Kupets (literally "merchant"), the large Western-style supermarket on *Ulitsa* [Street] *8 Marta* where I shopped for groceries, were devoted to alcohol, with a wide variety of vodka and beer.

Conspicuous Consumption

Did you hear the one about Sergey and Boris, who met for dinner at a sushi bar and discovered that they were wearing identical blue silk ties? "Where did you buy yours?" asked Boris. "At the

---

41. Miriam Elder, "Why spring in Moscow is utter hell," *The Guardian*, April 2, 2013.

Tsum [department store]," said Sergey. "I paid 1,600 *rubles* for it." "Oh, Sergey, you are such a fool," said Boris. "I bought mine at the *galstuk* (tie) store, and I paid 4,000 *rubles!*"

Both ties were probably over-priced, but the point of the story (told to me by my interpreter, Aleksey Zotikov) is that consumerism and status are well ingrained in the Russian middle class. The *nouveaux riches* prefer high-priced imported cars to Russian-made Ladas and Moskviches. The only socially leveling influences are the traffic jams and the mud, so the Mercedes and Lexuses get just as dirty as other vehicles. The central shopping district, a few minutes' walk from my first apartment, was full of upscale clothing and consumer electronics stores, and the streets lined with ads and billboards. One showed a young man (with a mobile phone, of course) and his doting parents: "I live in the U.S.A. and I worry about my poor parents back home in Russia. I send them money every month. I can always trust Western Union." English-language phrases and commercial signs are popular—Winemania, where Aleksey bought his Merlot, the Doctor Scotch Pub and the Rosy Jane Pub and Whiskey Bar.

I knew Russia would not be cheap, but I was taken aback by the cost of living. In a café, it was US $4-$5 for a small espresso, and a restaurant meal set you back at least US $25-$30 (not including a beer). Happily, at each university where I taught, I could pay US $3-4 for a filling, if carb-heavy meal at the *stolovaya*, the student canteen. On my stipend, self-catering was the only way to go so my trips to Kupets became more frequent. With help from my consulate liaison, Lada Tikhonova, I even applied for and obtained the Kupets supermarket discount card. The only cheap deal was public transportation. For eight *rubles* (about 32 cents) I could travel anywhere in the city on buses, streetcars, and trolley buses.

Mining History

My first apartment was near one of the main east-west drags, *Prospekt Lenina*. From the seventh floor, I looked out over the downtown and the *Gorodskoy prud* (city pond), where the Iset River was dammed to form a man-made lake. In late March, it was still partly covered with ice floes.

This small dam, now crossed by *Prospekt Lenina*, marks the site of Yekaterinburg's first industrial enterprise—an iron forge, powered by water from the dam. In the early eighteenth century, during the reign of Peter the Great, explorers discovered the vast mineral wealth of the Ural Mountains—coal, iron ore, copper, and precious stones. Yekaterinburg, founded in 1723 and named for Peter's wife, the Empress Yekaterina (Catherine I), emerged as the center of the mining industry with iron forges and machine plants. By the early nineteenth century, the industry supplied almost all the iron produced in Russia and exported to European markets. Urals iron and copper went into the Statue of Liberty and the roof of Britain's Houses of Parliament.

The city, bisected by the Iset River, a tributary of the Tobol, a major river in Siberia, was built on a grid pattern with iron works and residential buildings at the center. These were surrounded by walls, making Yekaterinburg both a manufacturing center and a fortress. Situated at the continental boundary, 1,000 miles east of Moscow and 2,000 miles west of Irkutsk, the city became Russia's gateway to Asia.

In 1924, the city was renamed Sverdlovsk in honor of the Communist party leader Yakov Sverdlov, Lenin's right-hand man until his death in the flu epidemic of 1918. In the Stalin era, heavy industry was developed; Sverdlovsk became the leading industrial city of the Urals region, a center for the manufacture of armored vehicles and munitions. During World War II, as the Nazi armies advanced, the Soviets relocated about 60 factories from Central Russia and Ukraine to Sverdlovsk, diversifying its industrial base. After the war, most of them stayed, along with the engineering and technical institutes that were also moved.

Industrial growth continued in the 1950s and 1960s, with the Khrushchev government building hundreds of prefabricated apartment blocks—the so-called *khrushchevkas*—to meet the post-war housing shortage. During the Cold War period, Sverdlovsk was a closed city because of the armaments industry and military bases. In 1960, a surface-to-air missile fired from Sverdlovsk brought down the U2 spy plane piloted by Gary Powers. He bailed out and was captured, tried as a spy, and imprisoned, before being swapped for a Soviet spy in 1962.

In 1991, with the collapse of the Soviet Union, the new Russian Federation president Boris Yeltsin, facing an attempted coup d'état, had a decision to make: where should the government move if the situation in Moscow became too dangerous? The choice was obvious—his home city of Sverdlovsk where he had served as the regional Communist Party boss in the late 1970s before being summoned to Moscow by Mikhail Gorbachev to take up a series of positions and join the Politburo. Yeltsin enjoyed widespread popular support in Sverdlovsk, so the city was designated as a temporary reserve capital of the Russian Federation. With the failure of the coup, the government stayed in Moscow. Sverdlovsk regained its historical name of Yekaterinburg on September 4, 1991.

Today, with a population of more than 1.5 million, Yekaterinburg is the fourth largest city in Russia and has diversified its economy into the retail, service, financial and telecommunications sectors. With its stylish nineteenth century architecture, museums and arts scene, Yekaterinburg is now a major tourist destination.

A Bloody History

The top sight for Russian tourists is the massive Byzantine style (and grimly named) Church of the Blood, next to the site of the house where Tsar Nicholas II, his wife and five children were murdered. After the 1917 Revolution, the Romanovs were moved from Petrograd (St. Petersburg) to Yekaterinburg, where they lived in the home of a local merchant, Nikolay Ipatiev. On July 16, 1918, with the Czechoslovak legions of the White Army closing in on the city, local Bolsheviks, believing the forces were on a mission to rescue the Romanovs, executed the family in the basement of the house. The legions captured the city less than a week later and it remained under the control of the Whites until the Red Army retook it a year later. In an effort to erase historical memory, the Soviets converted the house into a museum of atheism, but everyone knew about its bloody history. In 1977, Yeltsin, as regional party boss, had the house demolished to prevent it from being used as a rallying point for monarchists.

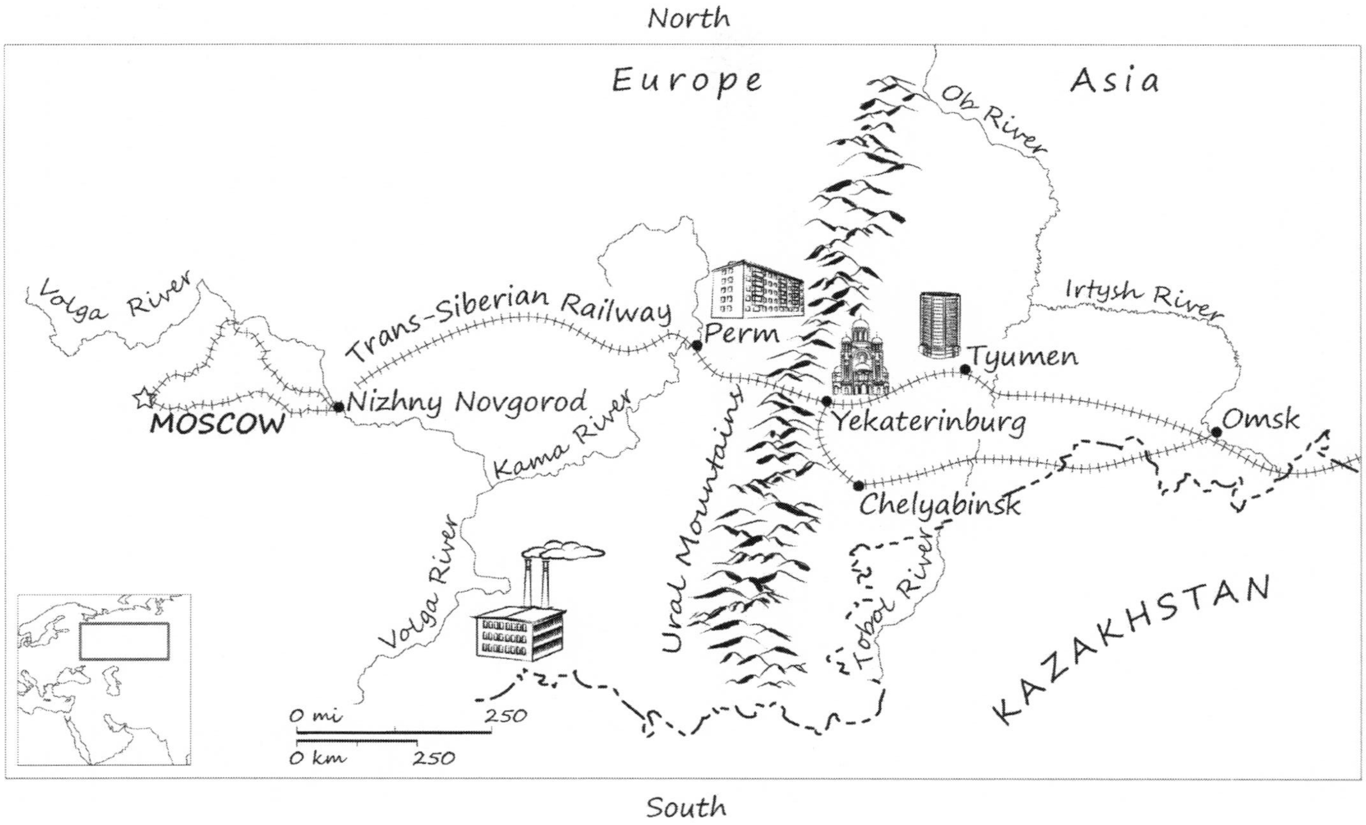

North

Europe   Asia

KAZAKHSTAN

South

Ob River

Irtysh River

Omsk

Tyumen

Yekaterinburg

Chelyabinsk

Tobol River

Ural Mountains

Perm

Trans-Siberian Railway

Kama River

Nizhny Novgorod

MOSCOW

Volga River

Volga River

0 mi   250

0 km   250

Today, the site is marked by two crosses, one dating from 1998 when the Romanovs' remains were removed to St. Petersburg for burial in the family vault. In an ironic historical twist, the major public event was presided over by Yeltsin, now President of the Russian Federation; sensing public opinion and the growing influence of the Russian Orthodox Church, he chose to celebrate the Romanovs rather than pretend they had never existed.

The Russian Orthodox Church of the Blood—a monument to the Romanovs and the top tourist destination in Yekaterinburg.

After paying their respects at the cross, visitors head straight for the Church of the Blood. To me, it seemed a garish modern monument, full of marble pillars and elaborate Orthodox icons, and a large gift shop selling expensive religious kitsch. It contains interesting photographs of the Romanovs, and memorabilia from their brief stay in the city. No one knows how much the Church of the Blood cost to build, or exactly where the money came from, but it's on every tourist itinerary. It's also a popular stop for wedding couples. As I was leaving, I passed a limousine that had pulled up at the front steps. Not just any limousine—a Humvee limousine. The Russian *nouveaux riches* at their most ostentatious. I'll bet the groom paid over the odds for his tie.

I saw a different side of the Russian Orthodox Church as I was leaving the Museum of Architecture and Industry a few hours later. The ticket-taker urged me to *slushat muziku* (listen to music) and pointed me towards what looked like the gift shop. It *was* the gift shop, but also a chapel where an Orthodox service was going on with about 30 worshippers, mostly women wearing head-scarves, a priest, and a choir of five women. I didn't understand a word, but the acoustics were perfect and the singing beautiful. It was a nice antidote to the ostentatious Church of the Blood.

I spent an hour or so at the Natural History and Geological Museum. The displays featured rocks from all geological eras and precious stones, along with stuffed animals in aggressive poses, devouring their prey. I could not make much headway with the captions, either the Russian or Latin equivalents. I did better, dictionary in hand, at the Museum of Architecture and Industry, although it helped that I already knew the Russian words for iron, coal, mine, factory, and industry. There were evocative archival photographs of the coal and iron mines and factories, together with elaborate architectural plans, and some heavy-duty vintage steam-powered mining equipment. In the early pictures, the settlements looked like Western boom towns, but as the timeline moved forward to the late nineteenth century they had developed and boasted impressive public buildings, wide boulevards, and many churches.

Crumbling Images of Soviet History[42]

For Leonid Lyubimov, the visual history of the Soviet Union is literally crumbling away.

Lyubimov spends his days among stacks of film cans at the Sverdlovsk Film Archive in Yekaterinburg, one of the largest archives in Russia. Lyubimov, the archive's deputy director, reels off the statistics, "more than 10,000 newsreels, 7,000 documentaries, 200 feature films and 50 animated films."

The collection is housed in five cramped rooms on the second floor of a nondescript city center office building. The archive long ago ran out of metal shelving, so film cans and paper records

---

42. Originally published in *History Today*, 58:1 (January 2008).

are stored in the corridor and in almost every nook and cranny.

Leonid Lyubimov in the stacks at the Sverdlovsk Film Archive.

Lyubimov has a bigger problem than storage space. Only one room, where the features and animated films are stored, is climate-controlled, with appropriate temperature and humidity for film storage. In the other rooms, documentaries and newsreels are slowly decaying. The problem is what archivists call "vinegar syndrome." Over time, with exposure to moisture and heat, a film's base starts to break down, releasing acetic acids. This process causes shrinkage, brittleness, fading, and a vinegary smell. Some films from the 1940s have already decomposed so badly that they cannot be screened.

The issue is funding. Until the early 1990s, the archive was part of the Sverdlovsk Film Studio. For half a century, with subsidies from Moscow, the studio produced a wide range of films, and stored them in climate-controlled rooms. Everything changed with the fall of the Soviet Union. Subsidies from Moscow ended, and the film studio was privatized. It is now a commercial business, competing with newer concerns for TV commercials and program production. The archive is still officially a state enterprise but receives no government funds. Its only assets are the films, to which it holds copyright. It licenses features for TV airing and sells some footage to documentary filmmakers, but the revenue barely covers the electricity bill and the salaries of the small staff. Russia's copyright term is 50 years, so some films are now in the public domain.

How did an industrial city, founded to exploit the mineral wealth of the Urals region and best known for its steel mills and coal mines, end up as major film center? "We have Hitler to thank for that," said Lyubimov.

In late 1941, as the German armies besieged Leningrad and advanced on Moscow, the government ordered film studios to close. Directors, cinematographers, set designers and artists moved east to Sverdlovsk, where the Soviets had located many of their war munitions plants. The Sverdlovsk Film Studio, founded in 1943, became the fourth largest in the USSR. It produced popular feature films such as *Privalov's Millions*, *Suva*, and *The Ugryum River*, but built its reputation on animated cartoons, documentaries about science, nature and ethnography in Siberia and the Far East, and training films.

For half a century, the studio turned out weekly 10-minute newsreels, shown in cinemas in the Urals region and later on television. The newsreels, most of which were shot on 35 mm black and white stock, provide a fascinating historical chronicle, not only of Soviet-era propaganda—the choreographed parades in honor of Communist leaders and celebrations of industrial production—but of everyday life.

The lead item usually featured the comings and goings of party leaders. In a December 1960 edition, cinemagoers saw Premier Khrushchev whipping up enthusiasm among delegates at the 21st session of the Communist Party Congress in Moscow. Scenes of economic progress in the Urals followed: the pipe factory in the city of Chelyabinsk, construction of an atomic power station in Sverdlovsk, and the reassuring Cold War news that "The USSR produces more milk than the USA."

It was not all ideology and industry. Soviet audiences wanted to be entertained, and the last three or four newsreel subjects featured sports, celebrations, or youth and children's activities. In December 1960, the newsreel featured the selling of New Year items, the marriage of two young people, and a couple moving into a new apartment. It is these images of the lives of ordinary Soviet citizens—their homes, family celebrations and daily routines—that will be lost if the newsreels are not preserved.

Some films were produced for foreign audiences. The "10 Minutes Around The USSR" series, with titles in English, French and Spanish, often featured art, architecture, nature, and science. One 1975 film on folk art shows the oldest log-built church in Siberia, intricately carved wood designs on houses and public buildings, and traditional painted window shutters. It was an exercise in "soft diplomacy" with not a missile or aging Soviet leader in sight.

Lyubimov worries this history will be lost if the archive cannot provide climate-controlled storage. He would also like to have the collection digitized to provide easier access, but as an archivist he knows that's not the ideal option. Digitizing will save the historical images, but not physically preserve the films.

"It's a tragedy," he said. "Whatever people in Russia today may think of the Soviet era, it's part of our history. Most of what's in these newsreels and documentaries was recorded only on film—it's not in any other medium. How will future generations know how we lived if we don't preserve it?"

Dr. Zhivago and Me

Lada Tikhonova, my consulate liaison, told me there were two simple ways to spot foreigners, even if they spoke good Russian (which I did not). First, they've seen too many re-runs of *Doctor Zhivago* and *Reds* and wear (or at least talk about wearing) fur hats. No one in Yekaterinburg, she said, had worn fur hats for years; indeed, I'd seen only two or three since I arrived. Second, they dream of traveling on the Trans-Siberian Railway. Lada just does not understand how the name conjures up mystery, romance, and danger. To her, it's just a train. Indeed, most Russians I met were blasé about long-distance train travel. I asked the wife of a university colleague where she was from, and she named a small city in Siberia. "Only 44 hours by train," she added. Only 44 hours?

Well, Lada pretty much pinned me. I had carefully packed the rabbit fur hat I bought on the bazaar in Bishkek, Kyrgyzstan, 10 years earlier, but it never came out of the suitcase. I had been nagging Lada since I arrived for that Trans-Siberian Railway trip. My first trip out of Yekaterinburg was to Perm, an industrial city in European Russia about six hours to the north-west. Lada said we would be travelling by car, but the return journey three days later would be on the Trans-Siberian. I began having *Doctor Zhivago* fantasies. If I colored my greying mustache, could I pass for Omar Sharif as Yuri Zhivago? My interpreter Aleksey could stand in for Alec Guinness as my half brother, the Bolshevik leader Yevgraf Zhivago. Who would be my Lara? In Slavic mythology, *Lada* is the goddess of beauty, love and marriage, but I did not think Lada wanted the role. Where was Julie Christie when I really needed her?

Straddling Two Continents

About 10 miles west of Yekaterinburg, along the *Moskovsky trakt* (Moscow highway), a roadside monument marks the official boundary between Asiatic and European Russia. Its location, in the middle of a pine forest on a level stretch of road, seems rather whimsical, but the sign states that scientists had studied geological records and water flow patterns to confirm the spot. It officially replaced a marker erected in 1837 on top of a hill that for many years had been a popular destination for picnickers and newlyweds. It was close, but not close enough. The scientifically correct boundary point offers no views—except for trees, trees and trees—but first-time travelers rarely resist the temptation to stop and strike the obligatory photo pose, standing on the painted line marking the boundary, one foot in Asia and one in Europe. In this region of the southern Urals, there's no perceptible difference between the two continents. From the road, in all directions, it was a landscape of hills, lakes, and forests of pine and white birch.

Russia is not only the largest country by land area in the world, but the only one that is dramatically transcontinental. Technically, other countries meet the transcontinental criterion. European Turkey and Istanbul face Asiatic Turkey across the Bosphorus Strait. Northwest Kazakhstan, west of the Uralsk River, is geographically in Europe, allowing the country's teams to compete (and usually lose) in European football competitions. Egypt's Sinai peninsula is technically in Asia; southern Panama in South America; Spain's Moroccan enclaves in Africa; some eastern Indonesian islands are in Oceania, not Asia. But only Russia impressively straddles two continents with a significant land mass in both.

Lada and I step across two continents.

Almost three quarters of Russia's land area is in Asia: at 5.1 million square miles, it's almost the size of the continent of Antarctica. European Russia is the largest country in the continent, a little less than half the size of the continental United States. The population distribution is almost exactly reversed, with almost three quarters of Russia's 146 million people in Europe. East of the industrial region of the Urals, the urban population is concentrated in a line of cities in southern Siberia, most of them along the Trans-Siberian Railway and its branches—Omsk, Tomsk, Krasnoyarsk, Novosibirsk, Irkutsk, Chita, Khabarovsk, and finally, on the Pacific Ocean, the port of Vladivostok. To the north are vast deciduous forests of birch and poplar, and further north, the taiga, the swampy coniferous forests of pine, spruce and larch. Then it's the tundra and finally the Arctic Sea. On average across its vast expanse, Siberia has a population density of eight per square mile, but the southern Siberian cities skew the statistic. Except for remote mining camps—and, in the Siberian context, remote is a relative term—the only people in some areas are hunters and herders who are passing through.

The Ural Mountains, whose watershed forms the dividing line between Asia and Europe, stretch 1,250 miles from the Kara Sea in the Arctic north to Kazakhstan in the south. As mountain ranges go, the Urals are in the minor leagues; the highest peak, Mount Narodnaya (People's Mountain), barely clears 6,000 feet, and in places the Urals are no more than large hills. For centuries, the region was mostly hunting country and lightly populated. The first large-scale settlements came in the early eighteenth century during the reign of Peter the Great when vast mineral resources were discovered. By the nineteenth century, the region, with its seemingly endless reserves of coal, iron and copper, as well as gold and precious metals, was the industrial heart of the expanding Russian Empire, with half a dozen large manufacturing cities.

Lada, Aleksey and I arrived in Perm, an industrial city of more than one million on the south bank of the Kama River, in time for lunch with my host Nastia (Anastasia), a faculty member at Perm State University. She drove us around the city in the afternoon. If it wasn't for the Soviet-era apartment blocks and Cyrillic signs, we could have been in an Ohio River city. Indeed, Perm's twin city is Louisville, Kentucky.

The Banks of the Ohio?

Since the late eighteenth century, the Kama, like the Ohio, has been an important transportation route, shipping salt and agricultural produce, and today coal, iron ore, petroleum, and chemical products. The Kama (1,122 miles long) is the largest tributary of the Volga, which flows into the Caspian Sea. And just as the Ohio was connected (in the early nineteenth century) by canal to Lake Erie and, via the Erie Canal, to the East Coast of the US, canals connect the Kama to rivers flowing into the Black Sea and the Barents Sea in the Arctic North. By the 1860s, the city had major ironworks and paper factories, and built steamboats for the Kama and Volga river trade. In the 1930s, Perm grew as aviation and chemical plants were built. During World War II, the Soviets moved industries east ahead of the advancing German army, and Perm became a center for artillery and munitions production.

Today, Perm's industrial output exceeds that of larger cities in the Southern Urals, including Yekaterinburg, Chelyabinsk and Ufa, with steel, oil, natural gas, chemicals, lumber and food processing the major sectors. Two large plants manufacture engines for the Russian aircraft industry. Perm is an important junction on the Trans-Siberian Railway with lines radiating to Central Russia, the northern Urals, and the far east. It is still a major river port, with barge traffic and a busy freight rail line.

For much of its history, Perm's image was that of a bland, industrial city. It provided literary inspiration for the playwright Anton Chekov, but not in the right way: it was the dreary place that the Prozorovs—the *Three Sisters*—were so desperate to leave. As a *New York Times* travel writer, who visited in 2011, put it: "Perm used to be the last stop to nowhere, the transient point where criminals, political prisoners and other people deemed undesirable by the czars and the Soviet regime passed through on their way to forced exile and later the *gulags*, often never to be heard from again. During the Cold War Perm itself disappeared from Soviet maps when it became a closed city, off limits to outsiders thanks to its military production facilities."[43]

With investment from the city government, Perm has experienced a cultural and economic renaissance, with new art galleries, theatres, and a lively music scene; in summer, the restaurants and cafes are crowded with Muscovites on weekend getaways. The *Times* described Perm as "Russia's emerging cultural hotspot." The riverfront looked rundown, but Nastia told us there were plans to convert older buildings (including the former headquarters of the regional nuclear missile unit) to hotels, restaurants, and apartments.

Although Soviet urban planners demolished many nineteenth century buildings to make way for factories and apartment blocks, some fine log-built merchants' homes have survived, and are designated as historical sites, with plaques and small museums. They include houses built by members of the Stroganov family, which rose to prominence during the reign of Ivan the Terrible in the

---

43. Finn-Olaf Jones, "A Bilbao on Siberia's Edge?" *New York Times*, July 22, 2011.

sixteenth century. The Stroganovs were Russia's first oligarchs, making their fortunes in salt manufacturing, mining, industry and shipping and using their political connections at court to gain land, mineral rights and tax breaks. They were elevated to the nobility by Peter the Great and went on to help bankroll the Russian army as the empire expanded west and east.

Nineteenth century log-built merchant's house in Perm.

Or Are We in Africa?

"Welcome to Africa!" Nastia laughed at her own joke as we passed another row of Soviet-era apartment blocks, indistinguishable from the rows I had seen from the car window for the last 15 minutes. She slowed down and pointed out the street sign.

I mentally transliterated the Cyrillic. "*Ulitsa* [Street] Kwame Nkrumah." Ghana's first prime minister after the country gained independence from the British in 1957 was an influential advocate of Pan-Africanism and a founding member of the Organization of African Unity. The Soviets awarded him the Lenin Peace Prize in 1962. "We also have *Ulitsa* Julius Nyerere, *Ulitsa* Patrice Lumumba." Nastia reeled off a short list of socialist-leaning, anti-colonial African leaders who had sought support from the Soviet Union during the Cold War. Moscow's soft diplomacy funded students from its African allies to study at universities in the Soviet Union, and Perm hosted many, mostly in social science and technical disciplines. The universities provided dormitories, cafeterias and, I trust, some warm winter clothing. The students were supposed to return to their home countries with a thorough dose of Marxist-Leninist principles on top of their agriculture or engineering degrees and become the educated elite in government, industry, and higher education. To try to make them feel at home, the Soviets renamed the streets where they lived, creating a heroes' gallery of African socialist leaders among the apartment blocks.

Pasternak's City

Perm residents are proud to point out that the old quarter of the city provided literary inspiration for Boris Pasternak, who lived there for seven months in 1916. Yuriatin, the town to which Zhivago and his family escape from the civil war, is said to be modeled on Perm. A well-known merchant's home, the Art Nouveau-style Gribushin House, built in 1907, offers an extravagant façade of wreaths, garlands, rosettes, and the bas-reliefs of female heads. This is "The House with the Figures," a prominent setting in the novel. Just around the corner in the Pushkin Library is the reading room where Pasternak worked and where he based the fateful reunion between Zhivago and his great love.

Nastia enthusiastically related scenes from the novel where our hero catches brief glimpses of Lara through windows or doorways and pointed out the locations. It all seemed rather conjectural, but certainly good for tourism. On Monday night, we had dinner at the appropriately-themed Zhivago restaurant, with a bust of Pasternak in the courtyard.

History Destroyed, History Preserved

Soviet urban planners made a mess of Perm. The two main east-west streets in the city center still carry their Soviet-era names—*Lenina* and *Kommunisticheskaya*. The Soviets lined both with huge apartment blocks, not only to provide much-needed housing but to block the view of the city's two main churches.

They demolished old wooden houses to make way for a central mall for parades and processions. At one end stands the drama theatre, at the other a triumphal monument, with statues of Mother Russia, a soldier and a worker striking appropriately heroic poses. Locals have the usual jokes about what the statues symbolize. The worker is trying to hail a cab. The soldier is blocking the approach to the drama theatre saying, "Culture stops here!" And Mother Russia, with her arms outstretched, is asking "Where's the money?"

The highlight of our tour was the Cathedral of the Transfiguration of the Savior, overlooking the Kama and completed in 1832. The cathedral with its neoclassical bell tower was built next to the Transfiguration Monastery, founded in 1560 by the Stroganov family. The cathedral and monastery buildings now house the city's art and regional history museums. The art museum is famous for its collection of painted wooden sculptures, religious figures from villages in the Prikamye (near the Kama) region of the western Urals dating from the seventeenth century. The indigenous population combined animist art forms with Christian figures to create remarkable sculptures including several depicting Jesus Christ in prison, his arm raised to signify his resistance. The sculptures are definitely not orthodox enough for the Russian Orthodox church which does not accept them as religious icons, but they provide a fascinating glimpse into the merging of cultures and belief systems. The museum also features a collection of Soviet-era table settings, with appropriate slogans ("Proletarian work will liberate you") on the plates. Some breakfast-time inspiration before another day at the collective farm or the munitions factory.

Aleksey, Lada and I stayed at the Urals Hotel, at the junction of *Lenina* and *Komsomolski Prospekt* (known locally as Komproz), one of those huge Soviet-era hotels found in most cities. It had been nicely modernized, and at US $60 a night (including breakfast) was a good deal, at least in comparison with Yekaterinburg hotel prices. Close by was an Uzbek restaurant. Unfortunately, it was Russians doing Uzbek cuisine. The meat was overcooked and lacked the distinctive spices used in Central Asia, and the *lipioshki* flat bread stale; the best dish was the so-called "Salad Exotica," but it was definitely Russian, not Uzbek. Aleksey and I had a better, but also ethnically questionable, meal at a "Czech restaurant," part of a local chain with the surprising (and ethnically inaccurate) name of Bob. "We brought the recipes from a cooking expedition to Moravia," boasted the menu. It did have a good Czech beer and was decorated with banners from English Premier League Clubs with minor misspellings (Angfield for Liverpool).

TV Time

Unlike many Russian universities, where academic buildings are scattered around the city, Perm State University has a real campus. Because of the harsh winters, the main buildings are connected by enclosed walkways. It was a bit of a maze and I never quite figured out how to get to my classroom in the three days I was at the university, but there was always a faculty member or student to serve as guide.

Foreign lecturers were still a novelty, so my visit attracted attention. Indeed, the university security service instructed the chair of the journalism department, Vladimir Abashev, to provide a full report on everything I said to the students. This seemed a futile exercise, because Vladimir would have been foolish to include anything controversial or critical in his report. But old habits die hard.

The title of my opening lecture, "The End of Television As We Know It," did attract attention, including that of the local TV stations. I did several TV interviews during my stay, including a recorded half hour show at Uralinform TV, owned by a regional telecommunications company. Although the program aired in the evening, it felt like a morning show with cutaway segments to the host Ivan (who looked as if he had not missed many meals) in the studio "kitchen" with his perky co-host. Aleksey and I did the interview sitting on the sheepskin-covered couch. The interviewer, Stepan, was well prepared, and things were going well until he turned to camera and announced that he was going to take calls from viewers. "What's going on?" I wondered. This was a recorded show, and no one was watching. It was the co-host, who had popped out of the kitchen to the make-up area to

261

make the call. She was back on the line five minutes later, trying to sound different from the first caller. "Very unethical," fumed Lada as we left the station. "They would never do this on local TV in Yekaterinburg."

Looking for Lara

At last it was time for my long-anticipated Trans-Siberian experience on the night sleeper from Moscow to Yekaterinburg. It was Aleksey's birthday. We celebrated with a few shots of vodka and I asked him about his life. He was the former head of the foreign languages department at the Agricultural Academy, and fluent in English and French. In Soviet times, he was sent as a "technical advisor" (he said that with a sly grin) to Algeria. Later, he worked with foreign companies investing in Russia and with the BBC on training programs. He also seemed to have an endless stock of Soviet-era jokes. Traveling around Yekaterinburg, he pointed out buildings that were government and military establishments when Sverdlovsk was a closed city. One was called the House of Industry. "Lots of military there," he said. "We used to call it the Pentagon."

The trip to Yekaterinburg took 10 hours, with frequent stops. For someone who rarely dozes in cars and planes I enjoyed a good night's sleep and woke up to morning views of forests of white birch and pine and small towns with log-built houses.

"Are you accompanying the foreigner?" someone asked Aleksey as he took a smoke break outside the compartment. "He seems fascinated by everything he sees." Well, I suppose that if I did this trip a few times, it would not have the same magic. Just trees, trees and more trees. But it was my first time and I began to daydream. I was on the Trans-Siberian and the guy opposite me in the compartment was Yevgraf Zhivago. Would he guess my identity? Would we fight hand-to-hand as the train roared through a tunnel? Would Lara be waiting on the platform at the next station?

Gateway to Siberia

The Latin word *Caesar* is linguistically well traveled, cropping up in many languages as the title for an emperor or ruler. In German, it's *Kaiser*, in Turkish it's *Kayser* or *Cezar*, in Arabic it's *Qays'r*. In Russian and Eastern Slavic languages, it's *Tsar*. It was first adopted by Ivan IV in 1546 when, at the age of 16, he emerged from the chaotic regency of his mother to have himself crowned as "Tsar of all the Russias."

Ivan IV is better known as Ivan the Terrible. After his wife Anastasia died in 1560, Ivan, believing she had been poisoned, embarked on a reign of terror, eliminating all rivals, real or suspected. In a fit of rage, he even killed his eldest son and heir. He took the "all the Russias" part of the title seriously, expanding the Kingdom of Muscovy's territory and power. To the east, he defeated the Tatar khanates of Kazan and Astrakhan, acquiring the Volga region and part of the Caspian Sea coast, and setting the stage for Russian expansion into Siberia.

After Ivan's death from poisoning in 1584, his second son, the religiously devout but feeble Fyodor I, became Tsar. Power was effectively wielded by a regent, Boris Godunov, who set about consolidating Ivan's territorial gains. He built towns and fortresses along Russia's borders to keep the Tatar and Finnic tribes under control and began colonizing western Siberia, establishing military posts at strategic locations. The fort of Tobolsk, which became Siberia's first capital, was built at the confluence of the Tobol and Irtysh Rivers. Tyumen was founded on the high bank of the Tura River, a tributary of the Tobol. The name comes from the Turkish and Mongol word *tumen*, meaning ten thousand, a term often used to apply to a military unit.

By the beginning of the eighteenth century Tyumen, 1,600 miles east of Moscow and on a historical trade route between Central Asia and the Volga region, had developed into an important commercial center. In 1836, the first steam boat in Siberia was built in its shipyard. The Trans-Siberian Railway reached the city in 1885, and for some years, it was Russia's easternmost railhead, where cargoes were on and off-loaded to cargo boats on the Tura, Tobol, Irtysh and Ob Rivers. By the end of the nineteenth century its population exceeded 30,000, surpassing that of the regional capital Tobolsk, which had been bypassed by the Trans-Siberian. The Soviets developed industries including shipbuilding, furniture, and the manufacture of fur and leather goods. In World War II, as in Yekaterinburg and Perm, industrial enterprises were relocated from central and western Russia, almost doubling Tyumen's population.

From the eighteenth century, the city's prosperity was celebrated by the building of Orthodox churches with onion domes and spires, in the so-called Siberian Baroque style. Several survived the Soviet era and have been restored, including the *Spasskaya Tserkov* (Church of the Savior). The central part of the city is still dotted with log-built one and two-story merchants' houses from the eighteenth and nineteenth century. As real estate prices have risen, some have been demolished and others are now overshadowed by glass and steel high-rises. A historic preservation commission is charged with reviewing all proposals for real estate development but feels the pressure from business and political interests. Tyumen's wealth will likely enable it to preserve the best of its traditional architecture, but only in a carefully protected and segregated historic quarter.

Colder than Houston

Until the early 1960s, Tyumen was a mid-sized city that most Soviet schoolchildren could not easily find on the map. Then rich oil and gas fields were discovered in the north of Tyumen *oblast*. Although most lay hundreds of miles away, Tyumen was the nearest railroad junction and became the supply base while the line was extended northwards. Over the next 20 years, workers arrived from across the Soviet Union. By the end of the 1980s, the city's population had doubled to almost half a million. Although its economy suffers when oil and gas prices fall, the city no longer depends exclusively on the energy sector. Tyumen now positions itself as a regional hub for finance, higher education, and medical care.

The city center looks like an American downtown with banks, commercial and government office buildings. The major oil and gas companies—Russia's Lukoil and Gazprom, and multinationals such as BP and Shell—have regional headquarters here. Flush with energy tax revenue, the city government has built a central mall with gardens, a circus, theaters, and sports facilities. It fixes the potholes and quickly clears the snow and mud from the streets and sidewalks. To me, the city felt rather bland and soulless. At night, most businesses, cafés and restaurants were closed, and few people were out on the streets. The kiosks that stay open late in other cities rolled up the shutters at eight o'clock at night. This is Russia's Houston, prosperous and conservative, but with much worse winter weather. I wasn't surprised to learn later that Houston, which has more than four times the population of Tyumen, is its twin city.

The energy boom has boosted every sector of the economy, including the media. A well-to-do radio station owner, Vladimir Bogodelov, drove us out for a late-afternoon meal at what he disarmingly called his "ranch" in the village of Guseva ("goose" in Russian). He apologized for the construction work, and explained that until his new house was built, his summer home was the "bath house." The bath house was as large as many American suburban homes (and much larger than the average Russian apartment). It had a small indoor swimming pool, a Russian sauna, a Turkish bath, a large living room (to be converted into a pool room once the new house was finished), a good-sized kitchen and two bedrooms. It was already the largest and most expensive house in the village, which is why Vladimir had hired a guard who lived in a more modest dwelling on the premises. Guseva is being transformed from a typical Siberian village into a summer retreat for the "new Russians" of Tyumen.

A Spy in the Classroom?

Tyumen State University (TSU) has benefited from the oil and gas boom. Unlike other universities where the administration struggles to repair aging buildings, all TSU's buildings are well maintained, and the university (enrollment 15,000) opens one or two new buildings each year. The expensively designed glass-and-brick law school looks like a corporate HQ, which it probably is anyway (there's good money to be made in oil and gas law).

There had been less investment in the university hotel, where Aleksey and I stayed. The first thing I do when I check into

Soviet-era accommodation is to inspect the bathroom, the most common source of problems. I was not surprised to find I had no hot water. The friendly staff promised to fix the plumbing the next day, and then the next day, but it never happened. Fortunately, there was hot water in Aleksey's room, so I was able to shower. It was an inconvenience, but in a sense, I was relieved to discover that not everything in Tyumen worked efficiently and smoothly. Russian cities just don't seem quite right without a little post-Soviet decay.

My university classes were attended by a man in his mid-thirties who described himself as a part-time teacher "doing research." He sat at the back of the room, listening and taking notes. If he was a spy for the local authorities, as Aleksey surmised, he wasn't a very good one because it was clear he knew little about media and journalism. The only question he asked was, according to Aleksey, "incredibly stupid." In any case, his presence didn't seem to bother the students or inhibit our discussion on business reporting. Perhaps he noted that I said that Gazprom is a monopoly with ties to the government. This is not news to anyone.

The only ominous event occurred when I was stopped by two cops as I walked back to the hostel one evening. They inspected my passport, asked where I was staying and then insisted on accompanying me back. I knew there was one dark street between the main drag and the hostel, so I politely refused. They kept insisting that it was dangerous to be out at night alone, and that they would protect me. I called Aleksey and stayed on the line for 10 minutes, pretending to talk to him, while he got dressed and walked over to meet me. Perhaps the cops were genuinely concerned about my safety, but I couldn't be sure. I knew that if I stayed on the line and something happened, Aleksey would hear it.

Back on the Trans-Siberian

We traveled to Tyumen and back by train, through a flat landscape of fields and forests of silver birch. The train from Yekaterinburg was an *electrichka* or commuter (a four-hour journey is a commute by Siberian standards). The return trip was on an older long-distance train, where all the cars were sleepers. For some passengers, Tyumen was the mid-point on a two-day journey to Saratov in Central Russia and most had stocked up on provisions. All the cars had an attendant, and free hot water for tea and coffee.

Aleksey and I decided to risk the drunks in the dining car and have dinner. It was not exactly the Orient Express, but the car had a certain faded ambience, with fake grapevines running along the top of the windows, above the green drapes. The *solyanka* (a thick, spicy soup with meat, mushrooms, pickled cucumbers, potatoes, cabbage, and sour cream) was excellent, and the drunks apologized for disturbing our meal.

I looked out of the window. Trees, trees and trees. I found myself checking my watch and looking forward to arriving at Yekaterinburg. The romance of the Trans-Siberian Railway was starting to fade.

Chapter 18

The Borders of Our Minds

★ ★ ★

Now that I've reached the conclusion, it's time to confess my cartographic crime. I have violated Article 1, sub-section 2, of India's 1961 Criminal Law Amendment Act, which states:

"Whoever publishes a map of India, which is not in conformity with the maps of India as published by the Survey of India, shall be punishable with imprisonment, which may extend to six months, or with fine, or with both."

Like most white collar criminals, I started small scale. My first offense occurred in 2012 when I arrived in Delhi carrying a copy of *The Economist*. It included a story about China's Belt and Road Initiative with a map showing that Pakistan administers part of Kashmir. It was an innocent oversight. I had failed to note the first category on the list of prohibited items on the customs declaration: *Maps and literature where Indian external boundaries have been shown incorrectly.* Fortunately, I was not apprehended.

Since then, I have scaled up my cartographic criminal activities. I have published (or rather republished) "incorrect" maps of India in articles and presentations and in my second book on travel, history and culture, *Monsoon Postcards: Indian Ocean Journeys.* If I am arrested by the map cops, I suppose I'll claim I didn't know what I was doing, although ignorance of the law is no excuse. If convicted, I will ask the judge to let me serve my prison term in Kashmir so that I can truly appreciate that this beautiful region is, and always has been, part of India.

The princely State of Jammu and Kashmir was split between India and Pakistan at partition in 1947. India administers about 55 percent of the region, a land area a little smaller than the United Kingdom, which is home to about 70 percent of the population. Pakistan controls about 30 percent, China 15 percent. On official maps, the whole province is shown as being part of India, even though everyone knows the reality is different. It would seem silly if the stakes were not so high. Thousands of troops face each other along the tense Line of Control (LoC) that forms the *de facto* border. India and Pakistan have fought three wars over the region, and border raids and skirmishes are frequent. India will always claim sovereignty over the whole of Kashmir, even if it does not control it.

On that trip in 2012, I should have known better than to be reading *The Economist*, a serial cartographic offender. The previous year, customs officials impounded 28,000 copies of the magazine, and ordered that stickers "correcting" India's borders be manually applied before they were released. In 2015, Al Jazeera was forced to stop broadcasting in India for five days after the surveyor general reported that "a portion of Indian territory has not been shown as part of India in some of [Al Jazeera's] maps."[44] Most maps acknowledge the territorial dispute by showing the LoC as a dotted line. India cannot force other governments to recognize its claim, but at least it can make them show that the border is fuzzy. In 2011, India complained that maps on the US State Department website ignored India's claims while recognizing Pakistan's; the maps were amended to show the region's disputed status and the LoC.[45] In May 2020, India got into a diplomatic tiff with Nepal when its government issued a new national map that included a 115 square mile area on its northwest border between India and China. Nepal had long claimed that the area was within its territory under the 1816 border treaty with the British; India offered a different reading of the historical map and, more to the point, had stationed troops there since the 1962 war with China.

---

44. Max Bearak, "Cartographers beware: India warns of $15 million fine for maps it doesn't like," *The Washington Post*, May 6, 2016.

45. "US state department removes India-Pakistan maps," BBC News, November 22, 2011.

The dispute was reignited by the inauguration of a new 50-mile road built by India through a mountain pass to provide a route for Hindu pilgrims traveling to a sacred site in Tibet. Thousands of Nepalis took to the streets in protest, burning effigies of Indian Prime Minister Narendra Modi. "This is our land and we will reclaim it," declared Nepal's Prime Minister, KP Sharma Oli.[46] India, which has always included the area on its maps, dismissed the claim as lacking in "historical facts and evidence." It's unlikely Nepal can do any more than huff and puff and publish more aspirational maps. As India has shown in the past, it has the means to strangle commerce to its landlocked neighbor.

In 2016, the Modi government briefly floated a draft law that would punish cartographic criminals with up to seven years in jail or fines ranging from US $150,000 to $15 million, and require individuals and companies producing maps to obtain a government license. The legislation was shelved, but it indicates the paranoia over borders. In that issue of *The Economist*, the editors noted that the offending map would probably be cut from India editions: "Sadly, India censors maps that show the current effective border, insisting that only its full territorial claims be shown. It is more intolerant on this issue than either China or Pakistan."

There's a difference between printed maps, which can include text and images to signify disputed borders, and online maps where dotted lines, symbols and footnotes may clutter the image. As Greg Bensinger noted in an analysis for *The Washington Post*, Google Maps, with an 80 percent market share and more than a billion users, "has an outsize impact on people's perception of the world." Where borders are in dispute, the company may decide to "localize" the map, bending to the will of a government so that it can continue to do business in the country. "From Argentina to the United Kingdom," writes Bensinger, "the world's borders look different depending on where you're viewing them from. That's because Google—and other online mapmakers—simply change them." Google told the *Post* that it remains "neutral on issues of disputed

46. Ashok Sharma, "India–Nepal territorial dispute flares over road to Tibet," Associated Press, May 21, 2020; Sugham Pokharel, "Nepal issues a new map claiming contested territories with India as its own," CNN, May 21, 2020.

regions and borders" but added that in countries where there are "local versions" of Google Maps, "we follow local legislation when displaying names and borders."[47] India, China, South Korea, Russia, and other countries issue official guidance on how maps should be presented, with penalties to cartographers for "incorrect" versions. There are two Google Maps of Kashmir—one for Indian users showing the whole region as part of the country, and one for everyone else showing the LoC and Pakistan-administered Kashmir.

India also has territorial squabbles with China which controls Aksai Chin, the area of Kashmir it seized after India's humiliating defeat in the 1962 war. Since then, troops have faced each other across the 2,100-mile Line of Actual Control (not to be confused with the Line of Control with Pakistan). As borders go, the line is on the fuzzy side; as rivers and snowcaps shift, it is difficult to demarcate. For more than half a century, the dispute has occasionally boiled over with scuffles between border patrols that wandered, deliberately or accidentally, across the line. In May 2020, tensions rose after India completed construction of a new road in the Galwan Valley in the Ladakh region that would speed up the movement of forces to the border. After a military build-up on both sides, Chinese troops crossed the border in at least three places, destroying posts and bridges and brawling with Indian troops. In a more serious clash on June 15, at least 20 Indian soldiers died, some after tumbling into an icy river; the Chinese did not report their casualties. Although, as *The Economist* noted, much of the India-China border is "too rugged and empty to fight over," the first deadly clash in almost half a century, combined with other skirmishes further east in the States of Sikkim and Arunachal Pradesh, have raised concerns about a wider war between the two powers. "The last thing the wider world needs," editorialized *The Economist*, "is an escalating slugfest between a dragon and an elephant over a lofty patch of frozen earth."[48]

---

47. Greg Bensinger, "Google redraws the borders on maps depending on who's looking," *The Washington Post*, February 14, 2020.

48. "Elephant v dragon: How to end the perilous Indo-Chinese border spat," *The Economist*, June 18, 2020.

In 2012, as I was flouting India's customs regulations, China was issuing its citizens a new e-passport with a map showing aspirational borders. The map of "Greater China" predictably included Taiwan, historically claimed by China, and islands in the South China Sea that are also claimed by Vietnam, the Philippines, Brunei, and Malaysia. Aksai Chin was included, as was most of Arunachal Pradesh, which China claims as "South Tibet." Taiwan and the Philippines protested. Vietnamese border officials refused to stamp the new passports.[49] Indian officials, who may have been running low on their stock of *Economist* map stickers, stamped their own version of the map on visas issued to Chinese citizens.

The lesson to be drawn from all the diplomatic pouting, map sticking and visa stamping is clear: each country, or at least its government, has its own idea of where its borders lie, and they usually encompass a larger area than it actually controls, certainly more than represented on maps drawn by other countries or supposedly neutral parties, such as international organizations. Occasionally, the need to make the border match the map leads to clashes where frontier guards and military units exchange fire or provocatively plant a national flag on the other side of the line. Sometimes, clashes spiral into what one country calls a righteous mission to reclaim its traditional homeland; the other country calls it an invasion.

In 2008, Russia claimed it was liberating its historic territories of Abkhazia and South Ossetia with their majority Russian-speaking populations from the tyranny of Georgia; to the Georgians, it felt very much like an invasion. The same claim and counter-claim were made with Russia's takeover of the Crimean peninsula in 2014. The annexation left cartographers with the challenge of how to represent the disputed region. Russian maps show a hard border between Crimea and Ukraine; for Ukraine and countries that condemned Russia's annexation, it's a dotted line. In 2019, under apparent pressure from Moscow, Apple revised its maps for Russian users to show Crimea as a territory of Russia, a change that led to protests from Ukrainian and

---

49. Max Fisher, "Here's the Chinese passport that's infuriating much of Asia," *The Washington Post*, November 26, 2012.

European officials. Like Kashmir, the borders change depending on who's viewing them.[50]

As You Possess under Law ...

Most often, border wars are "soft," fought out in diplomatic negotiations, international courts, policy institutes and the media. At the root of many disputes is the doctrine of *uti possidetis juris* (Latin for «as you possess under law»), a principle of international law which provides that colonial or internal administrative borders, whatever their origin, should be used to delineate new sovereign states. The doctrine originated in South America in the nineteenth century as the Spanish Empire was being dissolved. The new states used the colonial boundaries to ensure there was no *terra nullius* (nobody's land) between them and so reduce the likelihood of border wars. Peru and Ecuador patched up their squabble in 1998, leaving a dispute between Bolivia and Chile, the undefined border between Argentina and Chile in the Southern Patagonian Ice Field and the Argentine claim to the Falkland Islands (Islas Malvinas) as the major outstanding regional issues.

Most countries in Asia and Africa emerged with their colonial boundaries pretty much intact, with some, such as Malaysia, combining more than one former colony. Similarly, with the collapse of the Soviet Union in 1991, its 15 Soviet Socialist Republics (SSRs) became independent countries with their 1920s gerrymandered borders, enclaves, ethnic mixes, and all. Ethnic and national conflicts persist—for example, between Uzbeks and Kyrgyz in the Fergana Valley—and there have been some minor border grabs or nibbles, yet on the whole the Soviet-era artificial borders have held up pretty well. Not so in the Balkans, where the breakup of Yugoslavia into its six constituent republics unleashed violent ethnic and religious conflicts that lasted for more than a decade.

The alternative to *uti possidetis juris* is what is loosely called "self-determination" in which the people (or their elected or

---

50. *The Washington Post*, February 14, 2020.

self-appointed leaders) decide whether to keep the pre-independence borders or slice and dice the territory into smaller, usually ethnically or religiously-based, sovereign states. It's a messier nation-building process, given that each self-identified group may be dispersed over a large land area, or may simply be the majority group in a region. Some countries that inherited their colonial borders face secessionist movements by groups who feel oppressed by the regime and demand their own state. In countries such as Nepal, self-determination is played out in wrangles over the constitution, provincial borders, and the rights of ethnic groups.

British India was cobbled together, by conquest and alliance, over a century and a half. At the time of partition, it consisted of eight large provinces, five minor provinces and princely states. The latter were technically not under British rule; their rulers had treaties that allowed them to control domestic affairs, with the British responsible for external affairs, defense, and communication. After World War II, several princely states such as Hyderabad, with its Muslim ruler and majority Hindu population, lobbied to become constitutional monarchies, retaining their borders. The principle of *uti possidetis juris* might have worked for Hyderabad, which was almost as large as Britain, had an economy the size of Belgium's and a population of 16 million. However, if it had been applied across the board to princely states, almost 600 new countries would have been created, a political, economic, and cartographic train wreck. Instead, the princely states opted one by one to join either India or Pakistan, their rulers' decisions based primarily on whether the majority of inhabitants were Hindu or Muslim. The religiously mixed provinces of Bengal, Punjab and Kashmir were internally partitioned, dividing people who shared language and culture and had lived together, mostly peacefully, for centuries. The process of religious self-determination led to millions of people fleeing their homes and communal violence that persists today.

Before partition, Bengali politicians and intellectuals had called for the creation of an independent Bengal. The province had a rich history and culture, and a common language; in terms of land area, natural resources, and population, it would have made a viable country. Yet it was divided, according to the principle of self-determination, along religious lines between India and Pakistan. Bengalis, Hindu and Muslim, had more in common with each other than with other ethnic groups in India or with the peoples of West Pakistan, 1,400 miles away. A quarter of a century later in East Pakistan, resentment against the imposition of the Urdu language, lack of political representation and under-development finally boiled over in the nine-month Liberation War that ended with independence for Bangladesh. Could thousands of lives have been saved if *uti possidetis*, rather than religious self-determination, had been applied to the province of Bengal in 1947? We will never know.

There are close to 100 ongoing border disputes in Africa, with the number likely to rise as autocratic regimes give way to multi-party democracies in more countries. After World War II, as the European colonies gained their independence, *uti possidetis juris* was applied with the same rationale as in South America—to avoid border conflicts. Almost every country in Africa is multi-ethnic, so a policy of self-determination, allowing each ethnic group to decide on borders, would have been a recipe for chaos and conflict. In 1964 the Organisation of African Unity passed a resolution stating that the principle of stability of borders would be applied across the continent. Of course, the colonial borders drawn up in the half century after the Berlin Conference of 1884-85 were always artificial, paying no respect to the boundaries of pre-colonial states, topography, or ethnicities.

What would borders have looked like if the continent had not been colonized, or if its new leaders had tried to restore pre-colonial boundaries? The scenario is represented in the Alkebu-Lan 1260 AH map by the Swedish artist Nikolaj Cyon who drew boundaries based on a study of political and tribal units in 1844, on the eve of Europe's "scramble for Africa." Alkebu Lan, translated as "land of the blacks," is an old Arabic name for Africa. In old Islamic cartography, the South was often on top, subverting the traditional European orientation. The date, 1260 AH, represents the Anno Hegirae, the years since the migration of the prophet Muhammad from Mecca to Medina in 622 AD.

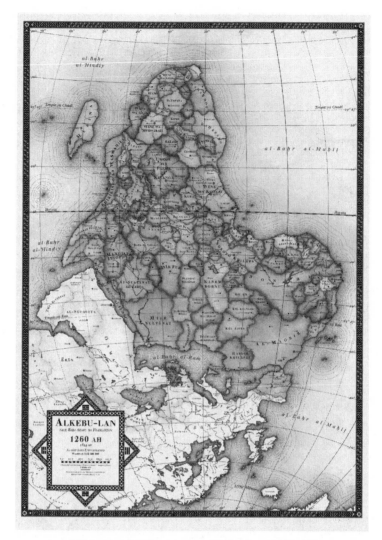

Africa as it might have been—Alkebu-Lan 1260 AH,
copyright Nikolaj Cyon, reproduced with permission.

Of course, this is a counterfactual. We will never know what might have happened if the boundaries of 1844—rather than those of 1944—had been used. Would there have still been border disputes? Probably yes. Would there still have been ethnic-based separatist movements? Probably yes. The fact remains that African border disputes are, according to Max Fisher, litigated on the basis of "whatever Europeans happen to have marked down

276

during the 19th and 20th centuries." In an essay for *The Atlantic*, he analyzes a 2002 ruling by the International Court of Justice on a dispute between Nigeria, a former British colony, and Cameroon, a former German colony, over the oil-rich Bekassi Peninsula. Each country's legal arguments were based not on "ancient cultural claims to the land, nor the preferences of its inhabitants, not even their own national interests." Rather, "they cited a pile of century-old European paperwork." In the end, Cameroon's "yellowed maps were apparently more persuasive" and it won the case.

Although conflict in Africa—the seemingly endless series of civil wars, coups, and counter-coups—has decreased since the 1970s, almost every country is made up of multiple ethnic groups, with distinct cultures and languages. As Fisher notes: "With tribal identities strong and national identities weak (after all, the former tend to be ancient and deeply rooted, the latter new and artificial), national cooperation can be tough." When you add religion, class divisions, corruption, migration and poverty to the ethnic mix, the potential for conflict is never far away. The continent currently has at least 20 separatist groups, fighting to establish their own states. The threat of secession, writes Fisher, "is a reminder of Africa's unique post-colonial borders, a devil's bargain sacrificing the democratic fundamental of national self-determination for the practical pursuits of peace and independence."[51]

Terra Incognita

Look at any European map from before the nineteenth century, and you're sure to find some areas with no place names or physical features such as mountains, rivers and lakes. Depending on the language of the mapmaker, they will be labeled *terra incognita* (Latin), *tierra desconocida* (Spanish), *terra desconhecida* (Portuguese), *terre inconnue* (French) or in English "parts unknown." Most maps of what was often referred to as the "known world" simply illustrated the development of the geographical knowledge of the

---

51. Max Fisher, "The Dividing of a Continent: Africa's Separatist Problem," *The Atlantic*, September 10, 2012.

West. Whether or not a particular region may be called unknown depends on whose knowledge is considered. Lands that were unknown to Europeans were familiar to the peoples who lived there, and often to peoples from other civilizations as well. Yet, throughout history, travelers—from medieval monks to conquistadors to merchants to nineteenth century missionaries—have been intent on filling in the blanks, mapping "parts unknown," their mountains, lakes, rivers, and trade routes, often to open the way for colonization and settlement. Such maps, of course, were not the exclusive domain of the West. Arab merchants and sea captains had their maps. The Chinese imperial bureaucracies had theirs. And so did other cultures

In some regions, maps from different civilizations overlapped, with common features and even borders. In others, they did not. What was a *terra incognita* to a Marco Polo, a Ferdinand Magellan, or a David Livingstone, might be well known to an Arab trader or Chinese bureaucrat, who would similarly draw a blank for Scandinavia or Northern Europe. By the mid – nineteenth century, the term had begun to disappear from European maps because both the coastlines and interior regions of all continents had been "explored" and mapped, with reasonable accuracy.

Mental Maps

I find the concept of *terra incognita* instructive because it indicates that everyone—from individuals to families to communities to societies and governments—constructs mental maps that consist of their personal and collective geographical knowledge. Within these maps, borders, real or perceived, exist. We may visit the same places as other people, but our perceptions and mental maps of them are shaped by who we are, our age, gender, race and ethnicity, our values and belief systems, as well as whether we had a good or bad experience in the place. We all set out on our journeys carrying mental baggage—national and cultural origins, economic interests, preconceptions about a place and its people. It is inevitable that views of the same places differ because we are looking at, and for, different things.

A simple, personal example. At a resort town on Spain's

Mediterranean coast, I will happily skip the beach, the shops, and the casino for a walking tour of the old town and the history museum. I do not expect everyone else to come along with me, literally or mentally. What I remember about the place—my mental map—will be different from another traveler who spent the day on the beach, with a break for shopping.

Another example. I like travelling in countries where things do not work efficiently or predictably and relish the challenge of figuring out how to get around. For someone else, that level of uncertainty is profoundly unsettling. Because of our different attitudes to travel and expected levels of comfort, our mental maps of the same place will differ.

In sum, there is no objective geographical reality to which all can subscribe. Each person looks at their surroundings from an individual and subjective perspective; we choose to see some things and ignore others. Each of us almost unconsciously constructs a personal geography, constantly storing and using data. We form impressions of places, and this "knowledge," coming from multiple sources, helps us to make decisions—on which route to take, on whether to walk or take the subway.

The study of spatial perception and mental maps is now well established in human and cultural geography and in disciplines such as anthropology, psychology and sociology that study human attitudes and behaviors. The first systematic articulation of the concept was by the scholar and urban planner Kevin Lynch in *The Image of the City* (1960) and *What Time is This Place?* (1972). Lynch asked groups of people in Boston, Jersey City and Los Angeles about their perceptions of landmarks, areas and borders of the city, and their driving routes. He asked each participant to sketch a map, saying: "Make it just as if you were making a rapid description of the city to a stranger, covering all the main features. We don't expect an accurate drawing—just a rough sketch." From these sketches, he identified five elements of the city—nodes, edges, districts, paths, and landmarks. Mental maps reveal how people find their bearings and, often unconsciously, plan their routes. For example, in rural Mongolia, herders are able to navigate across the steppe because of their precise memory of physical features—rocks, stream beds, slight hills or depressions;

in Ulaanbaatar, people use landmarks, not street addresses or district names.

Mental maps indicate invisible borders that are not represented on official maps. They reveal areas that people believe are dangerous, or places where they would not normally go. Obviously, mental maps vary depending on age, gender, race, and socio-economic status. In an urban area with residential segregation, mostly-white neighborhoods may be *terra incognita* to people from other races, and vice versa. Mental maps will also change over time, as a city or district changes. For example, as older, industrial areas are revitalized, with loft apartments, restaurants, and wine bars, they may be perceived as safer or more welcoming; by the same token, older residential neighborhoods where crime and drug use has increased will be viewed differently. Mental maps are in constant flux.

Even for places where we have traveled, our perceptions are based not only on our personal memories but on what others have told us, and what we have learned, read, or watched. "Envisaged London," writes David Lowenthal, "is a composite of personal experience, contemporary media, and historical images ranging from Hogarth and Turner to Pepys and Dickens."[52] Outside our communities or familiar environments, our mental maps become sketchier. As Peter Gould and Rodney White note in their classic study *Mental Maps*, "We know more about the areas close to us, and they tend to become much more important than others about which we know little." They cite studies which demonstrate, with logarithmic coordinates, that "people's emotional involvement, the degree to which they really care about what happens at a place, falls off in an extremely regular way with their estimates of how far the places are away from them."

The Maps in Our Heads

Such perceptions have been parodied in numerous maps and cartoons. Gould and White cite Daniel Wallingford's classic maps

---

52. David Lowenthal, "Past Time, Present Place: Landscape and Memory," *The Geographical Review* 65 (January 1975), p. 6.

from the late 1930s of the New Yorker's and Bostonian's views of the United States. In the New Yorker's map, the boroughs of Manhattan and Brooklyn occupy most of New York State, with the Bronx cast off to the north; the vacation land of Florida is just south of Staten Island; Boston is merely a village on Cape Cod; to the west, the map becomes more distorted as "states exchange names and wander to outlandish locations."[53] In the Bostonian's map, the city and Cape Cod assumes their proper cartographic places as the centers of culture and commerce, with upstart cities such as New York and Washington, DC, pushed to the hinterland.

If New Yorkers and Bostonians have skewed mental maps of the United States, how do they perceive the rest of the world? A 1976 *New Yorker* cover cartoon, "The View from 9th Avenue," humorously reinforces the conclusions of the academic studies that people's emotional involvement in a place decreases in proportion to its perceived distance. The cartoon briefly acknowledges "Jersey" and then compresses the rest of the continental US into an amorphous blob. The Hudson River—the western boundary of the civilized world as we know it—is half as wide as the Pacific Ocean. Japan, Russia, and China are vague shapes on a far horizon.

My most prized possession from more than a quarter century of travel is a laminated Soviet-era middle school historical map of the United States for the period from the end of the nineteenth to the early twentieth century. I bought it at a bookstore in Bishkek, Kyrgyzstan, in December 1995. At Almaty airport, the customs officials solemnly informed me that the export of historical maps was prohibited but that, if I really wanted to take it with me, they would need to charge a special export license fee. We argued for a few minutes. I pointed out that maps such as this had hung on schoolroom walls throughout the Soviet Union for years; it was neither rare, not valuable. It was also a map of the US. What was I going to do? Use a historical map to plan an invasion? They got the joke, confiscated a knick-knack from my suitcase, and sent me on my way.

---

53. Peter Gould and Rodney White, Mental Maps (Boston: Allen & Unwin, 1986), pp. 17-23.

At that time, my Russian was limited, and it was not until two years later, after returning from my Fulbright Fellowship in Kyrgyzstan and a year of study with a native speaker, that I studied the map in detail. It focused mostly on economy and population, with symbols indicating coal, oil, and iron deposits. I was puzzled by large red flags that seemed to pop up randomly, sometimes in cities, sometimes in rural areas. Below each was a year, and that was my clue. Cities in the northeast and Midwest such as Buffalo, Pittsburgh, Philadelphia, Chicago, and St. Louis had two years listed, 1877 and 1886—these were the years of railroad strikes, that were brutally suppressed. Pittsburgh, 1892—the Homestead Strike. Ludlow, Colorado, 1913—the miners' strike. And so on. The history of the United States was being taught to Soviet schoolchildren through the ideological lens of strikes and labor unrest. The red flags were the most prominent symbols on the map, larger than the circles that denoted the population sizes of cities. Shaded areas indicated Native American reservations, where presumably the indigenous peoples were being exploited. An inset map, entitled "Imperialist Aggression" showed Central America, the Caribbean and East Asia, with a lot of nasty-looking black arrows indicating military operations.

The map is interesting, not only because of the contrast it offers to the maps that were used to teach American middle-school students about their country's history, but because of the not-so-subtle message it sends about borders. State borders are marked, but the states are simply classified into two groups: those that were part of the Union before 1870, and those that joined later, with no text explaining when or why they became states. The real borders on this map, as represented by the red flags and shaded areas, are class borders—between the capitalist bosses, supported by the federal, state, and local governments, and the working classes, between settlers and ranchers and the Native Americans, confined to their reservations.

It is a selective, ideological history, although perhaps no more so than the history of the Soviet Union as taught to US students (if it was taught at all). I started working in Central Asia four years after the fall of the Soviet Union and met many people whose view of US history was largely a catalog of class warfare, strikes and

282

racial oppression. Lessons learned in middle and high school were amplified and reinforced by Soviet newspapers, TV, and films. In a March 1983 speech to the National Association of Evangelicals, President Ronald Reagan famously described the Soviet Union as the "Evil Empire," a label that fit well with the preconception of many Americans at that time. They might be surprised to learn that many Soviet citizens also thought of the US as an evil empire, even if they did not use that phrase. In both countries, education and the media shaped the mental maps of its citizens.

Nepal Is "Frozen India," Bangladesh "Poor Immigrants"

What are the perceptions of the countries featured in this book and their borders? For assistance, I turn to the non-scientific but intriguing mental maps by the graphic artist Yanko Tsvetkov, part of a long-term project on mapping stereotypes and featured in his best-selling 2017 collection, *Atlas of Prejudice*. I would like to feature some here, but I asked, and he said he would not allow republication. Because I'm already in trouble in India for my "incorrect" maps, I'm not going to risk nicking intellectual property. All I can do is give you Yanko's website address, www.atlasofprejudice.com and you can look for yourself. It's worth the trip.

Some borders on Tsvetkov's maps roughly correspond with political borders, but more often stereotypes sweep across regions, summing them up in a few words. In what is perhaps his most-viewed map, "The World According to Americans" (2012), most of sub-Saharan Africa is a blob labelled "AIDS." In Asia, India absorbs Bangladesh as "Yoga" and Malaysia is lumped in with Indonesia as "Obama's Schoolmates." Tsvetkov also skewers the stereotypes of other nations about each other. In "Asia According to China" (2015), the aspirational map of Greater China is writ large: the South China Sea is "Our Sea" and the Pacific Ocean "Water From Our Rivers," The Philippines are "Catholic China" and Malaysia "South China." Myanmar is "Our Mexico," and Indonesia "Our Middle East."

Depending on where you are in the world, Pakistan is perceived differently. To the Chinese, it is "Friendly Indians," to India, it's "Suicide Bombers" ("Asia According to India, 2015") To India, Russia is the "Weapons Supermarket"; the US labels Russia as "Commies," yet the Chinese regard it as the "People Who Fucked up Communism." India's small neighbors, who usually do not merit stereotypical labels on other maps, are all tagged: Nepal ("Frozen India"), Bhutan ("Happy People with TVs"), The Maldives ("Sinking Islands") and, most pointedly, Bangladesh ("Poor Immigrants").

It's easy to laugh—or feel slightly uncomfortable—with these labels, but it's worth noting that even in a fast-changing world, national and regional stereotypes remain remarkably stable. Wherever we live, it's tempting to see large countries, diverse in race, ethnicity, culture and landscape, through a single lens. In a radio interview about *Monsoon Postcards*, the host asked me a leading question which seems to reflect that narrow view. Of the countries featured in the book—Madagascar, India, Bangladesh, and Indonesia—which, he asked "is the most desperate?"

The End of Borders as We Know Them?

It's become fashionable in some academic, journalistic and intellectual circles to dismiss political borders as a passing phase in human history. After two centuries, surely the nation state has existed long past its expected shelf life. The decolonization process began in South America in the early nineteenth century; in the space of 15 years, from 1811 to 1826, all the Spanish colonies and Brazil (a Portuguese colony) gained independence. Meanwhile, nationalism was rising in nineteenth century Europe, leading to the unification of Germany and Italy. After World War I, new nations emerged with the breakup of the Austro-Hungarian and Ottoman Empires. Nationalism entered a new phase after World War II as Britain, France, Belgium, and the Netherlands surrendered their colonies, along with the remnants of the Spanish and Portuguese empires. Over the next half century, as the last colonial tidbits in the world became countries, annually expanding the list of United Nations members, we defined, delineated and aggregated the world using the unit of the nation state.

Even as the number of nation states was growing, there were signs that some just did not make much sense, dependent as they were on other states or regional groupings for trade and security. Since the end of World War I, but especially since World War II, the growth of nation states was paralleled by the rise of international organizations such as the UN agencies, and defense pacts such as NATO. Other groupings that were launched to develop economies by breaking down trade barriers developed strong political, legal and administrative bonds; the European Coal and Steel Community morphed into the European Economic Community and finally, gathering up more member states, into the European Union. At the same time, global communication networks were developing at a fast pace. It was not only Marshal McLuhan, who coined the term "global village," who believed communication was making the world a smaller place. As Hollywood movies were distributed worldwide, and small countries without domestic media industries filled their evening TV schedules with syndicated American soaps, critics fumed about cultural imperialism but could do nothing to stop the free flow of *Santa Barbara*.

Today, more than 30 years since the Internet was introduced, the country-with-national-borders-is-dead argument goes something like this. Global trade, financial markets and communications technologies have made the nation state largely irrelevant. Multinational corporations such as Google, Amazon and Ali Baba have more resources and money than many national governments, and more influence over people's attitudes and behaviors. For the global economy, the future lies in tariff-free trade, the opening of markets, and the reduction of regulations on foreign direct investment.

At the same time, the Internet and social media are revolutionizing how we learn, what we think, and how we envisage our community or neighborhood. To put it another way, perhaps the principal border in my personal world is between the people who claim to be my Facebook friends, who come from at least 30 countries but most of whom I have never met in person, and those who are not, who include people who live across the street in Charleston, West Virginia. That's silly, of course, because I know and like many people who are not on my dropdown list of "Friends," but the point is worth making. Technology has

285

enabled people to create vital, vibrant virtual communities that know no national borders. Attempts by governments to restrict information within borders, by blocking websites, shutting down social media, or censoring content deemed dangerous to public order (or to the reputation of rulers), have become increasingly sophisticated, yet have failed to prevent flow. For every cyber cop at a guard post along the Great Firewall of China, there's a teenage hacker in Hong Kong who knows how to break through or leap over the wall. Only in a handful of authoritarian regimes where the information networks are owned and managed by the government can such restrictions be enforced.

Yes, borders are disappearing. Or are they? As I write this in mid-2020, roughly one third of the world's population is still in some form of lockdown because of the coronavirus pandemic. One of the first steps by governments was to shut down their national borders and halt air travel to prevent the spread of the virus. Even Europe's landmark Schengen Agreement was put on hold—it was no longer possible to drive from Portugal to the Baltics, or from Greece to Norway, with or without a passport. How effective the travel restrictions were in curbing the spread of the virus may never be known, but the speed at which governments closed their borders, with all the economic consequences to trade and travel, indicates that borders still matter. It's too early to write the obituary for nation states and borders.

Dhaka Doctors and Other Acknowledgements

It was late April 2019. I was in Bangladesh's capital, Dhaka, with my colleagues Andrew Carlson and Nicola Christofides, on assignment for UNICEF. For the past 2½ years, our team had been working with faculty members at public and private universities to introduce curriculum on communication for development and improve their skills in applied social research. We had spent months planning a research conference to be held at the Bangabandhu International Conference Centre and a curriculum symposium. It was my seventh visit to Bangladesh since February 2017. It was almost my last.

Monday, April 22, was a public (religious) holiday. Andrew, Nicola and I decided to take advantage of the temporary lull in the notorious Dhaka traffic to do some sightseeing. We decided on a visit to the old city of Dhaka, with its narrow, winding streets and colorful markets, and the busy waterfront of the River Buriganga. I had been there on a previous visit and found it fascinating.

Our Uber driver dropped us off at Saidirghat, the bustling ferry terminal. Four-deck launches were lined up, waiting to take on passengers and cargo for destinations in the delta region. Small cargo freighters steamed upstream and downstream. Porters were unloading motorized wooden *nouka*, carrying sacks of onions, garlic, potatoes, chilis, coconuts, mangoes and other fruits and vegetables to the wholesale market. Narrow *nouka*, with one man paddling or poling, transported passengers, bicycles, and the odd farm animal across the river. On the other side of the Buriganga, freighters and launches were hauled up on the beach for repairs; workers clambered over the hulls and decks, the sparks from their acetylene torches flashing.

We moved from the riverfront to the maze of streets of Old

Dhaka, to the spice market, to nineteenth century red-brick merchants' houses, built in British Raj style, where the stucco crumbled from the columns and façades and small trees sprouted out of cracks and gutters. We visited the Shakari (weavers') bazaar, the predominantly Hindu neighborhood that was a primary target for the Pakistani army during its operations to crush resistance in the 1971 Liberation War.

It was hot, and we stopped several times to buy water. I started feeling light-headed and had to pause every five minutes or so to sit on a bench or rest against a wall. We decided we had had enough fun in the sun and headed back to the hotel. I figured that I'd recover after drinking more water and having a few hours' rest. By evening, I felt a little better, and we joined a Bangladeshi faculty colleague for dinner. When, after breakfast the next morning, I still felt unsteady, I sensed that I was suffering from more than dehydration. I called my UNICEF colleague Yasmin Khan. "I'll leave work now and drive you to the hospital," she said without hesitation.

United Hospital in the Gulshan-2 district was close to the hotel. Within an hour I was in the office of Dr. Taimur Nawaz, a family friend of Yasmin's. I recounted my symptoms and he did a quick examination. "I'm sending you for an EKG," he said. Within 30 minutes, he had the results. He reported that my heart rate was dangerously low—26 beats per minute. I had told him that I already knew the electrical system on the left side of the heart was not working (a left bundle branch blockage) and that my cardiologist had said I'd eventually need a pacemaker. "Looks like the whole electrical system is not working," said Dr. Nawaz. "It's your decision, of course, but I want you to see the cardiologist now. I don't want you walking. I'm ordering a wheelchair."

My mind raced as Yasmin and I moved through the hospital corridors. I had spent months preparing for the conference and symposium and had been in contact with many faculty who would be presenting. I was scheduled to give opening remarks at both events and knew I would have to deal with logistical issues. I decided that my role, while useful, was not essential. Andrew, Nicola, Yasmin, and others could step in for me. When the cardiologist, Dr. Reyan Anis, advised immediate admission, I agreed.

A small army of nurses prepared me for the operation to have a temporary pacemaker inserted in the groin. I learned later that my heart beat had dropped even further—to 19 beats per minute. The operation proved challenging, as Dr. Anis worked to insert the pacemaker into a vein. "It's a little difficult," she said, somewhat offhandedly. Later, I learned that my heart had stopped completely a couple of times—that's the flatline on the heart monitor that's the mini-climax in TV medical series. Then the pacemaker kicked in, and my heart rate went up. I was returned to the Coronary Care Centre, festooned like a Christmas tree with IVs and heart monitor leads dangling from appendages. The next day Dr. Anis and a colleague installed the permanent pacemaker in my chest. The operation was performed with only a local anesthetic. Dr. Anis and her colleague casually chatted away as they worked—an encouraging sign, showing that this was a routine procedure for them.

I spent the next five days in hospital. The post-operative care was excellent, the hospital food awful. At some point (perhaps as I was coming out of anesthetic) I was asked what I wanted to eat. I must have said something about chicken, fish and rice because that's what I got for both lunch and dinner along with soggy vegetables and a sliced apple. Stephanie, alerted by a phone call from Andrew, talked with Dr. Anis and made flight arrangements. Dr. Anis's assistant, Dr. Asif Iftikhar, visited me at least once a day. His cheerful face and good humor helped me believe I could enjoy a full recovery. Dr. Nawaz, who had diagnosed the low heart rate, also visited. Yasmin had told me he was somewhat reserved, and cautious in judgment. In other words, he does not joke around. "It was good you came in when you did," he said. "You would have not made it through the afternoon." He smiled, but I knew he was not joking. After I was released from hospital, Stephanie and I spent a week at the apartment of my UNICEF colleague and friend, Neha Kapil. I returned to the hospital for a check-up by Dr. Anis who cleared me to fly home to the US.

My first acknowledgements are to Dr. Anis, Dr. Iftikhar, the United Hospital surgical team, Dr. Nawaz, and Yasmin Khan for saving my life. Simply put, if they had not done what they did, and done it well, I would not be writing this now. Nine months later, on my next trip to Dhaka, I stopped by the hospital to thank them again, and donate blood. Dr. Anis invited me to join her, her husband and son for dinner at their apartment. I was happy Dr. Iftikhar was also at the table. The traditional Bangla food was sumptuous, the conversation lively. I felt so privileged to be with the people who had saved my life.

While I was still in hospital, I recounted my experience in what may be my most-read travel essay sent to family and friends and posted on Facebook. I always try to have an attention-grabbing title or subject line. "I didn't come to Dhaka to die, but I almost did" did the trick. I heard from people who had not contacted me in years, all concerned for my health. I wrote back to say that I expected to make a full recovery and hoped to travel again soon. "I'll do almost anything for a good travel story," I joked. I made two trips to India later in 2019 and was in Bangladesh for three weeks in early 2020, before the coronavirus started to spread across Asia.

My second acknowledgement is to all those who are regular readers of my travel essays and blogs. I'm not sure how many of them there are, but I hear from enough on a regular basis to encourage me to keep writing.

For the last decade, I've had the privilege to work with a talented group of faculty members and consultants on a series of projects, most of them for UNICEF. In Dhaka, I was with Andrew, from Metropolitan State University in St. Paul, Minnesota, and Nicola, from the School of Public Health at the University of the Witwatersrand in Johannesburg. Suruchi Sood from Drexel University in Philadelphia worked with me on the Bangladesh project and others, and has helped me to understand the history, politics, and culture of South Asia. I'm also grateful to my colleagues Ami Sengupta, an independent consultant, Sara Nieuwoudt from the University of the Witwatersrand, Karen Greiner (now with UNICEF) and anthropologist Luke Freeman of University College, London.

At UNICEF, I owe a special debt to Neha Kapil, currently regional communication for development (C4D) advisor for the Middle East and North Africa, with whom I worked for five years on a global learning course for UNICEF staff and later, when she was C4D chief in Bangladesh, on the university project. On the learning course, I developed a wonderful working relationship with Waithira Gikonyo, who served as Senior Learning Advisor at UNICEF HQ in New York until her recent retirement. In Bangladesh, I owe more than I can say to C4D manager Yasmin Khan—not only for getting me to the hospital on time, but for helping me to better understand the country and its culture.

Because *Postcards from the Borderlands* spans many countries and years, it's impossible to list all the people who have helped me in the places I've visited, so I'll apologize in advance to anyone I've missed. Most of my overseas assignments before 2010 were for UNESCO and the Asia-Pacific Institute for Broadcasting Development (AIBD), based in Kuala Lumpur. For my experiences in Central Asia, my thanks go to Tarja Virtanen, head of UNESCO's Almaty Cluster Office, and my good friend, programme officer Sergey Karpov. AIBD program officer Manil Cooray sent me on training assignments to Malaysia, India, Pakistan, Nepal, Thailand, The Maldives, Cambodia, Kazakhstan, and Mongolia. In Malawi, I was privileged to work with Deborah Mesce from Population Reference Bureau, consultant Sandra Mapemba and the staff of the Malawi Institute of Journalism. My Ohio University colleague, Drew McDaniel, and his wife, Nancy, hosted Stephanie and me on our first visit to Malaysia; my colleague, Adrian Budiman, hosted me on my last visit. On three visits to Mongolia, I learned much from the staff of Mongolian National Radio and Television and my guide and interpreter, Batzorig. When, on my second visit, I briefly fell ill, my colleague Chuck Ganzert from Northern Michigan University stepped up admirably to take over management of the project. I wish he had been able to join me on other assignments, but unfortunately he died in 2016 at a much too young age. I miss him.

I'd like to thank two fellow writers for reading an earlier draft of this book and providing valuable comments. I've known travel writer Alan Wilkinson, now living in Durham, UK, for most of my life because we've been friends since the age of 11. I wholeheartedly recommend his books on travelling in the American West. West Virginia writer Cat Pleska has been an admirable mentor, helping me hone my skills in memoir writing.

With so many countries featured in this book, I knew the maps would be vital to orienting readers. I was lucky to be able to work with Ana Mojika Myers, instructor of cartography at Ohio University, and her talented team of students—Benjamin Bryan, Anna Stover, and Hunter Uhl. They faced a challenge: the maps had to be cartographically accurate, yet have a rough-and-ready look, as if I'd sat on a rock by the river and sketched them. They captured my design concept superbly in the labelling of places, the representation of seas, lakes, mountains, and deserts, and in slightly quirky images of buildings, vehicles, ships, wildlife and so on.

This is my first (but perhaps not my last) venture with Open Books, a boutique small press with an impressive list of authors and genres. It's been an excellent experience working with David Ross and Kelly Huddleston, who have handled the publishing and marketing process expertly and collaboratively.

As I write this, the world is in the grip of the coronavirus pandemic. I have no idea when or even if I will be able to travel again, but if it is not to be I'm thankful to all those who have made my travel writing possible. Most of all, I thank my wife, Stephanie Hysmith, for putting up with my absences and for being the best companion for travel and life I could ever have hoped to have.

INDEX

A

Abkhazia, 12, 235, 237, 272, map, 236

Afghanistan, 91, 180, 181, 183

African National Congress (ANC), 58, 61, 70

Afrikaners, history of, 44, 68-69, 70, 71

aimag (Mongolian province), 200, 206, 207

Air Malawi, 29, 30

Aksai Chin (Chinese-controlled region of Kashmir), 271, 272

Albuquerque, Alfonso de, (Portuguese general), 152

Alexandra (Johannesburg township), 65

Ali, Khan Jahal (Muslim administrator), 102

Alkebu-Lan 1260 AD, 275, map, 276

Almaty, Kazakhstan, 1, 2, 3, 281

Alor Setar, Malaysia, 156, 157, 158, map, 142

Anchiskhati Basilica of St. Mary, Tbilisi, 239

Andrews, Roy Chapman (naturalist), 209,

Antananarivo, Madagascar, 20, 22

Apartheid, 8, 14, 25, 26, 64, 65, 70; Freedom Charter (1955), 61-62; history and impact of, 57-59, 61-62, 63, 68-69

Apartheid Museum, Johannesburg, 57-58, 63, 68-69

Arunachal Pradesh (Indian state), 13, 271, 272

Arusha, Tanzania, 50, 54, 55, 56, map, 53

Assam (Indian state), 75, 76, map, 77; Assam Accord (1985), 89-90; Assam Movement, 88-89; Citizenship Amendment Act (2019), 90-92; migration to, 87-90; National Register of Citizens, 89-92

Atlas of Prejudice, (Yanko Tsvetkov), 283-84

Autorickshaws, 100, picture, 101

Ayutthaya (ancient Thai capital), 162

B

Baaran, Purevdash (Mongolia radio manager), 206-07

bag (Mongolian sub-district), 200, 201, 204

Bagerhat Mosque City, Bangladesh, 102

Bakiyev, Kurmanbek (president of Kyrgyzstan), 222

Banda, Hastings (president of Malawi), 26-27, 33

Banda, Joyce (president of Malawi), 30, 33-36

Bandipur, Nepal, 132, map, 118

78, 80, 82, 83, 86, 89, 92, map, 77

Witwatersrand, University of, South
Africa, 29, 63, 66, 290

Y

Yao (Malawi tribe), 30, 31, 32, 34,
49, 51

Yekaterinburg (Sverdlovsk), 243-50,
254, 257, 262, 264, map, 248;
climate, 243-44; cost of living,
245; industrial history, 246-47;
Romanovs, murder of, 247, 249

Yeltsin, Boris (Russian Federation
president), 247, 249

Z

Zaisan Memorial, Ulaanbaatar, 202

Zambezi (river), 31, 32, map, 28

Zambia, 26, 27, 30, 36, 41, 64

Zanzibar, 31, 32, 50, 51, 52, map, 53

Zhivago, Dr. Yuri, 253-54, 259, 262

Zimbabwe, 61, 64, 66, 70-71

Zomba, Malawi, 26, 27

Zotikov, Aleksey (interpreter), 245,
254, 261, 262, 266, 267

Zulus, 30, 68-69